D0433895

HOSTAGES TO
FORTUNE

HOSTAGES TO FORTUNE

WINSTON CHURCHILL and the Loss of the *PRINCE OF WALES* and *REPULSE*

ARTHUR NICHOLSON

FOREWORD BY
ADMIRAL OF THE FLEET
SIR HENRY LEACH

SUTTON PUBLISHING

First published in the United Kingdom in 2005 by
Sutton Publishing Limited · Phoenix Mill
Thrupp · Stroud · Gloucestershire · GL5 2BU

Copyright © Arthur C. Nicholson III, 2005

All rights reserved. No part of this publication may be reproduced,
stored in a retrieval system, or transmitted, in any form, or by any
means, electronic, mechanical, photocopying, recording or otherwise,
without the prior permission of the publisher and copyright holder.

Arthur C. Nicholson III has asserted the moral right to be identified as
the author of this work.

British Library Cataloguing in Publication Data
A catalogue record for this book is available from the British Library.

ISBN 0-7509-3948-6

Typeset in 11/13.5pt Photina MT.
Typesetting and origination by
Sutton Publishing Limited.
Printed and bound in England by
J.H. Haynes & Co. Ltd, Sparkford.

To Sandy, James and Audrey

Contents

Part III: Decisions at Sea – Where to Go and Whom to Tell

Part IV: Aftermath

List of Illustrations

Foreword

Much has been written about the sinking of *Prince of Wales* and *Repulse* by Japanese aircraft off the east coast of Malaya in December 1941, some by eminent historians, some by survivors of the action itself. There exists a mass of data concerning this disaster, but it is somewhat fragmented. Here for the first time all the multiple threads have been drawn together into a single, comprehensive tapestry. It is confined to fact, and any conclusions drawn result from meticulous analysis of available evidence – to the exclusion of opinion and hindsight.

The work does not dwell on the reality that the whole concept of the operation was one of Churchill's greatest blunders, on the feebleness of the First Sea Lord of the day in failing to maintain his professional opposition to such ridiculous arrogance, on the shameful underrating of the threat of air attack to ships at sea (despite the recent débâcle off Crete), on the impossible position in which Admiral Phillips was placed or on his mishandling of that situation, or on the supine shambles emanating from the Higher Command at Singapore.

It is a benevolent book and a valuable, honest contribution to history. It is also easy to read and quite fascinating.

Admiral of the Fleet Sir Henry Leach

Preface

Warships and naval history have fascinated me since my childhood. Before I was ten, my godfather, Jim Kishi, gave me several volumes of H.T. Lenton's *Navies of the Second World War*, including one with a photograph of the battleship Bismarck, I saw the movie *Sink the Bismarck!*, with its unforgettable scene of the bridge of HMS *Prince of Wales* after she had been hit by the *Bismarck*, and I learned that my new step-grandmother, Mrs Hermione Alcock, belonged to a real Royal Navy family. This fascination has been a part of me ever since, and has continued to receive new inspiration each year since 1992 from my volunteer work with historians and veterans at the National Museum of the Pacific War in the home town of Fleet Admiral Chester Nimitz, Fredericksburg, Texas.

Still, nothing about naval history has fascinated me so much as the story of 'Force Z' and what the Japanese call *Malay oki kaisen*, 'the Battle off Malaya', when the famous British battleship *Prince of Wales* and the battlecruiser *Repulse* were sunk by Japanese bombers on 10 December 1941. It is hoped that the reader will shortly share that same fascination, if he or she does not already.

Before I begin to tell the story, it is important for the reader to understand several points to avoid any unnecessary confusion. First, Japanese names are given in the Japanese tradition with the surname first, e.g. Tojo Hideki. Secondly, a 24-hour clock is usually used. Thirdly, since this story involved people and events all over the world, it has often been necessary to give times in reference to a specific time zone. During the Second World War, the Royal Navy divided the world into 24 time zones, designated from A to Z, leaving out the letters 'I' and 'O' to avoid confusion. Normally, London was within Zone Z, which is also Greenwich Mean Time (GMT), but in December 1941, London used British Summer Time (BST), one hour ahead of GMT, or Zone A.[1] Singapore was in Zone GH, 7½ hours later. The Imperial Japanese Navy always used Tokyo time, Zone K, 1½ hours later than Singapore time, but in this book the times given in the Official Japanese History have been converted to Singapore time (GH) to avoid confusion. Fourthly, with absolutely no consideration for posterity, the Japanese and British failed to coordinate their clocks before the battle, so the times given in the Official Japanese History sometimes vary from the times given in British sources for the same events. Finally, the events in this story occurred on both sides of the International Date Line, but the date of the location in question is always used. Singapore and Tokyo are on the other side of the International Date Line from Pearl Harbor, Washington, DC and London.

To illustrate all this foolishness, at the same moment the time and the date in these places would be:

London: 0100 Zone Z (1.00 a.m.), 8 December
Singapore: 0830 Zone GH (8.30 a.m.), 8 December
Tokyo: 1000 Zone K (10.00 a.m.), 8 December
Pearl Harbor: 1430 Zone RS (2.30 p.m.), 7 December
Washington, DC: 2000 Zone V (8.00 p.m.) 7 December

The reader can well appreciate the difficulties that this must have caused in 1941 and that it causes even today in trying to understand what happened in 1941.

While the story of Force Z has been well told before,[2] this work is an attempt to take a fresh and balanced look at the story, often using information not previously considered or discovered from interviews and correspondence with survivors and the families of those lost in the battle, and from letters and documents in private papers and archives. Although living in Texas, I have been fortunate in being able to make frequent visits to Britain and to haunt the Churchill Archive Centre in Cambridge, the Imperial War Museum, the Liddell-Hart Centre for Military Archives at King's College, London, and the National Archives at Kew. I was also able to find new information from Admiral Geoffrey Layton's papers at the British Library, from Admiral Thomas C. Hart's papers at the US Naval Historical Center in Washington, DC, and from the Royal Archives. I also commissioned a very helpful translation of that portion of the Official Japanese History of the Second World War that deals with the Battle off Malaya. I have had the distinct pleasure of meeting and talking to men of the Prince of Wales & Repulse Survivors' Association.

I am very grateful to my wife Sandy, who has helped with this book in innumerable ways and has put up with this obsession of mine for enough years. Almost needless to say, this book would not have been possible without a tremendous amount of generous assistance from the many individuals and organizations listed in the Acknowledgements. Of course, any errors in this book are my sole responsibility.

Arthur Nicholson
San Antonio, Texas

Notes

1 Stephen W. Roskill, *Churchill and the Admirals*, New York, William Morrow & Co., 1978, at 15.
2 Some of the finest accounts of the story are Martin Middlebrook and Patrick Mahoney, *Battleship: The Loss of the Prince of Wales and Repulse*, London, Allen Lane, 1977, and Arthur J. Marder, *Old Friends, New Enemies: The Royal Navy and the Imperial Japanese Navy, Vol. 1: Strategic Illusions 1936–1941*, Oxford, Clarendon Press, 1981. Professor Marder had intended to call his book 'Reluctant Enemies', but before publication he changed the title, perhaps after learning that the two navies were not such reluctant enemies after all. A second volume was published after Marder's death with Mark Jacobsen and John Horsfield, *Old Friends, New Enemies, Vol. 2: The Pacific War 1942–1945*, Oxford, Clarendon Press, 1990.

Acknowledgements

I am deeply indebted to the following people and organizations. I sincerely apologize to anyone I might have inadvertently omitted.

Lieutenant-Commander K.G. Armstrong, RNR
Lieutenant J.G. Blackburn, RNVR
Paymaster Commander W.T. Blunt, RN
Colonel James Boling, US Army
Lieutenant-Commander Geoffrey A.G. Brooke, RN
Churchill Archive Centre, Churchill College, Cambridge (Ms Carolyn Lye and Mr Sam Bartle)
Lieutenant-Commander W.J.T. Crozer, RN
Mr Brian Cull
Mr Michael Davis of Dallas, Texas
Mr Gary L. Fuller
Mr I.D. Goode, Ministry of Defence (UK)
Imperial War Museum, Departments of Documents (Mr Roderick Suddaby), Photographs, Film and Video, Journals, and Sound Archive
Professor James Ivy
Mr Daniel H. Jones
Mr Steve Kirby
Mr Christopher Langtree
Admiral of the Fleet Sir Henry Leach, GCB, DL
Liddell-Hart Centre for Military Archives, King's College, London (Ms Kate O'Brian)
Mr Patrick Mahoney
Mr Alan Matthews
Mr L.O. 'Chuck' Maurer
The National Archives (formerly the Public Record Office), Kew
The National Maritime Museum at Woolwich Arsenal

The National Museum of the Pacific War (Ms Helen McDonald and Mr
   Richard Koone)
Naval Historical Branch, UK Ministry of Defence (including Messrs
   David Brown, Stephen Prince, Michael McAloon, and David Ashby)
US Naval Historical Center (Mr Mike Walker)
Sir Michael Palliser, GCMG, PC
Mr John Parkinson, South Africa
Mr Ronald E.F. Peal
Mrs T.V.G. Phillips
Mr Anthony J. and Mrs Elizabeth Price, formerly of Prestwood, England,
   and Singapore
The Prince of Wales and Repulse Survivors' Association (Ken Byrne,
   Chris Rhodes, *et al.*)
San Antonio Public Library, San Antonio, Texas, Reference and Inter-
   library Loan Departments
Mr P.F.C. Satow
Mr Roland Smith, Naval Video Time Capsules
South African Museum of Military History
Trinity University Library, San Antonio, Texas
University of California at Irvine, Special Collections
United States Naval Institute, Annapolis, Maryland (Ms Ann Hassinger
   and Mr Paul Stillwell)
Whitehall Library, UK Ministry of Defence (including Ms Jennifer
   Wraight)
Vice Admiral D.B.H. Wildish, CB
Commander Alastair Wilson, Secretary-Treasurer of the *Naval Review*

Abbreviations

It would have been difficult to write this book without any abbreviations, but an attempt has been made to keep them to a minimum. The principal ones used are as follows:

Adm	Admiralty
BAD	British Admiralty Delegation (in Washington, DC)
C-in-C	Commander-in-Chief
Cab	Cabinet
CNO	Chief of Naval Operations (US Navy)
COS	Chiefs of Staff
FO	Foreign Office
HMAS	His (or Her) Majesty's Australian Ship
HMS	His (or Her) Majesty's Ship
Opnav	Chief of Naval Operations (US Navy)
PM or Prem	Prime Minister (Premier)
SO	Senior Officer (as in SO, Force G)
Spenavo	US Special Naval Observer in London
TNA	The National Archives (formerly Public Record Office (PRO), Kew)
WO	War Office
W/T	Radio (Wireless/Telegraphy)

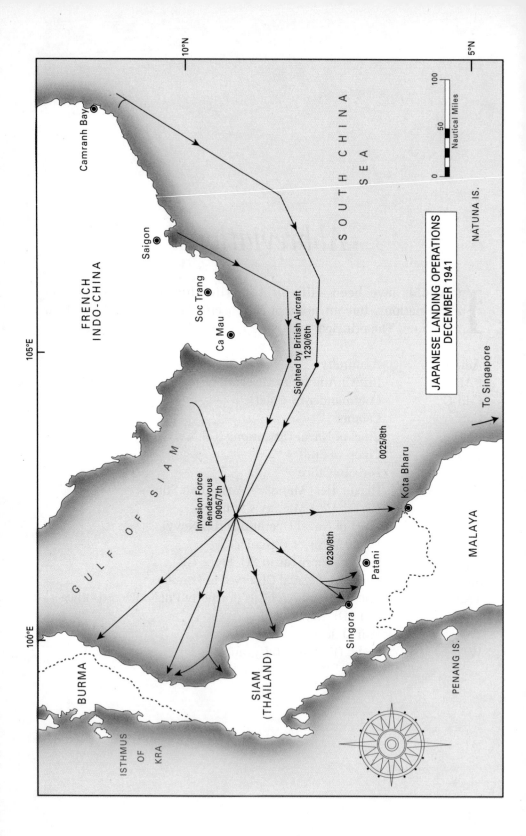

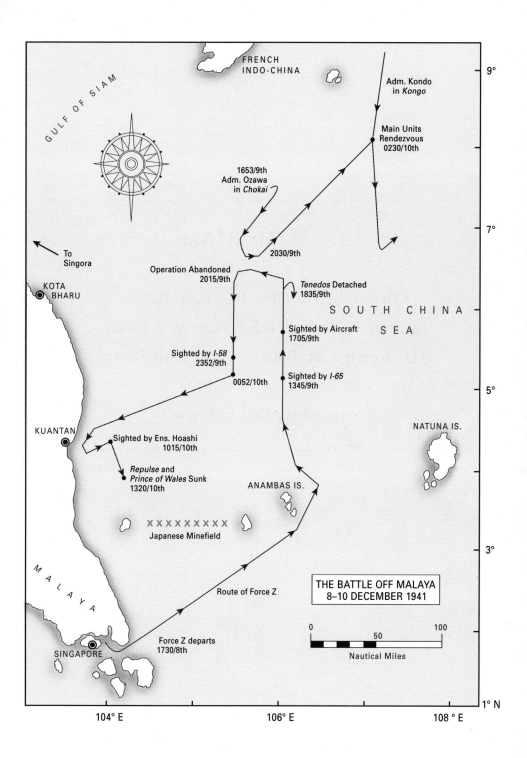

THE BATTLE OFF MALAYA
8–10 DECEMBER 1941

In Memoriam

Christopher Rhodes, F.L. 'Bim' Hardy,
Graham L. Kipling, R.E.F. Peal, W.T. Blunt,
J.D. Brown, C.R. Bateman and John Sharp

May They Rest in Peace

Introduction

We in Plans and Operations Foreign [in the Admiralty] were solidly against sending out *Prince of Wales* to the Far East, as it were almost by herself, as also was the First Sea Lord, who argued strongly against the unwisdom of despatching a wholly [*sic*] unbalanced force into an area where we did not know the strengths or capacities of the potential enemy. We suggested that such action would make *Prince of Wales* a hostage to fortune.

Admiral Sir William Davis[1]

In the early afternoon of 10 December 1941, in the South China Sea off the east coast of Malaya, Sub-Lieutenant Paul Satow took a moment away from his duties on the bridge of the destroyer HMS *Express* to pull out his Brownie camera to photograph the massive ship lying alongside. The ship was the battleship *Prince of Wales*, the flagship of Force Z of the British Eastern Fleet. In the skies above, Japanese bombers, which minutes before had sunk the battlecruiser *Repulse*, were silently watching their handiwork without interfering; in a few minutes they would be chased away by RAF fighters arriving too late to save the ships.

One of Sub-Lieutenant Satow's photographs, shown in the plate section and on the book jacket, was taken at this moment, the climax of the battle. It captured the haunting tragedy and drama of the moment, and became one of the most famous photographs of the Second World War. One can see the smoke from the Japanese bomb that had exploded in the cinema flat under the catapult deck just yards away and minutes before. Years later, at a reunion of survivors, Reginald Coker could see himself in a helmet at the far left of the photograph, and a son could see his father, Petty Officer William C. Uren, in a white anti-flash hood outside one of the forward 5.25in turrets.

Only moments after the photograph had been taken, the *Prince of Wales* would begin to capsize to port and sink. As she did, the *Prince of*

Wales gave the *Express* a bump that caused her to heel before she could get clear. Little did the crew of the *Express* realize, as we shall see, that the bump, so alarming at the time, would later save their ship and probably their lives as well.

This is the story of how and why the terrible moment captured by Sub-Lieutenant Satow's photograph came to be, of how and why a few warships, forming a powerful yet vulnerable force called Force Z, were sent to the Far East at the behest of Prime Minister Winston Churchill, in a desperate attempt first to deter, and then to halt, the expansion of the Japanese Empire. It is also the story of how these great ships became hostages to fortune.

The story of the *Prince of Wales* and *Repulse* is an endlessly fascinating one. It is first the story of a voyage around the world that ended in a hard but cleanly fought battle, a story of great and heroic men, powerful and graceful ships, and cruel twists of fate. It is also very much the story of a voyage and a battle brought about by a series of momentous and difficult decisions, decisions that have caused controversy over the years and that still raise questions begging to be answered.

The story of the voyage and the battle and the analysis of the decisions are told together in chronological order in successive chapters, which are grouped into four parts: first, the events that led to the decision to send the ships to Cape Town and then Singapore, without an aircraft carrier, and to have Admiral Phillips lead them; secondly, the outbreak of war in the Pacific and the decisions made in London and Singapore on whether and when to send the ships out against the Japanese; thirdly, once the ships had sailed, the story of the battle and the decisions made by Admiral Phillips on where to go and whom to tell about it; and fourthly, the aftermath of the battle, followed by an analysis of the men and machines that fought the battle, including the tale of how the *Prince of Wales* came to suffer crippling hits in the first torpedo attack on her, an examination of the many factors, including fortune, that led to the outcome of the Battle off Malaya, and an assignment of responsibility on the British side, especially that of Winston Churchill. After the Conclusion, the Appendix sets out in chronological order an extensive collection of British signals and messages that are so important to understanding the full story of Force Z and the Battle off Malaya.

Seven decisions on the British side are examined in detail: first, the choice of Admiral Phillips to be C-in-C of the Eastern Fleet; secondly, the decision to send the *Prince of Wales* and *Repulse* to Cape Town and then to Singapore; thirdly, the decision not to attack the Japanese convoys at sea;

fourthly, the decision to take Force Z to sea to attack the Japanese off the landing beaches; fifthly, the decisions to continue and then to abandon the operation; sixthly, Admiral Phillips's decision to divert to Kuantan after receiving a report of a Japanese invasion there; and seventhly, Admiral Phillips's decision not to break radio silence and call for air cover, and how it may have been influenced by Royal Navy tactical doctrine of the time.

Most of these decisions were not easy ones, and all were made under wartime conditions, whether they were made in London, in Singapore, or on the bridge of the *Prince of Wales*. Every effort has been made to analyse and evaluate these decisions in the light of what the decision-makers knew at the time. Not everyone will be satisfied with the analysis of the decisions; the Battle off Malaya seems to engender strongly held opinions.

The story of the voyage and the battle and the analysis of the decisions are told using many British sources (and a few American ones) and a translation of the Official Japanese History. The story uses a number of eyewitness accounts, some never told before. There is new information on such matters as the circumstances behind Force Z's lack of an aircraft carrier, the mysterious tale of a high-level, late-night meeting in Singapore the night before the ships sailed, the cryptic signal sent to Admiral Phillips by the Admiralty just hours before the battle, the role played by Winston Churchill (and what he said and wrote about the subject over the years), and the surprising reason for the survival of the destroyer HMS *Express*.

This does not pretend to be the 'last word' on this fascinating story, as if there were ever a 'last word' on any historical subject. It is easy to be left with the feeling that there is more to the story, if only because of signals between London and Singapore that we know were sent but are not now available. The men who fought so hard on 10 December 1941, now more than sixty years ago, are becoming fewer and fewer as the years pass, and they surely deserve no less than the fullest possible telling of their story.

Note

1 'Loss of "Prince of Wales" and "Repulse" 10 December 1941: Notes from Diaries of Captain William Davis, Deputy Director of Plans, Admiralty', attachment to letter from Admiral William Davis to Arthur Marder of 3 April 1975. Arthur J. Marder Papers, Special Collections, University of California at Irvine.

Part I

Off to Cape Town – and Singapore

CHAPTER ONE

On the Road to a Showdown

The Battle off Malaya would not have occurred at all if the British Empire had not decided to send the battleship *Prince of Wales* and the battlecruiser *Repulse* to Singapore. The background for that decision begins many years before the momentous events of 1941.

At the beginning of the twentieth century, the British Empire faced little threat to its interests in the Far East, among which were Singapore and the Straits Settlements, Hong Kong, Australia and New Zealand. In 1902, Britain signed an alliance with Japan, the new rising power in the Far East. Britain had bet on the right horse, for Japan promptly defeated Russia in the Russo-Japanese War of 1904–5. The alliance with Japan was renewed in 1905 and again in 1911, when it was amended to keep Britain from becoming involved in a war with the United States.[1] Britain's prize possession in the Far East, Singapore, had not seemed so secure since the Anglo-Dutch Treaty of 1824 had made Sir Stamford Raffles' gamble a permanent British possession.[2]

The alliance with Japan did not long survive the First World War, which Japan had used to its advantage to extend its territorial ambitions, mainly at the expense of Imperial Germany and China if it had been allowed. Wary of Japan's territorial ambitions and its plans for building new battleships and battlecruisers, the British began to plan a new naval base in the Far East. The British settled on Singapore, which was called by Admiral David Beatty 'the finest strategical position in the whole world', and which Admiral John Jellicoe called 'the naval key to the Far East'.[3] The British Cabinet formally approved the building of the naval base in June 1921.

Soon afterwards the British alliance with Japan came to an end. In the first of a series of three important treaties, on 13 December

1921, the United States, Great Britain, France and Japan signed the Four-Power Treaty, each agreeing to respect the others' possessions in the Pacific Ocean region and ending the alliance between Japan and Britain.[4]

Japan was not pleased with the termination of its alliance with Britain, and was further displeased with the Washington Naval Treaty, signed on 6 February 1922.[5] This pact was designed to halt a hugely expensive naval arms race between its signatories, and set ratios in tonnage of 'capital ships'[6] that could be retained by the British Empire, the United States, Japan, France and Italy of 5:5:3:1.75:1.75, respectively. Japan had argued unsuccessfully for a ratio of 10:10:7, and deeply resented the defeat. Under the treaty, existing battleships could not be replaced for twenty years, and their replacements were limited to a displacement of 35,000 tons.

On the same day that the Washington Treaty was signed, the Nine-Power Treaty was signed by the British Empire, the United States, Japan, France, Italy, the Netherlands, Portugal and, last but not least, China.[7] The signatories other than China agreed to respect the territorial sovereignty, independence and territorial integrity of China, to forgo special rights and privileges, and to establish and maintain equal opportunity in commerce in China.

In addition to halting the arms race in major warships, the Washington Treaty also restricted Britain, the United States and Japan from building new naval bases and fortifications in designated parts of the Pacific, but did not keep Britain from completing the Singapore naval base. Construction proceeded over a number of years in fits and starts, mainly because of changes in government, the great cost of the project in a time of financial stringency, and disagreements over whether to base the defence of the naval base on heavy guns or aircraft. The naval base was finally opened in February of 1938 with the completion of the King George VI dry dock, although much remained to be done.[8]

In spite of the powerful 15in guns that were put in place to protect the naval base, Singapore was never a true fortress capable of withstanding a direct attack or a siege, and it could not be fully defended without the dispatch of capital ships from Britain, the 'Main Fleet to Singapore'. British politicians and the Admiralty were destined to struggle for years with the question of when to send capital ships to Singapore and how many could be sent. The planning on the subject was based on what has been described as a matter of 'the simple sums of seapower strategy' – how many capital ships did Japan have and how many British ones were needed to meet them.[9]

The question of the dispatch of a Main Fleet to Singapore was of great and continuing importance to Australia and New Zealand, which contributed to its construction costs, and they were to make their concerns known to London from time to time in the coming years. Over the years successive governments in London took considerable pains to placate their concerns with promises of what would be done in terms of the number of capital ships to be sent and the 'time before relief', the time it would take the ships to arrive. However, Australia and New Zealand were not always provided with the latest, most complete, or most candid information. Communication even came close to deception at the Imperial Conference in 1937.[10]

A key ingredient in the planning for sending a fleet to the Far East was an evaluation of the threat posed by Japan vis-à-vis the situation in Europe. Unfortunately, as the years passed the threat from Japan increased at the same time that the rise of Mussolini and Hitler threw the situation in Europe into doubt.

In 1930, however, the international situation was still quiet when the London Naval Treaty was signed by the British Empire, the United States, Japan, France and Italy.[11] The treaty's main accomplishment was to delay the construction of new battleships by Britain, the United States and Japan until 1937. Unfortunately, the treaty also resulted in the early disposal of three American and five British capital ships, including the battlecruiser *Tiger*, compared to the early disposal of only one Japanese capital ship, the battlecruiser *Hiei*. This left the Royal Navy and the United States with fifteen capital ships each to Japan's nine, and left the Royal Navy with but three battlecruisers, the *Hood*, *Repulse* and *Renown*.

As the years passed, militarists gained more and more control over the Japanese government. Japan began to expand its empire in 1931 with the effective annexation of the Chinese province of Manchuria. Censured by the League of Nations, Japan merely walked out. In 1932, the Japanese precipitated a crisis in Shanghai, which brought home to the British government its weakness in the Far East.

In December 1934, Japan gave the required two years' notice of termination of the Washington Naval Treaty, and commenced work on what became the super-battleships *Yamato* and *Musashi*. On 1 January 1937, as soon as allowed by the naval treaties, Britain began laying down new battleships to replace older ones, starting with the *King*

George V and the *Prince of Wales*. The new ships were designed to meet the Washington Treaty's limit of 35,000 tons displacement. In a portent of things to come, in 1938 the Australian government requested that one of the new ships be allocated to the Far East and even considered buying one.[12]

In July 1937, Japan embarked upon a full-scale war against China, which it referred to as 'the China Incident'. As it dragged on, Japan's war against China began to have greater and greater consequences. The war severely strained its relations with the United States and Britain; and matters were not helped when the Japanese sank the US gunboat *Panay* on the Yangtze river in December 1937, although Japan apologized and paid some reparations.[13] Eventually, the war in China caused the British and the Americans to begin to coordinate their war planning, led the Americans, the British and the Dutch to impose more and more severe economic sanctions on Japan, and finally led to diplomatic negotiations between the United States and Japan to resolve their seemingly irreconcilable differences over China.

All of this took place against the background of ominous events unfolding in Europe. Adolph Hitler became Chancellor of Germany in 1933, and he soon repudiated the Treaty of Versailles, reoccupied the Rhineland and began making territorial demands. In 1938, he marched into Austria and obtained the Sudetenland in Czechoslovakia as a result of the Munich Agreement. In March 1939, he marched into the remainder of Czechoslovakia, and then began demanding the Danzig corridor in Poland. For his part, Italy's Benito Mussolini began to invade other countries, first Abyssinia (now Ethiopia) in 1935 and then Albania in April 1939. The Spanish Civil War was fought between 1936 and 1939, and added to European tensions.

After concluding a non-aggression pact with the Soviet Union in August 1939, Germany invaded Poland in September 1939 and the Second World War began in Europe. At that time, Japan was still well embroiled in China, and at first remained on the sidelines, but new opportunities for it were opened up in May and June 1940, when France and the Low Countries fell to Nazi Germany and Italy entered the war against France and Britain. By July 1940, Britain stood almost alone, and it could no longer count on the French Navy to counter the powerful Italian fleet in the Mediterranean. Nor could she count on France and the Netherlands to keep the Japanese away from their prize colonies in the Far East, French Indo-China and the oil-rich Dutch East Indies, which were literally next door to the British in Malaya and Singapore.

Japan could not help but notice these new opportunities, and the temptation proved too much. On 22 September 1940, Japan succeeded in pressuring the Vichy French government into allowing the Japanese to move troops into northern Indo-China, ostensibly to keep supplies from the Chinese.[14] On 27 September 1940, Japan, Germany and Italy signed the Tripartite Pact,[15] which, although it did not mention the United States, clearly had it in mind.[16] On 13 April 1941, Japan signed a Neutrality Pact with the Soviet Union,[17] raising fears that its next move would be to the south, instead of to the north against the Soviet Union. Then there came the momentous German invasion of the Soviet Union on 22 June 1941, which once again raised the question of which direction Japan would move.

During this march of events, Japan received an extraordinary windfall. On 12 December 1940, the Germans provided the Japanese with the British War Cabinet's August 1940 'Far East Appreciation',[18] which evaluated in detail Britain's situation in the Far East vis-à-vis Japan at that time.[19] The German raider *Atlantis* had captured a copy bound for Singapore on the steamer *Automedon* on 11 November 1940, just days before the *Atlantis* was sunk by the British cruiser *Devonshire*.[20] The *Atlantis* sent the Far East Appreciation and other sensitive documents to the German naval attaché in Japan on the captured Norwegian tanker *Ole Jacob*,[21] which arrived in Kobe, Japan, on 4 December.

In the Far East Appreciation, which was marked 'Secret', the British Chiefs of Staff stated that the general policy towards Japan must be to avoid an open clash and to conclude a general settlement, but if that was not possible, to play for time, to cede nothing until it had to, and to build up British defences as soon as possible. Recognizing the temporary impossibility of dispatching a fleet to the Far East, the Appreciation called for reinforcement of army strength in Malaya until air strength there could be increased by the end of 1940 and then brought up to full strength of 336 aircraft by the end of 1941. The Appreciation evaluated Britain's interests in the Far East, and determined that Britain should not go to war if the Japanese attacked French Indo-China. Singapore was seen as 'the foremost of our vital interests in the Far East', and the Appreciation rated a direct attack on Singapore as 'a very formidable undertaking'.

The effect of the compromise of the Far East Appreciation is difficult to measure. There is no hard evidence that the British learned of the compromise at any time during the war.[22] In January 1942, they did learn that a document from a crashed Japanese aircraft in China estimated RAF strength in the Far East at exactly 336 aircraft by the end of 1941, the same number called for in the Appreciation,[23] but there is no evidence this was connected with the lost copy of the Far East Appreciation. Even if the British had known of the breach, they could have done little about it, except perhaps to publicize the dispatch of reinforcements to the Far East to counteract the impression of weakness left by the Appreciation. There is no evidence that knowledge of the breach led to the dispatch of the *Prince of Wales* and *Repulse* to the Far East.

As for the Japanese, they are said to have read the Appreciation 'with extraordinary interest', and Vice-Admiral Kondo Nobutake, the Vice-Chief of Staff of the Imperial Navy,[24] repeatedly expressed to the German naval attaché how valuable the information was for the Navy, saying that '[s]uch a significant weakening of the British Empire could not have been identified [from outward appearances]'.[25] The impression of British weakness left by the Far East Appreciation could well have made an important difference in Japanese calculations at a time when Japan had not yet decided which way to move. Of course, Japan eventually *did* decide to move south, among other directions, and when it did so it must have been pleasantly surprised to find only 182 RAF aircraft in Singapore and Malaya, instead of the 336 aircraft that should have been there.

Japan continued the war against China, and in July 1939 the United States gave Japan six months' notice of the abrogation of its 1911 Treaty of Commerce, and then began imposing economic sanctions against it, including restrictions on the export of petroleum products and scrap iron. The economic sanctions led Japan to initiate diplomatic efforts to resolve the situation, which began in earnest in April 1941 with the arrival of Japanese Ambassador Nomura in Washington.[26] A strange diplomatic dance ensued, with Japan negotiating at times in good faith, but never really willing to give up its designs upon China, and at other times negotiating just to mask its military moves, and with the United States, hoping to avert war but not willing to abandon China, negotiating with the benefit of having by that time broken the Japanese diplomatic code and being able to read Tokyo's communications with Ambassador Nomura.

Then, Japan went one step too far. In July 1941, it pressured the Vichy French into allowing it to move troops and aircraft into the southern part of French Indo-China,[27] putting it uncomfortably close to Siam (Thailand), Malaya, Singapore and the Dutch East Indies.[28] Japan did not expect a strong reaction from the United States or Britain to the move into southern Indo-China,[29] but it had badly miscalculated. On 26 July 1941, the United States imposed the harshest sanctions yet, the freezing of Japanese assets in the United States, and its sanctions were quickly matched by Great Britain and the Netherlands. The sanctions effectively meant an end to trade and led to rapidly dwindling stocks of oil and other vital raw materials in Japan. Japan was forced to choose between abandoning its ambitions in China and the Far East and reaching a diplomatic settlement with the United States, or going to war. It eventually chose war – with the United States, Britain and the Netherlands.

Japanese moves in the Far East in 1937 prompted discussions between the United States and Britain about coordinating their policies and their war plans. The discussions began in London in January 1938 between Captain Royal E. Ingersoll of the US Navy and a Captain Tom Phillips of the Royal Navy.

Then, after the outbreak of the war in Europe and the German victories of 1940, military and naval representatives of the two powers met from January to March 1941 at the ABC-1 Conference in Washington, DC. Singapore became a major area of disagreement: the British proposed that the United States base a fleet at Singapore, but the United States saw Singapore as expendable and did not want to split its fleet.[30] There was agreement on a Germany-first strategy in the event of war,[31] and on augmenting US Navy forces in the Atlantic so that the British could release necessary forces for the Far East.[32]

The ABC-1 Conference was followed by the ADB (American–Dutch–British Commonwealth) Conference in Singapore in April 1941,[33] which adopted a joint plan. However, the plan was rejected by the United States in July 1941, largely because it would have put the US Asiatic Fleet under British command when the British had committed hardly any ships to the defence of Singapore or the Malay Barrier,[34] the line running from Malaya through Sumatra and Java to northern Australia.[35]

Further discussions about the war in Europe and the situation in the Far East took place between Prime Minister Churchill and President Roosevelt and their staffs aboard the battleship HMS *Prince of Wales* at Placentia Bay, Newfoundland, from 9 to 12 August 1941. The meeting and the discussions were fruitful, and resulted in the largely symbolic Atlantic Charter. To the disappointment of the British, a declaration by

President Roosevelt afterwards was not as severe a warning to Japan as Mr Churchill had wanted, as it omitted the key word 'war' and any mention of Britain.[36]

In the end, there was only so much that could be accomplished at these conferences. Each nation had its own point of view and its own vital interests, and President Roosevelt could go only so far, limited as he was by American public opinion and by the United States Constitution, under which only Congress had the power to declare war.

Unfortunately, these conferences did not result in any reinforcement of US Navy strength in the Far East; instead, the Philippines were to be reinforced by the vaunted B-17 Flying Fortress bombers. At the ABC-1 conference, the British had requested that the United States send a carrier task force to the Far East,[37] but the United States refused. Shortly before the conference began, President Roosevelt had vetoed the US Navy's proposal to send the 'Asiatic Reinforcement', a task force centred on the aircraft carrier *Yorktown*, to defend the eastern end of the Malay Barrier.[38] The President did authorize a 'training cruise' by four cruisers and a squadron of destroyers to New Zealand, Australia, Fiji and Tahiti in 1941,[39] but this was not a reinforcement of the US Asiatic Fleet, much less of Singapore. What was even worse, the provision of the ABC-1 report calling for the augmenting of US Navy forces in the Atlantic meant that between April and June 1941 the US Navy transferred three battleships, the aircraft carrier *Yorktown*, four cruisers and a number of destroyers from the Pacific to the Atlantic.[40] This was supposed to free British naval forces for the Far East, but for the time being there was no reinforcement of British naval strength in the Far East.

The Japanese move into southern Indo-China in July 1941 and the Prime Minister's meeting with President Roosevelt on the *Prince of Wales* at Placentia Bay in August 1941 ignited a disagreement between Winston Churchill and the Admiralty's First Sea Lord, Admiral Sir Dudley Pound, over how to increase British naval strength in the Far East. Churchill, who as First Lord of the Admiralty in November 1939 had argued against keeping battleships 'tethered' at Singapore against a mere threat,[41] now wanted to send a small force of fast, modern capital ships to Singapore, while Pound wanted to send out a larger force of older, slower ships.

This disagreement was an outgrowth of the question of how many and which capital ships to send to Singapore. In 1921, Admiral David Beatty had proposed basing a battlecruiser squadron at Singapore, but the idea was dropped in 1927.[42] In March 1939, Admiral Reginald Drax proposed sending a 'flying squadron' of two fast battleships and two aircraft carriers with escorting cruisers and destroyers to the Far East.[43] The Naval War Memorandum (Eastern) was amended to allow for this as a possibility, but the word 'flying' was used rather broadly, as it was proposed to send battleships of the 'Queen Elizabeth' class,[44] which were at best capable of 24–25 knots. However, in June 1939 the Chiefs of Staff rejected the idea of sending a flying squadron, and in July the Deputy Chief of the Naval Staff, Rear-Admiral Tom Phillips, instructed the Admiralty's Director of Plans to omit all references to a flying squadron from the Admiralty's war plans.[45] The problem was that most of the British capital ships of the day were slow battleships, and in 1941 not enough of them could be sent to counter the ten capital ships that Japan had, counting the conversion of the *Hiei* from a training ship back into a battlecruiser in 1939. To meet that situation, Churchill was effectively reviving the idea of the 'flying squadron'.

The first round in the battle between Churchill and Pound was fired by Mr Churchill on 25 August 1941. Fresh from his voyage in the *Prince of Wales*, he opened, 'It should become possible in the near future to place a deterrent Squadron in the Indian Ocean. Such a force should consist of the smallest number of the best ships. We have only to remember all the preoccupations which are caused us by the *Tirpitz* . . . to see what an effect would be produced on the Japanese Admiralty by the presence of a small but very powerful and fast force in Eastern waters.' He proposed sending the brand-new battleship *Duke of York*, which he said could work up on her way, with a battlecruiser, either the *Repulse* or the *Renown*, and a fast aircraft carrier. 'This powerful force might show itself in the triangle Aden–Singapore–Simonstown. It would exert a paralysing effect upon Japanese naval action.' He proposed keeping the new battleships *King George V* and *Prince of Wales* with the Home Fleet.[46]

On 28 August, Dudley Pound replied, 'I fully appreciate the attractiveness of sending one of the 'King George V' class battleships to the Indian Ocean when fully worked up, but after considering this most carefully I cannot recommend it.' He went on to point out the impracticalities of having the *Duke of York* work up on her way to the Far East. In an accompanying memorandum on the disposition of capital ships and aircraft carriers, Pound made his key points. He pointed out that 'the Atlantic is the vital area as it is in that ocean and that alone in which we can lose the war at sea', and that as long as the

Tirpitz was in being, it was necessary to have three battleships of the 'King George V' class in home waters, so that at least two would be available if one was damaged or refitting. Instead, he proposed sending the older battleships *Nelson* and *Rodney* and the battlecruiser *Renown* to Trincomalee or Singapore, and the four very old battleships of the 'R' class into the Indian Ocean.[47]

Undeterred, Mr Churchill replied on 29 August, 'It is surely a faulty disposition to create in the Indian Ocean a fleet considerable in numbers, costly in maintenance and manpower, but consisting entirely of slow obsolescent or unmodernized ships which can neither fight a fleet action with the main Japanese force nor act as a deterrent upon his modern fast heavy ships, if used singly or in pairs as raiders.' He deprecated the usefulness of the 'R'-class battleships, referring to them as 'floating coffins' and 'easy prey' to an enemy fast modern battleship. He claimed that one of the true principles of naval strategy was to 'use a small number of the best fast ships to cope with a superior force'. He mentioned the Admiralty's concern about the *Tirpitz*, and suggested that she 'is doing to us exactly what a K.G.V. in the Indian Ocean would do to the Japanese Navy. It exercises a vague, general fear and menaces all points at once.' He did not think three KGVs were needed to contain the *Tirpitz*, considering it 'a serious reflection upon the design of our latest ships, which through being undergunned and weakened by hangars in the middle of their citadels, are evidently judged unfit to fight their opposite number in a single-ship action'. He did not want to keep three KGVs in the Atlantic, given American dispositions and the proved power of aircraft carriers to slow down a ship like the *Tirpitz*, and suggested that it was unlikely the *Tirpitz* would be withdrawn from the Baltic while the Russian fleet was still in being. He considered it unlikely Japan would face the combination of nations forming against her, but would continue to negotiate with the United States before making an aggressive move, adding that 'Nothing would increase her hesitation more than the appearance of the force I mentioned in my minute [of 25 August], and above all of a K.G.V. This might indeed be a decisive deterrent.' He then closed, saying, 'I should like to talk these matters over with you.'[48]

Churchill and Pound were indeed to discuss the matter again, but in the meantime pressure to send capital ships to the Far East was coming in from other quarters. Australia and New Zealand were very concerned about the situation in the Far East, and were making their concerns known, but were encouraged by a telegram from Churchill to their prime ministers on 2 September discussing the dispatch of heavy ships, including first-class units, to the triangle Aden–Singapore–Simonstown before the end of the year.[49] At the beginning of October, the Chiefs of Staff were urged to send at least one battleship to the Far East by the C-in-C Far East, Air Chief Marshal Sir Robert Brooke-Popham, and the C-in-C China, Vice-Admiral Sir Geoffrey Layton.[50]

On 12 October, the Prime Minister served notice to the Admiralty that the issue was still very much open. Churchill vetoed a decision to send four 'R'-class battleships and the battleship *Rodney* to the Indian Ocean 'and possibly farther East as soon as possible', with the battleship *Nelson* to follow as soon as repaired, tartly noting to the First Sea Lord, 'This major Fleet movement has not been approved by me or by the Defence Committee. No action must be taken pending decision.'[51]

Just days later, the debate over naval reinforcements for the Far East suddenly assumed much greater urgency. On 16 October 1941, Japan's relatively moderate premier, Prince Kanoye, resigned with his entire cabinet, to be replaced by the more extreme General Tojo Hideki. Prince Takamatsu, Emperor Hirohito's brother, wrote that Japan had 'finally committed to war and now must do all we can to launch it powerfully', but admitted that the Japanese had 'clumsily telegraphed our intentions'.[52] Prince Takamatsu was correct; the change in government was indeed viewed in Washington and London as an ominous sign.

Notes

1 Naval Historical Branch, *War with Japan*, vol. 1, London, HMSO 1995, at 3.

2 C.M. Turnbull, *A History of Singapore 1819–1975*, Singapore, Oxford University Press, 1977, at 29, 41.

3 W. David McIntyre, *The Rise and Fall of the Singapore Naval Base*, Hamden, CT, Archon Books, 1979, at 41, 22.

4 'Insular Possessions and Dominions in the Pacific (Four-Power Treaty)', US Treaty Series 669.

5 'Limitation of Naval Armament (Five-Power Treaty or Washington Treaty)', US Treaty Series 671.

6 At the time, the term 'capital ship' effectively meant battleships and battlecruisers. The Washington Naval Treaty defined a capital ship as a vessel of war, not an aircraft carrier, whose displacement exceeded 10,000 tons or that carried a gun with a calibre exceeding 8in. During the Second World War, the term came to include aircraft carriers.

7 'Principles and Policies Concerning China', US Treaty Series 723.

8 McIntyre, *The Rise and Fall of the Singapore Naval Base*, at 135.

9 *Ibid.* at 6–7.

10 See generally McIntyre, *The Rise and Fall of the Singapore Naval Base.*

11 'International Treaty for the Limitation and Reduction of Naval Armament'.

12 McIntyre, *The Rise and Fall of the Singapore Naval Base*, at 140.

13 S.E. Morison, *History of United States Naval Operations in World War II, Vol. 3: The Rising Sun in the Pacific*, Edison, NJ, Castle Books, 1948, at 16–18.

14 Marder, *Old Friends, New Enemies*, at 88, 136; Naval Historical Branch, *War with Japan*, vol. 1, at 22.

· 15 The text of the treaty and related documents are found in John Chapman, *The Price of Admiralty*, vols 2 & 3, Ripe, East Sussex, Saltire Press, 1984, at 504–7.

16 Marder, *Old Friends, New Enemies*, at 120.

17 *Ibid.* at 157.

18 The Appreciation was provided to the Japanese by the German naval attaché in Tokyo, Rear Admiral Paul Wenneker, and to the Japanese naval attaché in Berlin, Admiral Yokoi. Chapman, *The Price of Admiralty*, vols 2 & 3, at 336–7.

19 'The Situation in the Far East in the Event of Japanese Intervention Against Us', COS (40) 592 (Revised), 15 August 1940. TNA Cab 121/765 and Cab 80/15. The Appreciation is described in some detail in Marder, *Old Friends, New Enemies*, at 85–6. An earlier version, dated 5 August 1940, can be found in TNA Cab 66/10. According to Admiral Wenneker's diary, the captured Appreciation was dated 15 August 1940. Chapman, *The Price of Admiralty*, vols 2 & 3, at 327.

20 Peter C. Smith and John Dominy, *Cruisers in Action 1939–1945*, London, William Kimber, 1981, at 123–4.

21 Peter Elphick, *Far Eastern File: The Intelligence War in the Far East 1930–1945*, London, Hodder & Stoughton, 1997, at 255–67.

22 After the war, Air Chief Marshal Robert Brooke-Popham was informed that the ship carrying the Appreciation had been sunk by a German submarine, and that 'it was not until after the war ended that we discovered that the German Submarine Commander managed to obtain the secret documents from the ship before sinking it'. Letter from Squadron-Leader G. Wiles to Brooke-Popham of 15 July 1948. Brooke-Popham Papers, Liddell-Hart Centre for Military Archives, Kings College, London. In a highly controversial book, James Rusbridger claimed that the British learned of the capture of the *Automedon*'s mail through a crewman named Sam Harper and through Norwegian sailors captured by the *Atlantis*. James Rusbridger and Eric Nave, *Betrayal at Pearl Harbor*, New York, Simon & Schuster, 1991, at 99 n. 29, 104. As for Harper, Peter Elphick wrote that Harper was not even asked about the mail, but he still considers it certain that the British knew that 'at the very least there was a chance that her secrets had fallen into German hands'. Elphick, *Far Eastern File*, at 264. As for the Norwegian sailors, Rusbridger gave as his source an incomplete reference to a document at the National Archives ('ADM/1135'). The Japanese naval attaché in Berlin was given a copy of the Appreciation and sent a message to Tokyo about it on 12 December 1940, but the message was sent in a code called 'Coral', which was not read by the United States until 1943. *Betrayal at Pearl Harbor*, at 101.

23 Richard J. Aldrich, *Intelligence and the War against Japan: Britain, America, and the Politics of Secret Service*, Cambridge, Cambridge University Press, 2000, at 48, citing Far East Combined Bureau to Air Ministry, WX2021, 12 January 1942, TNA Air 20/2160.

24 Marder, *Old Friends, New Enemies*, at 104.

25 Chapman, *The Price of Admiralty*, vols 2 & 3, at 337. The explanation in brackets is Professor Chapman's.

26 Marder, *Old Friends, New Enemies*, at 157–8.

27 *Ibid.* at 165–6.

28 Admiral Tom Phillips regarded this as 'France's most dastardly deed', for which it could never atone. Letter from Michael Goodenough to Stephen Roskill of 8 May 1951, Roskill Papers 4/79, Churchill Archive Centre, Churchill College, Cambridge University. Even if the French had really had a choice in the matter, they might not have been inclined to help the British after their attacks on French warships at Mers-el-Kebir and Dakar after the French had signed an armistice with Germany in June 1940. We will never know if the French would have resisted the Japanese more firmly in Indo-China if the incidents at Mers-el-Kebir and Dakar had not occurred.

29 Marder, *Old Friends, New Enemies*, at 165.

30 Edward S. Miller, *War Plan Orange*, Annapolis, Naval Institute Press, 1991, at 265.

31 Naval Historical Branch, *War with Japan*, vol. 1, at 41.

32 Report, United States-British Staff Conversations, 27 March 1941, para. 12. Naval Historical Branch, *War with Japan*, vol. 1, at 126.

33 Morison, *The Rising Sun in the Pacific*, at 53–5.

34 Marder, *Old Friends, New Enemies*, at 209.

35 Naval Historical Branch, *War with Japan*, vol. 1, at 97. Put another way, it is the line from the Kra Isthmus, the neck of land on the border between Thailand and Malaya, to Timor. Morison, *The Rising Sun in the Pacific*, at 49.

36 John Costello, *Days of Infamy*, New York, Pocket Books, 1994, at 74–5.

37 Miller, *War Plan Orange*, at 265.

38 *Ibid.* at 262–3.

39 Morison, *The Rising Sun in the Pacific*, at 56.

40 *Ibid.* at 57.

41 McIntyre, *The Rise and Fall of the Singapore Naval Base*, at 162.

42 *Ibid.* at 29, 113.

43 Christopher Bell, 'The "Singapore Strategy" and the Deterrence of Japan: Winston Churchill, the Admiralty and the Dispatch of Force Z', *English Historical Review* 116 (June 2001), at 613.

44 TNA Adm 116/4393.

45 Bell, 'The "Singapore Strategy" and the Deterrence of Japan: Winston Churchill, the Admiralty and the Dispatch of Force Z', at 614, citing TNA Adm 1/9767.

46 '1941 Far East (Naval Situation (I))', TNA Prem 3/163/3. Reproduced with permission of Curtis Brown Ltd, London, on behalf of the Estate of Sir Winston S. Churchill, as are all subsequent quotations from Mr Churchill's writings, books and speeches.

47 *Ibid.*

48 *Ibid.*

49 TNA Prem 3/163/3.

50 Marder, *Old Friends, New Enemies*, at 223, citing TNA Cab 84/35.

51 '1941 Far East (Naval Situation (I))', TNA Prem 3/163/3, at 54.

52 Herbert P. Bix, *Hirohito and the Making of Modern Japan*, New York, HarperCollins Publishers, 2000, at 419, 430.

CHAPTER TWO

Showdown

The fall of the Kanoye government set the stage for a showdown between Mr Churchill and the Admiralty over the question of naval reinforcements for the Far East. On 16 October, Foreign Secretary Anthony Eden again raised the issue of capital ship reinforcements for the Far East with Mr Churchill, and asked that the matter be taken up the next day at a meeting of the Defence Committee of the War Cabinet.[1] Mr Churchill did not have to be asked twice.

At the meeting on 17 October, Churchill reiterated the arguments he had put in writing to Pound back in August, and was supported by Foreign Secretary Anthony Eden and Clement Attlee. From a distance, Churchill's position was supported by a telegram received just that day from the Prime Minister of Australia, John Curtin, who referred to the telegram from Churchill of 2 September and requested a modern capital ship.[2]

As the meeting continued, Anthony Eden argued that from the point of view of deterring Japan from entering the war, the dispatch of a modern ship such as the *Prince of Wales* would have a far greater effect politically than a number of the last war's battleships. Attlee argued that the Admiralty's arguments assumed Britain would be prepared to remain on the defensive in Malalyan waters if Japan attacked Russia, and that such action would be hard to justify. Churchill invited the Admiralty to consider a proposal to send a modern capital ship, together with an aircraft carrier, to join up with the *Repulse* at Singapore. Dudley Pound was absent that day, and the Admiralty was represented by the civilian head of the Royal Navy, First Lord of the Admiralty A.V. Alexander, and the Vice-Chief of the Naval Staff, Admiral Sir Tom Phillips. Alexander argued that in the Far East Britain needed to protect its own trade routes rather than raid Japan's, and that another reason to have three battleships of the 'King George V' class in home waters was to have one available in the Western Mediterranean. Phillips argued that the four 'R's, with the *Nelson*, *Rodney* and *Renown*, would with shore-based air cover be enough to counter the Japanese, who like the British had a mixture of old and new capital ships. A final decision was put off until 20 October, when First Sea Lord Dudley Pound was to be present.[3] After the meeting on the 17th, Admiral Phillips forewarned the First Sea Lord of the Prime Minister's scathing attitude toward the Admiralty's position on the subject.[4]

At the fateful meeting on 20 October, the Prime Minister recapitulated the arguments he had made at the earlier meeting 'in favour of sending a fast modern battleship to the Far East to act as a deterrent to the Japanese', and was again supported by Anthony Eden. Churchill said the War Cabinet was prepared to accept the loss of shipping if the German battleship *Tirpitz* came out, and that 'the only thing which would induce caution in the Japanese would be the presence in Eastern Waters of a fast striking force', though he did not believe the Japanese would go to war against the British and the Americans. Dudley Pound argued against the move, and pointed out that, in addition to the *Tirpitz*, they had to worry about the German battlecruisers *Scharnhorst* and *Gneisenau*, which were then at the French port of Brest, and that one fast battleship would not prevent the Japanese from moving southwards, since they could easily put four modern battleships with any big convoy headed southward. Pressed hard by the committee, Pound suggested a compromise: the *Prince of Wales* would be sent forthwith to Cape Town, South Africa, 'a decision as to her onward journey being taken in the light of the situation when she arrived at Cape Town'. The committee adopted the compromise, and agreed to take a decision as to the ship's subsequent movements when she had arrived at her destination.[5]

The decision to send the *Prince of Wales* away led to a heated protest from Admiral Sir John Tovey, the C-in-C of the Home Fleet. He argued that recent operations showed that the ships of her class were inadequately ventilated for hot climates and wanted her to remain with the Home Fleet to counter the *Tirpitz*.[6]

Admiral Tovey's protest came to naught.[7] The day after the committee's decision, the Admiralty sent a message informing the Royal Navy that the *Prince of Wales*, wearing Admiral Phillips's flag, would leave the UK shortly for Singapore via the Cape.[8] On 23 October, the

British Admiralty Delegation in Washington informed the US Navy,[9] and on 25 October, Admiral Sir Geoffrey Layton, the C-in-C China, so informed Admiral Thomas Hart, the C-in-C of the US Asiatic Fleet, but asked him to keep the information to himself for the present.[10]

Before leaving to join the *Prince of Wales*, on 21 October Admiral Phillips was briefed at a conference at the Admiralty.[11] Unfortunately, there is no record of what was said.[12]

Notes

1 Minute from Eden to Churchill of 16 October 1941, TNA FO 371/27906, quoted in Roskill, 'Political Decisions Relating to the Sending of the Prince of Wales and the Repulse to the Far East'. Roskill Papers.

2 TNA Prem 3/163/3.

3 TNA Cab 69/2, at 369–70.

4 Letter from Phillips to Pound of 17 October 1941, quoted in Roskill, *Churchill and the Admirals*, at 197.

5 TNA Cab 69/8, at 39–41.

6 C-in-C Home Fleet to Admiralty, 2251A/20/10/41. Ship's Covers for 'King George V' Class, National Maritime Museum, Woolwich Arsenal.

7 It has been argued that the dispatch of the *Prince of Wales* to the Far East mattered little to the Admiralty, and that Churchill was outwitted into letting the Admiralty build up the Eastern Fleet and base it at Manila. Ian Cowman, 'Main Fleet to Singapore? Churchill, the Admiralty, and Force Z', *Journal of Strategic Studies* 17 (June 1994), 79–93. This 'elaborate conspiracy theory' has been shown to be without foundation by Christopher Bell in 'The "Singapore Strategy" and the Deterrence of Japan: Winston Churchill, the Admiralty and the Dispatch of Force Z', at 628–31. It is hard to believe that Pound would have openly disagreed with Churchill if it meant little to him.

8 See Appendix, No. 1, relying on the Admiralty War Diary for October 1941, TNA Adm 199/2232.

9 Letter from Admiral Sir Charles Little to Admiral H.R. Stark, attachment to letter from Dean Allard, US Naval Historical Center, to Arthur Marder of 2 July 1979. Marder Papers.

10 Letter of 25 October 1941. Admiral Thomas Hart Papers, Box 2, US Naval Historical Center, Operational Archives Branch, Washington Navy Yard.

11 According to Admiral Layton's secretary, Paymaster Captain Dougal Doig, Phillips's secretary (Paymaster Captain Thomas Beardsworth) told him that there was a 'historic' conference at the Admiralty on 21 October at which Admiral Phillips was briefed. Doig, 'Misfortune off Malaya', attachment to letter of 8 September 1978 from Doig to Arthur Marder. Marder Papers.

12 According to one source, at 1215 on 23 October Phillips had a final meeting with the Prime Minister. David Irving, *Churchill's War, Vol. 2: Triumph in Adversity*, London, Focal Point Productions Ltd, 2001, at 140, citing the PM's card.

CHAPTER THREE

The Choice of Tom Phillips

O ne of the more controversial aspects of the story of the *Prince of Wales* and *Repulse* has been the choice of Admiral Sir Tom Phillips to be the C-in-C of the Eastern Fleet. The decision actually predated the decision to send the *Prince of Wales* to Cape Town and the Far East. On 18 May 1941, Phillips was 'nominated' to command the Eastern Fleet 'if Japan comes into the war', but the appointment remained dormant until just before he sailed in the *Prince of Wales*.[1] The Admiralty informed Admiral Layton of the appointment in May 1941.[2] Of course, there was no possibility of sending capital ships to the Far East in May 1941: the *Bismarck* chase was about to begin.

While there is no official record of the circumstances of the choice, First Sea Lord Dudley Pound later wrote to Admiral Geoffrey Layton that he never regretted 'for a moment having recommended him for the appointment . . . '.[3] Such an important appointment must have been approved by the Prime Minister, who took great interest in such matters.[4] Phillips was given the rank of acting Admiral for his new post as C-in-C of the Eastern Fleet, and was to replace Admiral Layton, who was then C-in-C China.

At the time it was made, the choice of Tom Phillips, who because of his height (about 5ft 2in) was known to some as 'Tom Thumb', was not popular with Admiral Layton, nor with two of the 'fightin'est' admirals in the Royal Navy at the time, Vice-Admiral Sir Andrew Cunningham, the C-in-C of the Mediterranean Fleet, and Admiral Sir James Somerville, the commander of Force H at Gibraltar.[5] The choice naturally became even more controversial after the loss of the *Prince of Wales* and *Repulse*.

Tom Spencer Vaughan Phillips was born on 19 February 1888, at Pendennis Castle in Falmouth, the son of Colonel T.V.W. Phillips of the Royal Artillery. He became a naval cadet at HMS *Britannia* in 1903, and specialized in navigation. After serving in HMS *Bacchante* in the Dardanelles campaign, he spent much of the rest of the First World War 'marooned', as he described it, in HMS *Lancaster* in the Far East. After the war, Tom Phillips married a widow, Gladys Metcalfe, and raised her two sons and as well as their own son. Between the wars, his naval service included both seagoing and Admiralty staff appointments. His seagoing commands included the sloop *Verbena* from 1924 to 1925 and the cruiser *Hawkins* from 1932 to 1935, when he was also Chief of Staff to the C-in-C East Indies. Captain Tom Phillips was Director of Plans at the Admiralty from 1935 to 1938. In 1938, he was promoted to commodore and posted to the light cruiser HMS *Aurora* to command the Home Fleet's destroyer flotillas. In January 1939, he was promoted to rear admiral, and in May he became the Deputy Chief of the Naval Staff. In February 1940, the post was renamed Vice-Chief of the Naval Staff, and he was promoted to acting vice-admiral. While Phillips had some seagoing experience, much of his career was spent ashore at the Admiralty.

Much of the controversy over the choice of Tom Phillips is inevitably linked to the controversies over the key decisions he made. If his decisions are seen as correct, the choice looks good, and if the decisions are viewed as incorrect, the choice looks bad. What is important in analysing the choice of Tom Phillips is not a look at his decisions with the benefit of hindsight, but what Churchill and the Admiralty knew of him when the choice was made.

There was actually much to recommend Phillips for the post of Commander-in-Chief of the Eastern Fleet. As Vice-Chief of the Naval Staff, he was Dudley Pound's deputy and was as up to date on the war situation and the thinking in the Admiralty on the war as one could be. According to Captain Bell, Phillips 'had a knack of getting along well with others outside the Navy: the Services, civil servants, diplomats, and particularly Foreign Naval officers'.[6] Captain Bell's judgement is borne out by the opinions of others: Field Marshal Smuts told Churchill that Phillips was an 'admirable choice',[7] and after Phillips's death, Smuts told Churchill that he had 'formed a very high opinion' of Phillips.[8] The C-in-C of the US Asiatic Fleet, Admiral Thomas C. Hart, wrote that he had acquired considerable respect for Phillips, who was 'as good an Englishman to work with as I have had for some time'.[9] As

Director of Plans at the Admiralty, he had in 1938 met US Navy Captain Royal Ingersoll to discuss the naval situation in the Far East.[10] From a distance, Phillips was even respected and admired by Admiral Ozawa,[11] who would be one of his chief opponents in the battle and who turned out to be one of the greatest Japanese admirals of the war.

Perhaps most importantly, Tom Phillips had the complete respect and confidence of First Sea Lord Dudley Pound and First Lord A.V. Alexander, who were sorry to see him leave the Admiralty. Phillips had once been close to Winston Churchill, but by 1941 their relationship had become strained,[12] perhaps by Phillips's opposition to two of Churchill's pet projects, the dispatch of British forces to assist Greece against the Italians and the retaliatory bombing of German cities. According to his friend Mildred Barker, 'He had the greatest respect for the P.M. but did not always agree with him and was outspoken enough to say so. . . . I remember his saying that he did not think the P.M. liked being opposed, but he had to do it.'[13] Although it is sometimes said that Churchill used the appointment of Phillips to the Eastern Fleet to get rid of him, as far as we know the appointment was prompted by Dudley Pound's recommendation, not by Churchill. Although Churchill may not have been sorry to see Phillips go, there is no evidence he actually tried to get rid of him, and Tom Phillips's willingness to oppose the Prime Minister should be seen as an admirable example of moral courage.

Personally, Tom Phillips was an exceptional and complicated man, with great strengths and a few notable weaknesses. As a leader, he inspired great loyalty and devotion in some of his subordinates, notably his Staff Officer (Plans), Michael Goodenough, his assistant secretary Lieutenant Kenneth Farnhill, and his flag lieutenant, B.R. Armitage, but he did not otherwise have the sort of inspirational personality one might expect in a C-in-C.[14] He could be difficult to get along with. No one could doubt that Tom Phillips was extremely intelligent: one of his contemporaries thought he was the most intelligent man in a term at HMS *Britannia* that produced six admirals, with an 'ingenious and restless mind'.[15] There were some in the Royal Navy, including Admiral Layton, who thought Tom Phillips tended to be more theoretical than practical,[16] a trait that may have had serious consequences in the Battle off Malaya.

Tom Phillips also tended to be opinionated and thought he was almost always right.[17] But he was right on some very important matters. For instance, he opposed the bombing of German cities and the dispatch of troops to assist Greece in 1940–1, which resulted in a costly reverse when the Germans invaded Greece. On 25 April 1941, he had urged the Chiefs of Staff to send tanks and battle-tested Hawker Hurricane fighters to Malaya, as he was prophetically unconvinced of the merits of an untested American-built fighter, the Brewster Buffalo. To his great bitterness, he did not prevail on either count;[18] no tanks were sent to Malaya, and hundreds of Hurricanes were sent to help the Soviet Union. If Phillips's advice had been followed on either count, things might have turned out quite differently in the Far East.

Regardless of whether Pound was aware of Phillips's weaknesses, there was another reason for Pound to have had reservations about Phillips's appointment. Phillips was a brilliant staff officer, but he had had little seagoing command experience, and had seen no combat so far in the war. Tom Phillips has been characterized as an 'old sea-dog', but, with no disrespect to old sea-dogs, he was really more of a 'Whitehall warrior', an Admiralty staff officer, and his detractors, Admirals Cunningham, Somerville and Layton, were the old sea-dogs. As we shall see, Tom Phillips was slower than some in the Royal Navy to accept the threat that aircraft posed to ships, and perhaps kept his faith in the power of the battleship longer than some others.

It has been suggested that Admiral Layton should have been designated C-in-C Eastern Fleet instead of Tom Phillips. Layton had been C-in-C China since September 1940, and an officer who served on his staff describes him as 'a seasoned, shrewd officer', who had been a submarine commander in the First World War, who had commanded the Fifth Cruiser Squadron in the North Sea early in the Second World War, and who 'knew the realities of modern sea warfare and the vital role of air power. . . . He was a rough, tough old man, of deep religious belief well disguised, not much liked, but he knew his onions.'[19] Geoffrey Layton's fighting qualities were not doubted by anyone, and he had a higher, and more realistic, opinion of the fighting qualities of the Japanese than the Admiralty and most senior officers.[20]

However, the post of C-in-C Eastern Fleet also required the ability to work with Britain's probable allies, the Netherlands and the United States, and the Admiralty would not have expected Layton to be the diplomat Phillips was. To Layton's credit, before the war US Admiral Thomas Hart wrote that Layton 'has my people's entire liking and respect – as a fine example of the blue-water school of the Royal Navy. He is direct, frank and forceful.'[21] Whether that impression would have held once the war began is open to question, since Layton was quick to be harshly critical of the Americans, as early as in an 18 December letter to Dudley Pound.[22] If Layton had been put in the same position as Tom Phillips, we will never know if he would have done anything differently, except that, having commanded ships subjected to air attack by the Germans earlier in the war, he might well have broken radio silence and called for air cover much earlier than Phillips.

Perhaps the difficulty with the appointment of Admiral Phillips is that the C-in-C Eastern Fleet was given two very different jobs – the strategic direction of the Eastern Fleet and cooperation with the Dutch and Americans as well as its tactical command at sea. In April 1941, Admiral Layton had warned the Admiralty against having the supreme naval command in the Far East afloat,[23] but his advice was not heeded. Phillips was well equipped for the former job, as Dudley Pound well knew, but perhaps he should have known that he was not as well equipped for the latter. It would have been better if Phillips had picked a staff that had already experienced combat at sea, but that was not the way it happened. Admiral Layton would have been better equipped for the latter job, but not so well equipped for the former. As it turned out, war in the Far East could not be avoided, and the C-in-C Eastern Fleet had to do both jobs.

When Phillips was nominated to be C-in-C Eastern Fleet in May 1941, Pound and Alexander must have thought his outstanding qualities far outweighed any less-outstanding ones. It certainly would have been hard to foresee in May 1941 that Tom Phillips would find himself in the middle of the South China Sea in December 1941 needing to call for air cover!

Once he was appointed, Phillips wanted to go out to the Far East in June of 1941 to get busy strengthening Singapore and the Far East, but that did not happen.[24] Instead, he was not able to leave until October 1941, when the decision was made for him to sail with the *Prince of Wales* to Cape Town – and beyond.

Notes

1 Letter from Captain L.H. Bell to Marder of 2 March 1975. Marder Papers.
2 That is essentially what the Admiralty told Admiral Layton. Layton, 'Supplemental Report on Events in the Far East, 1940/45', 25 April 1947. TNA Adm 199/1472B.
3 Pound to Layton of 12 February 1942. Layton Papers, British Library.
4 Roskill, *Churchill and the Admirals*, at 279–80.
5 Marder, *Old Friends, New Enemies*, at 365–6.
6 Letter from L.H. Bell to Marder of 24 March 1975. Marder Papers.
7 Telegram from Smuts to Churchill of 18 November 1941. TNA Prem 3/163/3.

8 Telegram of 12 December 1941. TNA Prem 3/162/3, at 34.

9 Hart diary entry, enclosure to letter from Kathleen Lloyd, Head, Operational Archives Branch, US Naval Historical Center, to the author of 30 July 2003.

10 James Leutze, *A Different Kind of Victory: A Biography of Admiral Thomas C. Hart*, Annapolis, Naval Institute Press, 1981, at 139–40.

11 Marder, *Old Friends, New Enemies*, at 447.

12 According to Admiral John Godfrey, Phillips had 'sorrowfully confessed that he had lost the PM's confidence, was held at arm's length, and had not seen him for two months'. Donald McLachlan, *Room 39: A Study in Naval Intelligence*, New York, Atheneum, 1968, at 350.

13 Letter from Mildred Barker to Commander T.V.G. Phillips of 22 March 1962. T.V.G. Phillips Papers, by Courtesy of Mrs T.V.G. Phillips.

14 Marder, *Old Friends, New Enemies*, at 370–1, 374.

15 Admiral J.H. Godrey, 'The Navy and Naval Intelligence 1939–1942: Afterthoughts', 1947. TNA Adm 223/619.

16 Layton told his secretary that he thought Phillips was a theorist who clung to his opinions even when all the facts were against him, and who lacked practical experience. Attachment to letter from Paymaster Captain Dougal Doig to Arthur Marder of 20 October 1978; letter from Commander H.N.S. Brown, Admiral Phillips's Fleet Gunnery Officer, to Arthur Marder of 5 January 1979 ('more theoretical than practical, e.g., he didn't handle his ship as a born seaman'); letter from Admiral John Litchfield to Arthur Marder of 14 May 1975 ('a theorist rather than a man of action, better in Whitehall than on the bridge'). All from Marder Papers.

17 Marder, *Old Friends, New Enemies*, at 370.

18 TNA Cab 79/11, at 72–3.

19 Letter from Paymaster Commander W.T. Blunt to the author, undated but in reply to the author's letter of 8 December 1998.

20 No one, however, is perfect, and even Layton underestimated the Japanese in what must have been one of the least prophetic signals of the war. On 13 February 1942, he informed the Admiralty that 'Evidence is accumulating which seems to confirm pre-war impressions that Japanese ships do not take kindly to night fighting. . . . [W]e should exploit this feature of Japanese to the utmost, and our policy should be to seek night actions by every means. . . .' Signal of 1302Z/13/2/42, TNA Cab 105/20. The Japanese were to prove Layton thoroughly wrong in the night-time part of the Battle of the Java Sea and in many night battles around Guadalcanal.

21 Leutze, *A Different Kind of Victory*, at 196.

22 Layton wrote, 'The Dutch are playing up 100 per cent. I wish I could say the same about the Yanks. I think the attack on Pearl Harbour has shaken them and in the end may prove to be a beneficial dose of medicine, but not now.' Letter from Layton to Dudley Pound of 18 December 1941. Layton Papers, British Library.

23 TNA Adm 199/1472B, at 6.

24 Letter from Lady Phillips to Captain Russell Grenfell of 28 November 1950. Grenfell Papers, Churchill Archive Centre, Churchill College, Cambridge.

CHAPTER FOUR

Off to Singapore

The *Prince of Wales* sailed from the Home Fleet's base at Scapa Flow in the Orkney Islands on 23 October 1941, escorted by the destroyers *Express* and *Electra*. On 24 October, the *Prince of Wales* was joined at Greenock, Scotland, by Admiral Sir Tom Phillips, the C-in-C of the new British Eastern Fleet, and his staff.

The Admiral's sizeable staff included Rear Admiral Arthur Palliser as his Chief of Staff, and Commander Michael Goodenough as his Staff Officer (Plans). Commodore Ralph Edwards was to be the seagoing 'Chief Staff Officer', with Admiral Palliser to remain ashore at Singapore,[1] but Commodore Edwards did not arrive in the Far East until too late. Instead, Phillips's seagoing Chief of Staff was to be another member of his staff, Captain L.H. Bell, the Captain of the Fleet. With Admiral Phillips and his staff aboard, the voyage to the Far East began on 25 October 1941, and the small force was known for the moment as 'Force G'.

On the voyage to the Far East, the men aboard *Prince of Wales*, *Express* and *Electra* found various ways to pass the time. Some studied for promotions, and most would have written home. Admiral Phillips wrote to his son Jerry, Midshipman T.V.G. Phillips, who was then in the destroyer HMS *Jackal* in the Mediterranean Fleet. He penned, 'We had a crossing the line ceremony on the way down – quite good – I had to meet Neptune and Amphitrite on the quarter deck [and] there were so many of the ship's company who had never crossed the line before.'[2] He also wrote, 'I am longing to hear of all your experiences in *Jackal*; they must have been pretty tough at times.' The younger Phillips could have given his father quite an earful: while in the *Jackal* during the Battle of Crete the previous May, the son had witnessed the German dive-bombing of the armoured aircraft carrier *Formidable* and the destroyer *Nubian*.[3] The letter's father-to-son closing, 'Bye, bye, Old Man, take care of yourself. . . . I look forward so much to seeing you again,' belies the popular image of the highly intelligent but impersonal Tom Phillips.[4]

The long voyage was not without its lighter moments, at least for the men of the destroyers. The gunnery officer of the *Electra* recalled:

> We were very light of heart during the voyage out, and quickly engaged in a good-natured duel with our betters, the officers of the Flagship. . . . Phillips had brought his own staff with him from the Admiralty, and as the 'staffies' could not be expected to keep up to date with every routine order affecting the day-to-day running of the Fleet, their instructions to us sometimes went awry, and gave us the opportunity – so dear to every seaman's heart – of scoring against the Flagship.[5]

After the *Electra* had pointed out yet another fleet order the Admiral's staff had missed, she was sent this signal from the *Prince of Wales*: 'I will catch you yet with your trousers down, you villain. So good luck to you, for you will be ruddy well needing it. Your inveterate enemy, Staffie.'[6]

The *Prince of Wales* first anchored at Freetown, and then from 16 to 18 November she docked at Cape Town, South Africa. The men of Force G were treated to a memorably friendly reception by the local population. Admiral Phillips flew to Pretoria to visit the legendary Field Marshal Jan Smuts, who was most impressed with Phillips, but worried that because the fleets based on Hawaii and Singapore were each inferior to the Japanese and could be defeated in turn, there was an opening for a 'first-class disaster' if the Japanese were really 'nippy'.[7]

On 18 November, the *Prince of Wales* and her destroyers left the Cape and entered the Indian Ocean. Even though the Chiefs of Staff Committee had not met again to decide her movements, there could be no doubt but that the *Prince of Wales* was sailing for Singapore.

The *Prince of Wales* and her escorts then crossed the Indian Ocean, and, after refuelling stops at Mauritius and the secret base at Addu Atoll,[8] reached Ceylon. There would be no dawdling there either: Admiral Phillips and some of his staff flew ahead to Singapore on 28 November, and the *Prince of Wales* and her destroyers rendezvoused with the battlecruiser *Repulse* off Ceylon. The *Repulse* had left Scapa Flow on 29 August 1941,[9] and proceeded to Cape Town, where her crew was addressed by Field Marshal Jan Smuts, and then to Mombasa in East Africa, before reaching Ceylon. Joined by the destroyers *Jupiter* and *Encounter*, which had been begged and borrowed from the Mediterranean Fleet, the ships headed for Singapore.

The Japanese were not unaware of what was coming. The appearance of the *Prince of Wales* at Cape Town was noted by the Japanese consul-general there, who commented on the *Prince of Wales*'s camouflage and on the authorities' allowing information to be published, suggesting that this was 'a warning from the democracies and an attempt to stimulate the morale of the South Africans who have special connections with this powerful and historic battleship'.[10] By 24 November, the Imperial Japanese Navy had learned that the *Prince of Wales* had left Cape Town on 18 November for the Indian Ocean. On 28 November, it was reported (not very accurately) that the *King George V*, the *Revenge*, the *Renown* and possibly the *Repulse* were in the Indian Ocean, and that the *Prince of Wales* was probably going to Singapore. On 2 December, the Japanese learned that the *Prince of Wales* had entered Colombo on 28 November and left the next day for Singapore.[11]

The long-awaited 'fleet' was about to arrive at Singapore.

Notes

1 So that Admiral Phillips could fly his flag afloat, he was to have a Chief of Staff to deputize for him ashore and a 'Chief Staff Officer' to remain afloat. TNA Adm 116/4877, at 87–8.

2 Tom Phillips played King Neptune in the ceremony. Letter from Lieutenant-Commander Dick Caldwell to Marder of 31 March 1975. Marder Papers.

3 John Wingate, *Never So Proud: Crete, May, 1941, The Battle and Evacuation*, New York, Meredith Press, 1966, at 132–6, 150–3.

4 Letter of 14 November 1941. T.V.G. Phillips Papers.

5 T.J. Cain and A.V. Sellwood, *H.M.S. Electra*, London, Frederick Muller Ltd, 1959, at 148.

6 *Ibid.* at 155.

7 Telegram of 18 November 1941. TNA Prem 3/163/3.

8 Geoffrey Brooke, *Alarm Starboard!*, Cambridge, Patrick Stephens, 1982, at 91.

9 Letter from David Brown, Naval Historical Branch, to Arthur Marder of 12 October 1978. Marder Papers.

10 Message to the Foreign Minister of 29 November 1941. TNA HW 1/296, by courtesy of Mr John Parkinson.

11 Ohtsuka Bunichi, trans., Military History Office, National Defense College, *Daitoa (Taiheiyo) Senso Kokan Senshi sosho (Greater East Asia War)*, Vol. 24: *Hito Mare kaigun shinko sakusen (Naval Advance Operations into the Philippines and Malay Area)*, Tokyo, Asakumo Shimunsha, 1969 (hereinafter Official Japanese History), at 116.

CHAPTER FIVE

The Decision to Send the Prince of Wales and Repulse to Singapore

There were really two crucial decisions leading up to the arrival of the *Prince of Wales* and *Repulse* in Singapore: the first was the on-the-record decision to send the *Prince of Wales* to Cape Town, and the second was the off-the-record decision to send the *Prince of Wales* and also the *Repulse* on to Singapore. The Prime Minister's memoirs are of little help in explaining the two decisions; after describing in some detail the exchanges between him and Dudley Pound on the matter in August 1941, he wrote,

> It was decided to send as the first instalment of our Far Eastern Fleet both the *Prince of Wales* and the *Repulse*, with four destroyers, and as an essential element the modern armoured aircraft carrier *Indomitable*. Unhappily the *Indomitable* was temporarily disabled in an accident. It was decided in spite of this to let the two fast capital ships go forward, in the hope of steadying the Japanese political situation, and also to be in relation to the United States Pacific Fleet.[1]

In using the passive voice – 'it was decided' – this rather sparse passage tells us nothing about the contentious meetings on 17 and 20 October. Nor does it tell us anything about how it was decided, and by whom, that the *Prince of Wales* would sail on from Cape Town to Singapore.

The on-the-record decision at the 20 October Chiefs of Staff Committee meeting was to send the *Prince of Wales* to Cape Town, with 'a decision as to her onward journey being taken in the light of the situation when she arrived at Cape Town'. In effect, the decision was a compromise between Churchill and Eden, who were determined to send a modern battleship to the Far East, and Dudley Pound and A.V. Alexander, who were opposed to just such a course of action. The compromise resulted from Pound finding himself backed into a corner where he could not use his usual strategy of not saying a direct 'no' to Churchill, but of delaying and pointing out the weaknesses in a bad idea until Churchill himself realized it was a bad idea.[2]

Unfortunately, the compromise proposed by Pound and adopted by the Chiefs of Staff Committee made no sense. There was no reason to send the new C-in-C Eastern Fleet and his staff to Cape Town, and at Cape Town the *Prince of Wales* would be far from anywhere that she could be of any real use. Since recalling her to the Home Fleet would have been admitting a mistake, and since no one was proposing to send her through the Suez Canal to join the Mediterranean Fleet, the Far East was the only possible realistic destination for the *Prince of Wales*.

The second and more important of the two decisions was the off-the-record decision to send the *Prince of Wales*, as well as the *Repulse*, on to Singapore. The question of the *Prince of Wales*'s ultimate destination was never submitted to the Chiefs of Staff Committee for a decision. The Chiefs of Staff did not consider the movements of the *Prince of Wales* again until a meeting on 6 December, after she had arrived at Singapore and after Japanese convoys had been sighted, and then not again until a meeting on the evening of 9 December, when she had already gone to sea.

It is amazing that such a critical decision was not recorded officially, at least not in any document that has survived, and naval historian Stephen Roskill could find no record of it in the Admiralty's or the Prime Minister's papers.[3] Since the decision was not in writing, one might have expected Mr Churchill to object to anyone pinning the decision on him, since when he became Prime Minister he had insisted that he would not accept responsibility for decisions he was alleged to have given unless they were recorded in writing.[4] However, in his memoirs he did not do so.

Indeed, there is reason to believe that Churchill *did* participate in the decision. According to Captain (later Admiral) Ronald Brockman, who was Pound's secretary at the time, 'I am pretty sure myself that the decision [to send the ships to Singapore] subsequent to the Defence Committee meeting was taken by the Prime Minister direct with Sir Dudley Pound.'[5] According to Colonel Ian Jacob, who was then on the Defence Committee staff, naval questions that were unresolved in Defence Committee meetings were pursued afterwards by Pound and

Churchill. While Colonel Jacob did not know if Pound had raised the question of the *Prince of Wales* with Churchill, he said the question was presumably settled by Pound and Churchill.[6] Indeed, it is hard to see how it could have been otherwise: since Dudley Pound was against sending the *Prince of Wales* to Singapore in the first place, he certainly would not have made the decision on his own.

Assuming the matter was settled privately between Pound and Churchill, it is not so easy to determine when it was so settled, because the messages we have on the subject are so mixed. For example, the Admiralty seems to have thrown in the towel right away, informing the Royal Navy on 21 October that the *Prince of Wales* was heading for Singapore via the Cape,[7] but Mr Churchill continued for a time to observe the decision of the Defence Committee. On 25 October Churchill told the Prime Minister of Australia, 'I must however make it clear that movements of *Prince of Wales* must be reviewed when she is at Cape Town.'[8] On 2 November, Dudley Pound told Mr Churchill that it was his intention to review the situation generally just before the *Prince of Wales* reached the Cape, to which Churchill noted 'Yes'. Churchill informed the Defence Committee on 5 November that the *Prince of Wales* was 'on her way to Cape Town and likely to proceed to Singapore'.[9] On 9 November, the Admiralty informed the naval base at Simonstown, South Africa, that the urgency of Admiral Phillips's arrival at Singapore necessitated 'the stay of *Prince of Wales* being as short as possible over 48 hours'.[10] That same day, Dudley Pound lunched with the Prime Minister at Chequers.[11]

The next day, 10 November, Mr Churchill gave a speech at the Guildhall banquet at Mansion House in London, and sent a veiled – but nevertheless clear – warning to Japan:

> I am able to go further and announce to you here at the Lord Mayor's annual celebration that we now feel ourselves strong enough to provide a powerful naval force of heavy ships, with its necessary ancillary vessels, for service if needed in the Indian and Pacific Oceans. . . . And this movement of our naval forces, in conjunction with the United States Main Fleet, may give a practical proof to all who have eyes that the forces of freedom and democracy have not by any means reached the limits of their power.[12]

One might well wonder what the Prime Minister meant by 'necessary ancillary vessels'! Mr Churchill chose to quote another part of the speech in *The Grand Alliance*, the third volume of his series on the Second World War, but left out this part.[13]

If the matter had not been settled by the time of the speech at the Guildhall banquet, it was certainly settled by 12 November. At a meeting of the War Cabinet on that date, the First Sea Lord effectively acknowledged that the *Prince of Wales* was going beyond Cape Town to Singapore when he said that by January/February 1942 'our Far Eastern Battle Fleet' would be composed of the *Prince of Wales*, one battlecruiser (*Repulse* or *Renown*), and four 'R'-class capital ships.[14]

Assuming the decision was taken by Churchill and Pound by 12 November that the *Prince of Wales*, and the *Repulse* as well, would go to Singapore, we can only speculate as to how the decision was made. Perhaps Pound realized how little sense it made to keep the *Prince of Wales* at Cape Town, and faced the reality that she must go to Singapore. Perhaps he realized that the Prime Minister's Guildhall banquet speech had effectively decided the matter: since the PM had publicly promised reinforcements for the Far East, the *Prince of Wales* would have to go to Singapore. On 18 November, Pound told Churchill that the *Prince of Wales*'s arrival at Cape Town, taken in conjunction with what Churchill had said in his speech at the Guildhall banquet, 'will leave neither the Japanese, nor our press, in doubt as to the eventual destination of the *Prince of Wales*';[15] that 'eventual destination' could only have meant Singapore.

Pound must eventually have agreed to the move, however reluctantly, since he later wrote to Churchill that he had been able to say 'quite definitely' that it was in accordance with his advice.[16] Pound told Admiral John Godfrey that Churchill 'wore him down'.[17] We will probably never know exactly how it went, since Pound fell gravely ill by August 1943 and died on Trafalgar Day, 21 October 1943, but that seems like a very plausible explanation.

As it was proposed by Mr Churchill, the decision to send the *Prince of Wales* and the *Repulse* to Singapore was based on two assumptions. The first was that the *Prince of Wales* was not needed to counter the *Tirpitz* in the Atlantic, and the second was that the news of the *Prince of Wales*'s voyage to the Far East would act as a deterrent on Japan. On the first assumption, Mr Churchill was either right or lucky, but the second assumption was fatally flawed.

With respect to the assumption regarding the *Tirpitz*, Mr Churchill fully realized he was taking a gamble, and the gamble paid off. *Tirpitz* was never sent into the North Atlantic, and when she sailed against two Arctic convoys to the Soviet Union, the *Prince of Wales* was not needed. On the first occasion, in March 1942, the Royal Navy was able to field the modern battleships *King George V* and *Duke of York* and the battlecruiser *Renown*. They were not able to bring the *Tirpitz* to battle, but she made port only after a very narrow escape from torpedo-bombers from the carrier *Victorious*. On the second occasion, in July 1942, the Royal Navy was able to field only the *Duke of York*, as the *King George V* had been damaged in a collision in June, thus demonstrating why the First Sea Lord had wanted three 'King George V' class battleships available in case of refit or damage to one of them. Nevertheless, because of the entry of the United States into the war in December, the modern US battleship *Washington* was sailing with the *Duke of York*, and the problem was not a lack of capital ships. When the *Tirpitz* finally sailed against Convoy PQ-17, the *Duke of York* and *Washington* were too far away to help, and the spectre of the appearance of the *Tirpitz* on the horizon prompted the Admiralty to order the convoy to scatter, and it was destroyed by German aircraft and U-boats. The *Tirpitz* was never again a threat; she was damaged by British midget submarines in 1943, then damaged again by Fleet Air Arm bombers in April 1944, and finished off by 12,000lb bombs dropped by RAF Lancaster bombers in November 1944.

As Pound pointed out, the *Tirpitz* was not the only threat. The battlecruisers *Scharnhorst* and *Gneisenau* were also a danger, but they were constantly harassed by the RAF in Brest, and sneaked up the English Channel to Germany in February 1942. They never combined with the *Tirpitz* in an operation of any importance: the *Gneisenau* was badly bombed by the RAF shortly after her arrival in Germany, and the *Scharnhorst* was sunk by the British off the North Cape in December 1943. In that battle, the *Duke of York* was the only battleship available, but she was enough.

If Churchill's gamble had not paid off, say if the Germans had been bolder in their employment of the *Tirpitz*, *Scharnhorst* and *Gneisenau*, the consequences for Britain could have been disastrous; as Dudley Pound suggested, the British could have lost the war in the Atlantic. In war, great risks must sometimes be taken, and this one paid off.

Before moving to the second assumption, it is worth noting that Churchill denigrated the ships of the 'King George V' class when the Admiralty proposed keeping three to counter the *Tirpitz*, but turned around and argued that one of the same ships would deter the Japanese from going to war. In neither case was Churchill accurately evaluating the ships; they were not too undergunned to fight the *Tirpitz* and did not suffer from any defect from having a catapult and hangar amidships. The Admiralty wanted three, not because the *Tirpitz* was three times more powerful, but to have two available for better odds in an engagement, and a third on hand in case one was unavailable due to refit or repair, as actually occurred with the *King George V* herself.

As for the second assumption in the decision to send the *Prince of Wales* to the Far East, that the dispatch of the *Prince of Wales* to the Far East would deter Japan from going to war, it turned out, for several reasons, that the news of her arrival at Cape Town and then Singapore had no deterrent effect on the Japanese at all. In the first place, the timing of the move was off. Japan decided on war at an Imperial Conference on 2 November, after the *Prince of Wales* had sailed but before she called at Cape Town and was first noticed by the Japanese, and Japan made the final decision for war on 1 December, the day before she arrived in Singapore but after Japan had received intelligence of her probable move to Singapore.

Even if the British timing had not been off, it was not reasonable to expect that Japan would be deterred by a single capital ship, even a modern one. Churchill, who had a habit of underestimating the Japanese, anyway,[18] overestimated the effect the *Prince of Wales* would have on Japanese plans in the light of Japan's determination to go to war. Even if battleships still retained some of their symbolic importance by 1941, the 'King George Vs' were not super-battleships; while the Japanese Navy had great respect for them, there was no reason to think the Japanese decision-makers would quake at the thought of one of them at Singapore, thousands of miles away. Churchill thought in terms of the effect the German battleships *Bismarck* and *Tirpitz* had on British naval strategy and deployments, but the situation in the Far East was totally different. Japan had ten capital ships of its own, all older than the *Prince of Wales* but considerably modernized, and with the super-battleship *Yamato* about to be completed. Although Japan depended on trade, it did not have a lifeline like the North Atlantic, and the *Prince of Wales*, with her limited range, like her sister ships, was no commerce raider.

In fairness to Mr Churchill, he was not the only man in Britain, or in the United States for that matter, who never dreamed that the Japanese would go to war with both Britain and the United States in the all-out way they did; it was thought by some that Japan would move cautiously, as she had to that point, and that a comparatively small reinforcement like the *Prince of Wales* and an aircraft carrier 'might tip the scales in favour of even more caution' on the part of the Japanese.[19] Nor was Churchill the only figure to push for the dispatch of a few capital ships to Singapore in the hope that they might influence Japan not to go to war. Still, that does not excuse the miscalculation on his part. Churchill did not appreciate Japan's determination to risk everything in the war; it believed its survival depended on doing so, and a single modern capital ship would not dissuade it when it was already ready to take on the entire United States Navy.

To expect Japan to be deterred by the *Prince of Wales* was little better than wishful thinking. Admiral John Godfrey, the Director of Naval Intelligence at the time the ships were sent out, later recalled,

> Undoubtedly we were badly at fault about the effect of the arrival of the 'Prince of Wales' and 'Repulse', the forerunners of a big Pacific fleet, on Japanese aggression in South-East Asia. We all got an idée fixe, and even went so far as to advertise their departure from the Cape. As part of a properly balanced fleet with its own anti-submarine and anti-aircraft, fighter protection, we might have impressed the Japanese, but the 'forerunner' idea was wishfulness pure and simple.[20]

The wishful thinking was not limited to the Prime Minister, and lasted up to the very last moment. On 6 December, presumably before Japanese convoys had been sighted, Admiral Pound wrote to Admiral Sir Charles Little, head of the British Admiralty Delegation in Washington:

> At the moment we are all wondering what the Japanese are going to do. I think it is quite possible that the arrival of PoW [*Prince of Wales*] at Singapore may have made them hesitate, as surely it will necessitate their sending an escort of capital ships with any expedition to the South.[21]

Thanks to the publicity of the *Prince of Wales*'s arrival at Singapore, the Japanese *had* provided an escort of capital ships with their southward expedition, and were not hesitating at all.

As it turns out, the threat of the *Prince of Wales* was dealt with not by Japanese political leaders, who had already made their decisions, but by the Imperial Japanese Navy, specifically Admiral Yamamoto Isoroku. This revealed a fatal flaw in the British plan.

No one seems to have considered the danger that if the Japanese declined to be deterred, all this publicity was equivalent to providing them with operational intelligence of the highest value.[22]

And so it did. The arrival and departure of the *Prince of Wales* at Cape Town and the announcement of the arrival of the *Prince of Wales* at Singapore caused Admiral Yamamoto to redeploy two battlecruisers to the Southern Force, and then part of the Kanoya Air Group from Formosa to Saigon. It was those bombers that ultimately made the decisive difference.

While it was little better than wishful thinking to send the *Prince of Wales* and *Repulse* to Singapore to deter Japan from going to war, it would have made a bit more sense *if* there had been some planning for what to do with the ships should deterrence fail and the Japanese went to war anyway, and *if* the ships had been made part of a more balanced force. Unfortunately, neither was done.

When the Japanese convoys were sighted at sea on 6 December, it should have been abundantly clear that Japan had not been deterred, but there seems to have been no plan for what to do with the *Prince of Wales* and *Repulse* in that eventuality. Instead, two very valuable capital ships were left in an uncomfortably forward area and were drawn into the battle for Malaya and Singapore. In an August 1941 minute to the Prime Minister on the disposition of capital ships and aircraft carriers, Dudley Pound wrote regarding the dispatch of ships to Singapore, 'If war eventuated they would have to retire to Trincomalee [in Ceylon]',[23] but that idea seems to have gone by the wayside by December 1941. Perhaps if the decision in October 1941 had been to send the *Prince of Wales* to Singapore instead of Cape Town, Mr Churchill and the Chiefs of Staff could have discussed what to do with the *Prince of Wales* and *Repulse* if Japan was not deterred by them; instead, because of the hackneyed compromise that was reached, no such discussion took place.

In addition to not planning what to do with the ships in case deterrence failed, Churchill and the Admiralty did not provide the *Prince of Wales* and *Repulse* with anything like a balanced force of modern warships. *The Times* reported on 6 December 1941 that the Eastern Fleet was 'fully constituted' and that at Singapore were 'some of the most modern cruisers and destroyers',[24] but it was just not so; Force Z sorely lacked modern cruisers and enough modern destroyers, not to mention an aircraft carrier.

If the *Prince of Wales* and *Repulse* had been made part of a balanced force, they would have been less vulnerable themselves and could have formed a fast striking force, which older and slower battleships could not have done. Such a force could have created major problems for the Japanese, who, instead of concentrating their forces in one place, as Field Marshal Smuts feared, attacked nearly simultaneously on a number of very widely separated fronts from Malaya to Pearl Harbor. It should not have taken much, even with the crippling of the battleships of the US Pacific Fleet, to disrupt the Japanese plan and timetable. For example, the Japanese attacked Wake Island on 11 December, but suffered a bloody nose at the hands of the US Marines there, and had to return with a much greater force on 23 December to overwhelm the garrison. Even at the Battle of the Java Sea, the Japanese did not muster an overwhelmingly superior naval force to defeat the Allies, and the presence of the *Prince of Wales* and the *Repulse* could have seriously altered the equation.

As for the lack of an aircraft carrier, Churchill wrote in his memoirs that an 'essential element' of the new Eastern Fleet, along with the *Prince of Wales* and *Repulse*, was the modern armoured aircraft carrier *Indomitable*,[25] and it has often been lamented that she went aground on 3 November 1941, while working up in the West Indies, and could not join Force Z in time. After the *Indomitable* had been quickly repaired in the United States, she was sent back to the West Indies to continue her work-up. The *Indomitable* was not actually ordered to sail for the Far East until 10 December.[26] When the *Indomitable* finally arrived in the Far East, she was used to fly off fifty RAF Hawker Hurricanes bound for Batavia in the Dutch East Indies on 27–8 January 1942.[27] After delivering a second batch of fifty Hurricanes to Ceylon, she joined Admiral Somerville's new Eastern Fleet at Addu Atoll.[28]

As it turns out, there is a bit more to the story of the *Indomitable* and Force Z than that. It has been suggested that, while the *Indomitable* was eventually destined for the Far East, she was never ordered to join Force Z, and because her working-up programme was not to finish until 22 November and she was due to arrive at Gibraltar by 29 November, she could never have made it to Singapore by 8 December anyway.[29] The record of what was written – or not written – about the *Indomitable* before and after the loss of the *Prince of Wales* and *Repulse* is far from clear.

At least initially, Mr Churchill intended to send an aircraft carrier with the capital ships to go to the Far East. At a lunch with Anthony

Eden on 12 September, the two agreed that it was a modern battleship, a battlecruiser and an aircraft carrier, or nothing.[30] Churchill, at least, knew this was not the Admiralty's plan: with his minute to Churchill of 28 August, the First Sea Lord enclosed a plan for the disposition of capital ships and aircraft carriers that called for the *Indomitable* to join Force H at Gibraltar in November 1941, and for the *Ark Royal* to arrive at Trincomalee in Ceylon by April 1942, after a refit, to be joined by the *Indomitable* in an emergency.[31] Then, at the Defence Committee meeting on 17 October, Mr Churchill proposed to send 'one modern Capital Ship, *together with an aircraft carrier*, to join up with *Repulse* at Singapore'.[32]

There was, however, no mention of an aircraft carrier in the minutes of the 20 October meeting at which it was decided to send the *Prince of Wales* to Cape Town, and there is no mention of the *Indomitable* or any aircraft carrier in the 21 October Admiralty message announcing the departure of the *Prince of Wales* and Admiral Phillips for Singapore. Nor is there any mention of the *Indomitable* or any aircraft carrier in the Prime Minister's cable to the Prime Minister of Australia on 25 October, in which he discussed the dispatch of the *Prince of Wales* to join the *Repulse*.[33] By 23 November, the Prime Minister had completely forgotten about, or given up, the idea of sending the *Indomitable* to the Far East. In a minute to the First Sea Lord, he wrote,

> What is the present plan about the distribution of the aircraft carriers? Since these telegrams were received we have lost the *Ark Royal*, but we still have four good new ones. I do not want to waste any one of them by sending it all round the Cape, unless such a voyage coincided with an inevitable working-up period. At present I am waiting to see what will happen in the Mediterranean. Of course, if Admiral Cunningham is going to take station in the Central Mediterranean, or if we get Tripoli or perhaps French North Africa comes out, it would be worth putting at least two aircraft carriers there. I suppose you will give one or two of the older ones to the Indian Ocean or the Pacific.[34]

Evidently by then the *Indomitable* was hardly an 'essential element' of the new Eastern Fleet, if she ever had been.

With respect to what was written about the *Indomitable* after the loss of the *Prince of Wales* and *Repulse*, First Sea Lord Dudley Pound did not mention the *Indomitable* in his January 1942 report to the Prime

Minister on the loss of the ships, which states only that there 'were no aircraft carriers available but *Victorious* who was working with the Home Fleet'.[35] On the other hand, in early 1943 Pound wrote to a friend of Tom Phillips that 'It was intended that he should have an aircraft carrier with his force, but unfortunately she ran ashore before joining him so did not arrive in Singapore with the two ships'.[36] First Lord A.V. Alexander recalled after the war,

> There was some difficulty because we had great arguments with the P.M. about air cover and Pound and I stood out against sending a battle squadron without a Carrier. On [sic] pressure we agreed to try and speed up the 'working up' of a new Carrier just completed, and on the understanding that after working up in the West Indies she would rendezvous with *Prince of Wales* at Cape Town. Unfortunately the Carrier was stranded on a reef in West Indies during a fog and it was too late to go back on the promise made to Australia and New Zealand. . . . I think the Carrier was the *Indomitable* but that could be checked.[37]

Tom Phillips had been hoping for an aircraft carrier, but it wasn't the *Indomitable*. In his meeting with Admiral Hart and General MacArthur on 6 December, Phillips was asked if the Admiralty was going to send him an aircraft carrier, and he replied, 'I hope so. I was going to get *Ark Royal*. Will have six capital ships – no carrier.'[38]

Perhaps this is what happened. When the decision was made to send the *Prince of Wales* to Cape Town on 20 October, there probably was an unrecorded agreement or understanding between Churchill, Pound and Alexander that that the *Indomitable* would be sent to join the *Prince of Wales* and *Repulse* in the Far East. Then the idea was almost immediately dropped, perhaps because it was realized that the brand-new *Indomitable* still needed to work up and could not possibly accompany the *Prince of Wales* and *Repulse* to Singapore. The August 1941 plan for the disposition of at least the aircraft carriers was kept in place, and the idea of sending the *Indomitable* to the Far East 'in an emergency' was not revived until after the war had broken out. In any event, Mr Churchill's statement that the *Indomitable* was an 'essential element' of the new Eastern Fleet seems, at best, a bit of an overstatement. Indeed, if the *Indomitable* had really been an essential element of the new Eastern Fleet, why were the *Prince of Wales* and *Repulse* allowed to go on to Singapore after the *Indomitable* went aground?

It is certain that, once the *Indomitable* went aground on 3 November, she could not have made it to Singapore in time, and there were no other aircraft carriers available, especially once the legendary *Ark Royal* was sunk by U-81 on 14 November 1941. The nearest aircraft carrier, the *Hermes*, had condenser troubles and had begun a refit in South Africa on 19 November that had her in dry dock from 6 December 1941 to 24 January 1942.[39] Even if she had been available, she was too old, small and slow, and carried only twelve Swordfish torpedo-planes.[40] Of the newest carriers, the *Victorious* could not be spared from the Home Fleet, and the *Illustrious* and *Formidable* were under repair in the United States until 12 December.[41] As regards the other older carriers, the *Eagle* and *Furious* began refits in October 1941 that would last several months each.[42] The *Prince of Wales* and *Repulse* were simply not going to have an aircraft carrier at any time in the near future,[43] but they were sent on to Singapore anyway.

Regarding cruisers to accompany the *Prince of Wales* and *Repulse*, the Royal Navy was very short of modern cruisers at that point in the war, and the few in the Far East were not available in time. The heavy cruiser *Exeter*, which had been repaired and modernized after the damage inflicted by the pocket battleship *Graf Spee* in 1939, was not ordered to join Phillips until the morning of 8 December,[44] and she did not arrive in Singapore until 10 December, too late to be of any help. The modern light cruiser *Mauritius* was already at Singapore, and would have been a most valuable addition to Force Z, but she was still completing a refit and was not available. Phillips decided not to take the old light cruiser *Durban* with him.

Apart from these vessels, the Royal Australian Navy had two heavy cruisers, the *Canberra* and *Australia*, two modern light cruisers, the *Perth* and *Hobart*, and the old light cruiser *Adelaide*; any of these but the *Adelaide* would have been a valuable addition. Phillips had hoped to have the light cruiser *Sydney*,[45] but she had been sunk with all hands on 19 November 1941, just two weeks before Force Z's arrival at Singapore, by the German raider *Kormoran*, which the *Sydney* sent to the bottom in the same action. The Royal New Zealand Navy had the modern light cruisers *Leander* and *Achilles*, which had also fought the *Graf Spee*. The Dutch made the light cruiser *Java* available, but she was as antiquated as the *Durban* and did not arrive in Singapore until 10 December. The Dutch also had the modern light cruisers *De Ruyter* and *Tromp* in the Dutch East Indies, but they were not made available. Any of the modern Australian or Dutch cruisers would have added considerably to the strength of Force Z against both ships and aircraft if they had been sent to join Phillips at Singapore in time, and it is unfortunate that they were not there in time to help.

With regard to destroyers to screen the *Prince of Wales* and *Repulse*, there was an even greater shortage of modern British ones in the Far East. As we have seen, at Singapore the *Encounter* and *Jupiter* were undergoing repairs, and the *Isis* was still undergoing a refit, and they could not be ready in time; there were simply no more modern British destroyers to be had. Admiral Hart was sending four older American destroyers, but they would not arrive until 10 December. There were no modern Australian destroyers in the Far East, although the *Nizam*, *Nestor* and *Napier*, sisters of the *Jupiter*, were detached from the Mediterranean Fleet in January 1942 to escort the *Indomitable* to the Far East.[46] There were also seven relatively modern Dutch destroyers in the Netherlands East Indies, but, unfortunately, none of them was made available to Force Z.

While Force Z was by any measure an unbalanced force, it may not have seemed so unbalanced to Churchill, Pound and perhaps Phillips, who were led to believe that the Japanese had only one capital ship, the *Kongo*, to match up against the two British capital ships, the *Prince of Wales* and *Repulse*, when in fact the Japanese also had the *Haruna*. By December 1941, there was much more to the balance of forces than the number of capital ships, but in an earlier era, one perhaps still subscribed to by Churchill, Pound and Phillips, a comparison of the number of capital ships was the most important measure of the balance of forces.

So the *Prince of Wales* was ordered to Cape Town in a compromise that made no sense, and then she and *Repulse* were sent on to Singapore, without further consideration by the Chiefs of Staff, in the wishful hope that they would deter the Japanese. The Japanese refused to be deterred, and adjusted their plans to prepare for them. When war came, the ships were in harm's way without a plan for what to do and without a balanced force to do anything.

Of course, it would not have mattered that there was neither a plan nor a balanced force for the *Prince of Wales* and *Repulse* if the RAF in Singapore and Malaya had been provided with the 336 front-line aircraft called for in the Far East Appreciation; if they had, it probably would not have been necessary for Force Z to sail against the Japanese at all. Instead, there were only 182 aircraft, many of them not by any means 'front-line'. It is no doubt true that Britain's resources were stretched very thinly indeed at that time, but, as shown by the hundreds of Hawker Hurricanes sent to the Soviet Union in the autumn of 1941 and the reinforcements that were rushed to Malaya and Singapore in the weeks following the Japanese attack, it was really a matter of priorities, and the Far East was simply too low in the pecking order,[47] with the notable exception of the dispatch of the *Prince of Wales* and *Repulse*.

Lacking either a plan of action or a balanced force, the *Prince of Wales* and *Repulse* should have been ordered away from Singapore and out of harm's way. That is not, however, what happened.

Notes

1　Churchill, *The Grand Alliance*, at 589.
2　Marder, *Old Friends, New Enemies*, at 235.
3　S.W. Roskill, *The War at Sea, Vol. I: The Defensive*, London, HMSO, 1954, at 557.
4　Minute of 19 July 1940, quoted in Winston S. Churchill, *The Second World War: Their Finest Hour*, Boston, Houghton Mifflin Co., 1949, at 17–18.
5　Letter from Ronald Brockman to Stephen Roskill of 31 December 1952. Roskill Papers.
6　Letters from General Ian Jacob to Arthur Marder of 23 November 1976 and 3 November 1977. Marder Papers.
7　See Appendix, No. 1, relying on Admiralty War Diary.
8　TNA Prem 3/163/3. This cable is quoted in Churchill's history of the Second World War, but without the first paragraph, 'Your [cable] 682. Tobruk. Relief is being carried out in accordance with your decision [i.e. to withdraw Australian troops from Tobruk] which I greatly regret.'
9　TNA Cab 65/24, at 9.
10　See Appendix, No. 5.
11　Irving, *Churchill's War*, vol. 2, at 143, citing to the Chequers registry for that date.
12　Robert R. James, ed., *Winston S. Churchill: His Complete Speeches 1897–1963, Vol. 6, 1935–1942*, New York and London, R.R. Bowker Co. and Chelsea House Publishers, 1974, at 6504.
13　Winston S. Churchill, *The Grand Alliance*, Boston, Houghton Mifflin Co., 1950, at 594.
14　TNA Cab 65/24, at 26.
15　Minute of 18 November 1941. TNA Prem 3/163/3.
16　Letter of 7 March 1942. Roskill Papers. In the letter, which concerned Lord Mountbatten, Pound was very concerned about the perception that Churchill had overridden his naval advisers on this and other points.
17　Marder, *Old Friends, New Enemies*, at 239, citing *Naval Memoirs of J.H. Godfrey*, vol. 8, privately printed, at 66.
18　Roskill, *Churchill and the Admirals*, at 196.
19　Letter from General Ian Jacob to Arthur Marder of 3 November 1977. Marder Papers.
20　J.H. Godfrey, 'The Navy and Naval Intelligence 1939–1942: Afterthoughts', 1947. TNA Adm 223/619.

21 Handwritten note, '1SL to Little, 6/12/41 (Vol. 9)'. Roskill Papers 4/79.

22 Sir Andrew Gilchrist, *Malaya 1941*, London, Robert Hale, 1992, at 43.

23 'Capital Ship and Aircraft Carrier Dispositions', at 4, attachment to Memorandum from First Sea Lord Dudley Pound to Winston Churchill of 28 August 1941. TNA Prem 3/163/3.

24 'With the Eastern Fleet', *The Times* (London), 6 December 1941.

25 *The Grand Alliance*, at 589.

26 See Appendix, No. 74.

27 S.W. Roskill, *The War at Sea, Vol. 2: The Period of Balance*, London, HMSO, 1956, at 8.

28 David Hobbs, *Aircraft Carriers of the Royal and Commonwealth Navies*, London, Greenhill Books, 1996, at 122.

29 Commander David Hobbs, Letter, 'Indomitable Out of the Picture', *Navy News* (November 1997), at 7; Hobbs, *Aircraft Carriers of the Royal and Commonwealth Navies*, at 122; David Brown, 'If Only the Indomitable Had Been There!', Memorandum S10571, March 1996, Naval Historical Branch, Ministry of Defence.

30 Eden Diary. Papers of First Earl of Avon, Special Collections, University of Birmingham, quoted in Bell, *The 'Singapore Strategy' and the Deterrence of Japan*, at 623.

31 'Capital Ship and Aircraft Carrier Dispositions', at 1, 3, 5, attachment to Memorandum from Dudley Pound to Winston Churchill of 28 August 1941. TNA Prem 3/163/3.

32 TNA Cab 69/2, at 370 (emphasis added).

33 TNA Prem 3/163/3, at 45.

34 Churchill, *The Grand Alliance*, Appendix, at 836.

35 Prem 3/163/2, at 9.

36 Letter from Pound to Mildred Barker of 25 February 1943. Roskill Papers.

37 Letter from A.V. Alexander to Prof. Butler of 14 November 1952. Roskill Papers.

38 Report of Conference, 6 December 1941, at 12. Admiral Hart Papers, Box 3, US Naval Historical Center, Operational Archives Branch, Washington Navy Yard.

39 Emails from John Parkinson to the author of 6 June 2000, and 23 September 2002, based on Mr Parkinson's research for a forthcoming book on the *Hermes*.

40 J.D. Brown, *Carrier Operations in World War II, Vol. 1: The Royal Navy*, London, Ian Allen, 1968, at 120.

41 David Brown, *Warship Profile 11: HMS Illustrious, Aircraft Carrier 1939–1956, Operational History*, Windsor, Berks., Profile Publications Limited, 1971, at 246.

42 David Brown, *Warship Profile 35: HMS Eagle*, Windsor, Berks., Profile Publications Ltd, 1973, at 265; C.A. Jenkins, *Warship Profile 24, HMS Furious, Aircraft Carrier 1917–1948, Part II: 1925–1948*, Windsor, Berks., Profile Publications Ltd, 1972, at 284.

43 It is indeed a moot point, but, even if the *Indomitable* had been able to join Force Z by 8 December, it is not at all clear how she would have been used by Admiral Phillips. Phillips could have used his force as a carrier task force and attacked the Japanese with the *Indomitable*'s aircraft, but she had few strike aircraft and Phillips would have found it difficult to resist employing the heavy guns of the *Prince of Wales* and *Repulse* in a surface action. On the other hand, it would have been unwise to risk a valuable and vulnerable aircraft carrier in a surface gun battle

with the Japanese; Admiral Cunningham had barely got away with having the aircraft carrier *Formidable* in his battle line until the last moment at the Battle of Matapan in March 1941. Phillips certainly had far too few escort ships to divide his forces into a carrier task force including the *Indomitable* and a surface action force including the *Prince of Wales* and *Repulse*.

44   See Appendix, No. 34.

45   See Appendix, No. 14.

46   L.J. Lind and M.A. Payne, *N Class: The Story of H.M.A. Ships NIZAM, NESTOR, NAPIER, NORMAN, and NEPAL*, Garden Island, NSW, Australia, Naval Historical Society of Australia, 1974, 1993, at 93.

47   See Roskill, *Churchill and the Admirals*, at 196–7.

Part II

To Sail or Not to Sail against the Japanese

CHAPTER SIX

The Countdown to War

The *Prince of Wales* and *Repulse* and the four destroyers finally arrived at Singapore just after 1730 on 2 December 1941.[1] With great fanfare, the British announced the arrival of the *Prince of Wales* and 'other heavy units' in Singapore. It would have been unusual and even unwise to have mentioned the names of the other ships that had arrived, since to do so would have given the lie to the press claim that 'it may be assumed [the Eastern Fleet] consists of a number of heavy ships and auxiliary vessels';[2] that, however, would have been little consolation to the proud men of the *Repulse*.

The ships' arrival was a major event in Singapore, and no doubt it raised morale. To dampen local expectations, Air Chief Marshal Sir Robert Brooke-Popham called a press conference, and warned the population of Singapore:

The arrival of the two capital ships in no way reduced the need for continuance of every effort being made to improve the defences of Malaya and Singapore; indeed, it enhanced the importance of this effort. Warships must not be tied down to their base; they must be free to operate to the full limit of their range of action and know that they can still return to a safe base when necessary. These ships would be of value to the Far East as a whole, but must not be regarded in any sense as part of the local defences of Malaya and Singapore. Further, in the same way as these ships had arrived from distant stations so, if the situation changed and they became needed elsewhere, we had to be prepared for them to be ordered away.[3]

The same theme was echoed by *The Times* in London, which noted that 'it is presumed that the *Prince of Wales*, and other ships that have been seen today, would be cruising far from here in the next few weeks'.[4]

Upon their arrival, the men of Force Z had to contend with the 'terrific, damp, enervating heat' of Singapore,[5] for which the *Prince of Wales* was inadequately ventilated, as Admiral Tovey had predicted. Ironically, a correspondent for *The Times* reported that the *Prince of Wales*'s 'modern construction and adequate ventilation are especially appreciated by the officers and crew, who would be far from comfortable in a vessel less well fitted'.[6]

There was more to contend with than just the heat. According to Lady Phillips, Tom Phillips was 'horrified at conditions in Singapore, the light-hearted way they were taking it all'.[7] He was not alone; when the ships' crews went ashore, they also found Singapore ill prepared for war, both militarily and mentally. According to the gunnery officer of HMS *Electra*,

> The frivolous attitude of the wealthy, social-conscious city, crammed with every luxury, came as a shock to us. There seemed to be little awareness among the people we met of the possibility that the disputes between Japan and the West might lead to something worse than a war of words. From the way in which some of the local folk reacted one would have thought the squadron had been despatched from the western theatre for no more than a social call.[8]

Admiral Phillips's force could not 'prevent the unpreventable';[9] it had reached Singapore just the day after the Japanese had made the final decision to go to war at a conference at the Imperial Palace in Tokyo.[10] Japan's armed forces were already on the move; Admiral Nagumo Chuichi's carrier attack force was already heading for Pearl Harbor, Admiral Kondo's Southern Force was moving south, and Japanese aircraft were massing in French Indo-China.

Diplomatic efforts to avert war were in fact doomed after 26 November 1941, when US Secretary of State Cordell Hull rejected Japan's proposal for a *modus vivendi*, and countered with a proposal that the Japanese were sure to find unacceptable. The Army and Navy chiefs, General George C. Marshall and Admiral Harold R. Stark, had argued in favour of the *modus vivendi* to buy time, but the President and Secretary Hull were incensed at Japanese warlike moves during negotiations, and were wary of making even the temporary concessions the *modus vivendi* required. In the end, Japan would not abandon its ambitions in China and beyond, and the United States would not let Japan have its way with China, but also wanted to keep Japan from turning north to attack the Soviet Union, whose survival was deemed so vital to the ultimate defeat of Nazi Germany.[11]

Although Admiral Phillips's force could not deter Japan from going to war, it did provoke a reaction from the Imperial Japanese Navy. The Commander-in-Chief of the Japanese Combined Fleet, Admiral Yamamoto Isoroku, decided to make changes in the Japanese order of battle. Yamamoto ordered two old but modernized battlecruisers, the *Kongo* and *Haruna*, to join the Southern Force, ordered twenty-seven bombers of the Kanoya Air Group from Formosa to Saigon, moved a submarine division to the Malay area,[12] and ordered the minelayer *Tatsumiya* to sow mines on the route between Singapore and the eastern coast of Malaya and Thailand.[13] Yamamoto, however, refused the idea of additional battleship reinforcements, saying, 'In this chess game with the United States and Britain, we can't afford the luxury of countering a battleship with a battleship. We have to use a pawn to get their king. I am confident our brave torpedo units will finish them.'[14]

At that late date, no redeployments of major warships could be made to help Admiral Phillips. The carrier *Indomitable* had only just returned to the West Indies from repairs in the United States. The battleship *Revenge* was in the Indian Ocean, but she was old and slow and would have been of little use to Admiral Phillips. The United States Pacific Fleet had three aircraft carriers, but it could ill afford to part with any of them, and a fourth, the *Yorktown*, had been transferred to the Atlantic months earlier. It was by then too late to revive the 'Asiatic Reinforcement' to unite the *Yorktown* and her escorts with *Prince of Wales* and *Repulse*, which would have formed a formidable force. At the time, the US Navy had two fast battleships, the *North Carolina* and *Washington*, which had been commissioned by June 1941, but they were still experiencing serious problems with machinery vibration,[15] and were in no shape to transfer to the Pacific even if there had been a desire for them to do so.

On 1 December, and again on 3 December, the Admiralty suggested that Phillips consider getting the *Prince of Wales* and/or the *Repulse* away from Singapore to disconcert the Japanese and to avoid Japanese submarines heading for Singapore.[16] Phillips was already thinking about getting his capital ships away from Singapore until reinforcements arrived, possibly to Port Darwin in Australia.[17]

Phillips did decide to send the *Repulse* and two destroyers, HMAS *Vampire* and HMS *Tenedos*, to visit Darwin to show the flag, since, as he told Captain Tennant of the *Repulse*, 'the Aussies were feeling sore that we never sent any RN ships to their waters'.[18] At the Naval Base in Singapore, the *Prince of Wales* started a long-overdue boiler cleaning and went into dock to have her bottom cleaned.

On 4 December, Admiral Phillips flew in a Catalina flying boat to Manila in the Philippines to confer with General Douglas MacArthur and Admiral Thomas Hart, the C-in-C of the US Asiatic Fleet. Admiral Hart was very impressed by Phillips, whom he described as 'good stuff' and 'decidedly the intellectual type with a first rate brain'.[19] After the meeting with MacArthur, the two admirals, neither more than 5ft 2in and 10 stone,[20] attempted to hammer out a joint operational plan, since none had replaced the ADB plan, or the subsequent ADB-2 plan, which had also been rejected by the United States.[21] The two admirals were able to agree upon a plan, which they sent to the US Navy and the Admiralty.[22] Ironically, after all the British attempts before the war to have the United States send warships to Singapore, the plan called for the British Eastern Fleet to operate with the US Asiatic Fleet from Manila. In any case, events were to overtake the plan before it could be implemented.

The entire situation changed dramatically at midday on 6 December, when Hudson bombers of No. 1 Squadron, Royal Australian Air Force, found and reported several large groups of Japanese merchant ships and warships heading from French Indo-China toward Thailand.[23]

The news soon spread around the world: the British in Singapore informed London, London informed the US Ambassador John Winant, Singapore informed Admiral Hart in the Philippines, and both Winant and Hart informed Washington.[24]

Upon hearing of the sightings, Admiral Phillips quickly left the Philippines, having obtained a last-minute promise of four US destroyers from Admiral Hart, and returned to Singapore at 1000 on 7 December.[25] Admiral Palliser, who was deputizing for Phillips in Singapore, ordered the *Repulse* and her escorting destroyers to return immediately to Singapore, which they did at 1200 on 7 December.[26] For better or worse, Air Chief Marshal Brooke-Popham and Admiral Phillips were not authorized by London to attack the Japanese convoys while they were at sea.[27] In any event, further efforts to locate the convoys were to no avail, and on 7 December the Japanese shot down one of the Catalina flying-boats sent to find them.[28] At 0905 on 7 December, the

Japanese invasion convoys made a rendezvous in the Gulf of Siam (now Thailand), and then began their voyages to landing points at Kota Bharu in Malaya and various points, including Singora, in Thailand.[29]

It is tempting to speculate on what might have happened if Force Z had been able to go to sea, and had been ordered to do so, right after the Japanese convoys had been sighted on 6 December. Indeed, several historians have actually been tempted to suggest some alternatives, such as throwing warships and aircraft against the Japanese convoys,[30] or a 'spoiling operation' in which the British would 'move their warships and aircraft as secretly as possible to within much closer striking distance of the Japanese convoys and their landing points than the naval base at Singapore, so that an immediate and devastating attack might be launched on the Japanese the instant war broke out'.[31] Certainly the Japanese Navy was very worried that their convoys would be attacked while still at sea, and expected the British to do so.[32] There were several very good reasons why this was not done.

The first reason was simply that, when the Japanese convoys were sighted at midday on 6 December, Force Z was in no position either to be sent out to attack the Japanese convoys or to be sent out for a spoiling operation. The *Prince of Wales* was at Singapore cleaning her boilers, Tom Phillips was away in Manila conferring with Admiral Hart, and the *Repulse* was on her way to Darwin with the *Vampire* and *Tenedos*. None of this should be laid at Tom Phillips's door. It was not his fault (or the fault of the captain and crew of the *Prince of Wales*) that the *Prince of Wales*'s boilers were long overdue for cleaning after arduous war service and a long voyage. The Admiralty knew and approved of Phillips going on an important trip to Manila to confer with Admiral Hart, and it was the Admiralty that had suggested that Phillips get the *Prince of Wales* 'and/or' the *Repulse* away to the eastward. Even if extraordinary efforts could have been made to ready the *Prince of Wales* for sea in time for such an operation – and nothing of the sort was ever ordered – it would not have done to send her out without Admiral Phillips or the *Repulse*, *Vampire* or *Tenedos*. Admiral Phillips did not return to Singapore until 1000 on the 7th, and the *Repulse* and her escorts did not arrive back until noon that day; by then, the original sighting reports were a day old and the trail was cold.

It has nevertheless been suggested that Admiral Phillips was 'insufficiently alert to the pressing realities of the strategic situation in which he was involved', and that he should have made extraordinary efforts to have the *Prince of Wales* made ready for sea.[33] Certainly, by his actions Phillips does not seem to have realized that war was so near, even though there was information available in Singapore by 3 December that the Japanese diplomats were being told to destroy their codes,[34] but British and American leaders in London and Washington had the same information and more, and were no more aware of how soon the Japanese would act than he was.[35] Admiral Phillips became very aware of the imminent outbreak of war when the convoys were sighted on the 6th, but, as we are about to see, for political reasons there was no reason to make extraordinary efforts to have the *Prince of Wales* ready for sea to attack the Japanese convoys, and it would have been too dangerous to sail into the South China Sea just to lie in wait for them. In the event, the *Prince of Wales* was ready to go to sea when the occasion demanded.

The second reason, completely apart from whether Force Z was ready to go to sea or could have been made ready to go to sea, was that attacking the Japanese convoys at sea would have meant war, and Admiral Phillips's standing orders simply did not include starting a war with Japan.[36] The signals exchanged between the Admiralty and Phillips show that he never had authorization to attack the Japanese convoys at sea. Although he was asked what action he could take against a Japanese expedition in the South China Sea, the same signal made it clear that no decision had been taken.[37] Although Phillips replied that an endeavour would be made to attack the expedition or to attempt a raid,[38] he and Brooke-Popham also signalled that 'Our reading of instruction is that Naval and Air action against such expedition is not at present authorised. Request confirmation.'[39] The Admiralty eventually replied, 'Further instructions will shortly be sent as to whether or not a Japanese expedition can be attacked at sea before any hostile act against the United States, the Dutch or ourselves or any Japanese entry into Thai territory has taken place,'[40] but by then the war with Japan had already begun. Admiral Phillips's orders did not preclude him from sending his ships into the South China Sea to be ready for a Japanese landing, but, as we have seen, he and his ships were in no position for such a move, even aside from how dangerous it would have been.[41]

Thirdly, the decision not to attack the convoys at sea was made in London, not Singapore, and it was based on the broader political and diplomatic situation facing Britain at the time. When the Chiefs of Staff Committee, then made up of Admiral Pound, Air Chief Marshal Portal, and General Alan Brooke, met at 1545 on 6 December to consider the situation, they noted that under existing orders Phillips and Brooke-Popham had no authority to attack the Japanese unless they actually attempted to land on the Kra Isthmus, and, more importantly, they suggested to the Prime Minister that, while militarily it would pay to attack the convoys at sea, politically Britain could not strike the first blow without an assurance of armed support from the United States.[42]

It is true that, at this, the Prime Minister remarked, 'If it is not physically possible, the political issue does not arise.'[43] The physical impediments to attacking the convoys at sea made no difference if it was not politically possible to attack, and it was not: whatever assurance of armed support President Roosevelt may have given the British, it did not include attacking Japanese convoys at sea before Japan had attacked anyone. Mr Churchill could have just as easily said, 'If it is not politically possible, the physical issue does not arise.'

It was with good reason that Force Z was not ordered to sea when the Japanese convoys were sighted. Force Z was sent to sea to attack the Japanese only after they had landed and war had broken out in the Pacific, but under the most puzzling of circumstances.

Notes

1 According to the log of HMS *Mauritius*, the *Prince of Wales* arrived at 1736, and the *Repulse*, *Express* and *Electra* anchored at 1750. TNA Adm 53/114646.
2 'Eastern Fleet in Being', *The Times* (London), 3 December 1941, at 3.
3 Sir Robert Brooke-Popham, 'Operations in the Far East, from 17th October 1940 to 27th December 1941', Supplement to the *London Gazette* of 22 January 1948, at 558. TNA ZJ 1/1028.
4 'With the Eastern Fleet', *The Times* (London), 6 December 1941.
5 Brooke, *Alarm Starboard!*, at 93.
6 'With the Eastern Fleet', *The Times* (London), 6 December 1941.
7 Letter from Lady Phillips to Captain Russell Grenfell of 28 November 1950. Grenfell Papers.
8 Cain and Sellwood, *H.M.S. Electra*, at 160.
9 Marder, *Old Friends, New Enemies*, at 251.
10 Bix, *Hirohito and the Making of Modern Japan*, at 431–3.
11 Mark A. Stoler, *Allies and Adversaries: The Joint Chiefs of Staff, the Grand Alliance, and U.S. Strategy in World War II*, Chapel Hill, University of North Carolina Press, 2000, at 55–60.
12 Official Japanese History, at 116–18.
13 Ministry of Defence, Admiralty Historical Section (Naval Historical Branch), 'The Loss of H.M. Ships *Prince of Wales* and *Repulse*, 10th December, 1941', Battle Summary No. 14, BR 1736(8)/1955 ('Admiralty Battle Summary'), at 9. TNA Adm 234/330.

14 Official Japanese History, at 118.

15 Norman Friedman, *U.S. Battleships: An Illustrated Design History*, Annapolis, Naval Institute Press, 1985, at 274–6.

16 See Appendix, Nos 10 and 11.

17 Letter from Michael Goodenough to S.W. Roskill of 8 May 1951. Roskill Papers.

18 Letter from Admiral William G. Tennant to S.W. Roskill of 4 January. Roskill Papers.

19 Leutze, *A Different Kind of Victory*, at 225, 226.

20 *Ibid.* at 225.

21 Marder, *Old Friends, New Enemies*, at 210–11.

22 Joint Committee on the Investigation of the Pearl Harbor Attack, *Hearings before the Joint Committee on the Investigation of the Pearl Harbor Attack*, vol. 4, Washington, DC, Government Printing Office, 1946, at 1933–5.

23 War Diary, General Headquarters Far East, TNA WO 172/15; Douglas Gillison, *Royal Australian Air Force 1939–1942*, Canberra, Australian War Memorial, 1962, at 200.

24 Gordon W. Prange, Donald M. Goldstein, and Katherine Dillon, *December 7, 1941: The Day the Japanese Attacked Pearl Harbor*, New York, McGraw-Hill Book Company, 1988, at 4–5.

25 See Appendix, No. 16.

26 War Diary of Admiral Geoffrey Layton, Part 1, at 8. TNA Adm 199/1185. According to Sub-Lieutenant R.A.W. Pool, the ships arrived at 1600. Richard Pool, *Course for Disaster: From Scapa Flow to the River Kwai*, London, Leo Cooper Ltd, 1987, at 54.

27 TNA Cab 79/55, at 325–7. See Chapter 12 for more on this.

28 According to the Naval Historical Branch account, this occurred about 1600, *War with Japan*, vol. 2, at 45, but according to a more recent account, it occurred shortly after 0845. Christopher Shores, Brian Cull and Yazuho Izawa, *Bloody Shambles, Vol. 1*, London, Grub Street, 1992, at 76.

29 Headquarters, US Army Far East and US Eighth Army (Rear), *Japanese Monograph No. 107: Malaya Invasion Naval Operations* (rev. edn), Washington, DC, Office of the Chief of Military History, Department of the Army, 1958, at 19.

30 Middlebrook and Mahoney, *Battleship*, at 91–2.

31 Gilchrist, *Malaya 1941*, at 104.

32 Official Japanese History, at 427.

33 Gilchrist, *Malaya 1941*, at 163, Chapter 12 and Appendix C. In Appendix C, Sir Andrew cites some examples of extraordinary efforts, such as the German efforts to keep the battlecruiser *Goeben* steaming in September 1914, the efforts to make the battlecruisers *Invincible* and *Inflexible* ready to sail to the Falklands in November 1914, and the efforts to make the USS *Yorktown* ready for the Battle of Midway in 1942, and at least implies that the same efforts should have been applied to ready the *Prince of Wales* for sea. Those examples were not only technically different from the one facing the *Prince of Wales*, but they involved much more desperate situations than the one faced by the British in Singapore on 6 December.

34 Ong Chit Chung, *Operation Matador*, at 230.

35 Perhaps Phillips would have been more aware of the imminent outbreak of war if

the Far East Combined Bureau had had an American 'Purple' machine for decoding Japanese diplomatic traffic, but the one that was sent did not arrive in time and was then misplaced; fortunately, the Japanese either did not find it or did not realize its significance. Ralph Erskine, Research Note, 'When a Purple Machine Went Missing: How Japan Nearly Discovered America's Greatest Secret', *Intelligence and National Security* 12, No. 3 (July 1997), 185–9.

36 A copy of Phillips's orders, which are not terribly helpful, can be found in Appendix 4 of Kirby, *The War against Japan, Vol. 1: The Loss of Singapore*, and in TNA Adm 116/4877 in a signal dated 28 October 1941.

37 See Appendix, No. 19.

38 See Appendix, No. 22.

39 See Appendix, No. 21.

40 See Appendix, No. 28.

41 A potentially tempting third option might have been a demonstration or feint, to sail Force Z into the South China Sea with the intention of being sighted and unnerving the Japanese, and then to return once sighted. Of course, once again, the *Prince of Wales* and *Repulse*, as well as the *Tenedos* and *Vampire*, were not available for such a course until well after noon on the 7th, and then only if the *Prince of Wales* could have been readied by then. Given the known presence of Japanese submarines in the area and the uncertain situation facing the British in Singapore on the 7th, such a course was probably not seriously considered.

42 TNA Cab 79/55, at 325–7.

43 Marder, *Old Friends, New Enemies*, at 404.

CHAPTER SEVEN

The World War Comes to the Far East

Although their mission of deterrence had failed, the *Prince of Wales* and *Repulse* had, for better or worse, arrived just in time for the beginning of the war in the Far East. The imminent possibility of Japanese landings raised the difficult question of what to do with the land, air and naval forces available to the British in Singapore and Malaya. On the evening of 7 December, Admiral Phillips met the British C-in-C Far East, Air Chief Marshal Sir Robert Brooke-Popham, and General A.E. Percival, the General Officer Commanding British Army forces in Malaya,[1] to consider the situation and then to communicate with London. When the Admiralty sent a message to Admiral Phillips asking what action it would be possible to take with naval or air forces against a Japanese expedition,[2] he replied that if the relative strength of the enemy force permitted, an endeavour would be made to attack the expedition, but that if his force were inferior in strength, a raid would be attempted.[3] He received no response.

Shortly before midnight in Singapore, Brooke-Popham informed London that he had decided not to execute Operation Matador,[4] a long-planned incursion by British Army units into southern Thailand designed to forestall a Japanese invasion of the Thai part of the Kra Isthmus.[5] The British government had given Brooke-Popham authority to execute Operation Matador[6] based on assurances of armed support from the United States if the Japanese attacked Malaya, Thailand or the Dutch East Indies, but not the United States. The assurances upon which the authorization to execute Matador was based were evidently oral ones given by President Roosevelt to the British ambassador, Lord

Halifax,[7] who conveyed the assurances to London.[8] It may well have been President Roosevelt's intention to provide armed support to Britain under the circumstances he discussed with Lord Halifax;[9] but the assurances, which were not only oral but probably beyond the President's war-making powers as limited by the US Constitution, were surely a slender reed upon which to base a potentially momentous decision to violate Thai neutrality. It is perhaps just as well Brooke-Popham did not order Matador, but the preparations for the execution of Matador left some of his ground forces badly out of position for the battle that ensued.

The assurances given by President Roosevelt took on another life of their own when the British evidently showed the message from London repeating the assurances to Captain John M. Creighton, the US naval observer in Singapore. Repeating the British message almost verbatim, Captain Creighton sent word of the assurances to Admiral Hart,[10] who was shown the same message by Admiral Phillips during his visit to Manila.[11] Understandably miffed at learning of the American assurances from the British, Admiral Hart asked Admiral Harold R. Stark, the Chief of Naval Operations in Washington, why he had received no word of such assurances,[12] but he received no reply. After the war, the Joint Congressional Committee investigating the attack on Pearl Harbor looked into the matter of the supposed assurances, but Captain Creighton suffered a severe case of amnesia as to how he had received word of the assurances.[13] There the matter died.

In addition to the meeting on the evening of 7 December with Brook-Popham and General Percival, Admiral Phillips may – or may not – have had another important meeting early the next morning, 8 December, in Singapore, at the Naval Base with Brooke-Popham, Governor Sir Shenton Thomas, Air Vice-Marshal Pulford, the Air Officer Commanding Far East, and others. A very detailed account of such a meeting appeared in 1981 with the publication of Professor Arthur Marder's book *Old Friends, New Enemies*.[14] According to this account, the meeting started between 0300 and 0330 and broke up shortly after the Japanese had begun bombing Singapore at 0400. By the end of the meeting, Phillips had manoeuvred Air Chief Marshal Brooke-Popham into stating that, 'if the Japanese intend to attack, your intervention is the only thing that can prevent the invasion succeeding'. Professor Marder's sole source of information on the meeting was Lieutenant-Commander James W. McClelland,[15] who at the time was in charge of the Changi wireless station and had an office at the War Room at the Naval Base.

There are a number of reasons to question McClelland's account of this meeting, quite apart from the sheer implausibility of having such a meeting with so many lofty participants at such an ungodly hour. First, there seem to be no other records or accounts of the meeting: it is not mentioned in the official histories or, for instance, in the postwar dispatch of Air Chief Marshal Brooke-Popham.[16] McClelland's account states rather implausibly that it was decided that no minutes of the conference should be recorded 'to save time at a future joint conference to coordinate the employment of Force Z' and to 'give the participants time to mull over their commitments'. Secondly, Shenton Thomas's war diary not only says nothing about the meeting, but says that he learned of the impending Japanese air attack in a telephone call from Air Vice-Marshal Pulford at 4.00 a.m.[17] Although McClelland claims that Pulford left the meeting near the end, it hardly seems likely that he would have called Sir Shenton in a meeting at the Naval Base instead of at his residence. Thirdly, McClelland told Professor Marder that the participants in the meeting did not know of the Japanese landings at Kota Bharu in north-east Malaya.[18] But that cannot be correct: at 0115 General Percival telephoned Sir Shenton with the news that the Japanese were shelling the beaches at Kota Bharu,[19] and at 0116 Admiral Layton informed London of the attempted landing there.[20] Fourthly, although McClelland claimed to have notes, and is even said to have shown them to one author,[21] he was evacuated unconscious from Singapore after a head injury, and could not have brought out any contemporaneous notes of the meeting.[22] McClelland's account would be more suspect than not if based upon memory alone, even aside from the possible effects of an intervening head injury. Fifthly, McClelland claimed he was there at the behest of Admiral Layton, but Layton's secretary and right-hand man, Paymaster Captain Dougal Doig, was in the War Room at the Naval Base all night but was not aware of the meeting. Although Doig did not actually deny that the meeting had taken place, he suggested that the decision to sail was taken by Phillips after he had returned to the War Room at 0630 that morning, that there was insufficient information to make a reasoned and informed decision at a meeting at the time suggested by McClelland because the landings at Singora had not taken place, and that he remembered complete calm during the air raid, not the scene described by McClelland of everyone diving under tables.[23] Whether Captain McClelland's memory failed him or he was acting from an ulterior motive, there is plenty of reason to question his account of the nocturnal meeting and the conclusion that

Admiral Phillips had manoeuvred the participants into urging him to sail against the Japanese.[24]

Meanwhile, in London and Washington, in the last days and hours of peace, the British and American governments were anxiously waiting to see when and where the Japanese blows would fall. The British were especially concerned that the Japanese would attack them and not the United States; without an ironclad guarantee of American support, that was their worst nightmare. Just hours before hearing the news of the attack on Pearl Harbor, Mr Churchill asked US Ambassador John Winant whether the United States would declare war on Japan if Japan declared war on Britain; the ambassador could only point out that only Congress could declare war under the United States Constitution.[25] As it turned out, the British need not have worried: the Japanese were about to take on everyone. Everyone, that is, except the Soviet Union. Tipped off by master-spy Richard Sorge that Japan would move south instead of north, the Soviets transferred divisions from the Far East just in time to halt the German drive before Moscow[26] on 6 December 1941, just as all hell was about to break loose in the Far East.

The uncertainty as to Japanese plans and intentions came to an abrupt end at about 0025GH in Singapore on 8 December, when the Japanese landed at Khota Bharu in Malaya.[27] Minutes later and thousands of miles away, on the other side of the International Date Line, at 0045GH, and 0645 local time in Hawaii, the destroyer USS *Ward* fired on and sank a Japanese midget submarine outside the entrance to Pearl Harbor.[28] Then at 0155GH, 0755 local time, Japanese carrier aircraft attacked the United States Pacific Fleet at Pearl Harbor and other American installations in the Hawaiian Islands. At 0400GH, Japanese bombers from the 22nd Air Flotilla based near Saigon bombed Singapore. There was some damage to the city and loss of civilian lives, but no damage to the naval base or the warships there, and the *Prince of Wales*, the *Repulse*[29] and the cruiser *Mauritius*[30] lent their anti-aircraft guns to the island's defences. At 0415, a signal was received from the Admiralty, 'Commence hostilities against Japan at once.'[31] At 0815, it was reported that the Japanese were landing in large numbers between Singora and Pattani on the Thai side of the Kra Isthmus.[32]

The world war had finally come to Singapore and the rest of the Far East and the Pacific. Diplomatic efforts to avert a war had continued to the very end, when a message from President Roosevelt reached Emperor Hirohito within an hour of the dropping of the first bomb on Pearl Harbor.[33] Japanese diplomats did not deliver their country's reply to Secretary of State Hull's last proposal until after the attack on Pearl Harbor had already begun.

At Kota Bharu, Indian troops at first offered fierce resistance to the Japanese landing, and Royal Australian Air Force Hudson bombers attacked the troopships off the coast, sinking the *Awagisan Maru* with ten bomb hits.[34] Despite this initial resistance, Japanese troops soon established a beachhead and began to move inland, forcing the withdrawal of the airfield at Kota Bharu. The British began losing many aircraft to Japanese fighters in the air and to attacks on airfields, and began losing other airfields in the north. The Japanese were enormously aided by a spy, an Indian Army officer named Captain Patrick Heenan, who was unfortunately posted as an Air Intelligence Liaison Officer in northern Malaya.[35] With the capture of northern airfields and heavy British aircraft losses, the Japanese soon established almost complete air superiority over northern Malaya. Meanwhile, on the east coast of Malaya, the airfield at Kuantan was hurriedly abandoned after an attack by nine Japanese bombers on 9 December.[36]

With Operation Matador cancelled and the battle beginning to go badly in northern Malaya, the burden of action fell upon Admiral Phillips, whose ships were the last weapon left to halt the Japanese onslaught. After news of the Japanese landings, at 0630 on the 8th he went to the War Room at the Naval Base and conferred with Admiral Layton and Admiral Palliser. At one point, Admiral Phillips was heard to say, 'I certainly can't go to sea until I have some more destroyers.'[37] Nevertheless, at 0934 Singapore time, 0304 British Summer Time in London, he sent a signal informing the Admiralty of his intention to proceed at dusk with *Prince of Wales* and *Repulse* and four destroyers on the 8th to attack enemy forces off Kota Bharu at daylight on the 10th.[38] As with his earlier signal about attacking the Japanese expedition, Admiral Phillips received no reply.

Admiral Phillips began making preparations to sail, and made repeated efforts to enlist a promise of air support from the RAF. At 1045, he met Air Vice-Marshal C.W. Pulford[39] to request reconnaissance ahead of his ships on the 9th, and reconnaissance and fighter protection off Singora on the 10th. Later that day, Phillips remarked, 'I am not sure that Pulford realizes the importance I attach to air cover over Singora,' and he had Captain L.H. Bell send a message to Pulford by staff car just as the *Prince of Wales* was casting off.[40]

At about 1230, after he had already sent a signal informing the Dutch and other commands in Singapore of his decision to attack the

Japanese,[41] Admiral Phillips had a meeting aboard the *Prince of Wales* with some of his staff and the captains of the *Prince of Wales* and *Repulse* and the destroyers *Electra*, *Express*, *Tenedos*, and *Vampire*. Phillips looked ill, his grey face damp with sweat, but in concise and sharp tones he outlined the situation and his plan, and asked those present what they thought of it.[42] Captain Tennant broke the silence, and said he thought the fleet could do nothing else but go out and have a try against the transports.[43] Supported by the men present, Phillips proceeded to outline his intentions. With what was now to be known as Force Z, Admiral Phillips hoped to use the usual poor weather of the season to avoid detection and to surprise and attack the Japanese landing force off Kota Bharu on the morning of 10 December. After the meeting, Captain Leach of the *Prince of Wales* told his Gunnery Officer, Lieutenant-Commander C.W. McMullen, 'I'm afraid we're in for a "sticky party", Guns.'[44]

Notes

1 Ong Chit Chung, *Operation Matador: Britain's War Plans against the Japanese 1918–1941*, Singapore, Times Academic Press, 1997, at 232; S. Woodburn Kirby, *The War against Japan, Vol. 1: The Loss of Singapore*, London, HMSO, 1957, at 181.

2 See Appendix, No. 19.

3 See Appendix, No. 22.

4 See Appendix, No. 23.

5 Mr Churchill later wrote, 'It was rightly decided, both on political and military grounds, that we should not complicate the course of events by striking first in a secondary theatre.' *The Grand Alliance*, at 601. This passage glosses over the fact that the authorities in London had given Brooke-Popham the authority to execute Operation Matador, but that it was Brooke-Popham, not London, who decided not to do so.

6 See Appendix, No. 15.

7 Costello, *Days of Infamy*, at 139–46. The British official history even states that Mr Roosevelt 'gave an *undertaking* that the United States would support, if necessary by force, whatever action Britain found it necessary to take in Siam'. J.M.A. Gwyer and J.R.M. Butler, *Grand Strategy, Vol. 3: June 1941–August 1942*, London, HMSO, 1964, at 293 (emphasis added). No *written* assurances from President Roosevelt have surfaced, although Anthony Eden's diary entry of 4 December refers to a 'good message from Roosevelt about the Far East'. Anthony Eden, Earl of Avon, *The Eden Memoirs: The Reckoning*, London, Cassell, 1965, at 314. The matter of the assurances is discussed in detail in Raymond A. Esthmus, 'President Roosevelt's Commitment to Britain to Intervene in a Pacific War', *Mississippi Valley Historical Review* 50, No. 1 (1963), at 28.

8 TNA Cab 121/114.

9 The Army and Navy chiefs, General George C. Marshall and Admiral Harold R. Stark, had recommended on 5 November 1941 that the United States go to war

under such circumstances, and President Roosevelt's Cabinet agreed on 7 November. Michael Gannon, *Pearl Harbor Betrayed*, New York, Henry Holt & Co., 2001, at 116–17.

10 *Pearl Harbor Hearings*, vol. 10, at 5082–3, reprinted in Layton, '*And I Was There*': *Pearl Harbor and Midway – Breaking the Secrets*, New York, Quill William Morrow, 1985, at 258–9. Compare the text of this message with the message from the War Office to Air Chief Marshal Brooke-Popham in Appendix, No. 15.

11 See Appendix, No. 25.

12 *Pearl Harbor Hearings*, vol. 10, at 4802.

13 *Ibid.*, vol. 10, at 5080–9. Captain Creighton was not asked if he knew Admiral Phillips or anyone on his staff; in fact, Captain Creighton knew at least Admiral Tom Phillips, see Appendix, No. 9, and Captain O.W. Phillips, the Fleet Engineer Officer. Memoirs of O.W. Phillips, at 338. Papers of Rear Admiral O.W. Phillips. Imperial War Museum, Department of Documents.

14 *Old Friends, New Enemies*, at 406–11.

15 Letters from McClelland to Marder of 6 February, 15 February, 3 March and 30 March 1979. Marder Papers.

16 Brooke-Popham, 'Operations in the Far East, from 17th October 1940 to 27th December 1941', Supplement to the *London Gazette* of 20 January 1948. TNA ZJ 1/1028, at 555.

17 Brian Montgomery, *Shenton of Singapore: Governor and Prisoner of War*, Singapore, Times Books International, 1984, at 83.

18 Letter from McClelland to Marder of 30 March 1979. Marder Papers.

19 War Diary of Sir Shenton Thomas, quoted in Montgomery, *Shenton of Singapore*, at 83.

20 See Appendix, No. 27.

21 Brian Montgomery, *Shenton of Singapore*, at 5n.

22 Author's telephone conversations with Captain R.I.A. Sarrell, a friend of McClelland, and with McClelland's daughter and son-in-law.

23 Letter from Paymaster Captain Dougal Doig to Arthur Marder of 16 May 1979. Marder Papers.

24 McClelland also claimed that after the meeting Phillips had him send a signal to the Admiralty about his intentions, but he was adamant that the one he sent was not the signal that Phillips sent at 0934 Singapore time, Appendix, No. 36. Letter from McClelland to Marder of 11 March 1979. Marder Papers.

25 John Winant, *A Letter from Grosvenor Square: An Account of a Stewardship*, Boston, Houghton Mifflin Co., 1947, at 196–7.

26 Elphick, *Far Eastern File*, at 240.

27 Naval Historical Branch, *War with Japan*, vol. 2, at 46.

28 Arnold Lott and Robert Sumrall, *USS Ward – The First Shot*, Annapolis, Leeward Publications, 1977, at 24.

29 Attachment to letter from Lieutenant-Commander O.M.B. de las Casas to Arthur Marder of 1 July 1976. Marder Papers.

30 Log of HMS *Mauritius* for 8 December 1941. TNA Adm 53/114646.

31 War Diary of Admiral Geoffrey Layton, Part 1, at 9. TNA Adm 199/1185. See Appendix, No. 30.

32 War Diary of Admiral Geoffrey Layton, Part 1, at 9. TNA Adm 199/1185.
33 Bix, *Hirohito and the Making of Modern Japan*, at 436 and n. 111. According to an Admiralty message to Admiral Phillips, the President's message to the Emperor recounted the long history of peace between the two countries, drawing attention to the unjustifiable concentration of troops in all parts of Indo-China and urging him to withdraw in the interests of peace. See Appendix, No. 28.
34 Gillison, *Royal Australian Air Force 1939–1942*, at 215 n. 5.
35 Peter Elphick and Michael Smith, *Odd Man Out: The Story of the Singapore Traitor*, London, Hodder & Stoughton, 1993.
36 Gillison, *Royal Australian Air Force 1939–1942*, at 247–9.
37 'Misfortune off Malaya', attachment to letter from Paymaster Captain Dougal Doig to Arthur Marder of 8 September 1978. Marder Papers.
38 See Appendix, No. 36.
39 TNA Air 23/4745.
40 Russell Grenfell, *Main Fleet to Singapore*, London, Faber & Faber, 1951, at 114.
41 See Appendix, No. 40.
42 Richard Hough, *The Hunting of Force Z: Britain's Greatest Modern Naval Disaster*, London, Collins, 1963, at 192–3.
43 Grenfell, *Main Fleet to Singapore*, at 112.
44 Letter from C.W. McMullen to Marder of 3 March 1976. Marder Papers.

CHAPTER EIGHT

The Decision to Send Force Z to Attack

Once the Japanese had attacked and the war had begun, the critical decision was what to do with the *Prince of Wales* and *Repulse*. The main options were, first, to stay in Singapore; secondly, to sail Force Z to attack the Japanese; thirdly, to sail elsewhere, such as to Colombo, Darwin, Manila, the Dutch East Indies or even Pearl Harbor; or fourthly, to wait for reinforcements and then sail to attack the Japanese. The first option was not very attractive, because of all the publicity given the ships' arrival and the negative effect on morale if the ships had done nothing in the face of an invasion of Malaya, and because the Japanese bombing of Singapore had shown its vulnerability as a base. The fourth option was not attractive for the same reasons, and because the reinforcements that were to arrive in a few days, the British cruiser *Exeter*, the old Dutch cruiser *Java* and four old American destroyers, were not worth losing the chance to disrupt the Japanese landings at the outset. The only real options were the second and third ones, to sail elsewhere or to sail to attack the Japanese, and somehow it was the latter option that was chosen.

The decision to send Force Z to attack the Japanese is usually portrayed as Tom Phillips's to make, and is said to have occurred in the meeting aboard the *Prince of Wales* at noon on 8 December. In fact, he had already made the decision, or, perhaps more accurately, the decision had already been made for him, and the meeting in the *Prince of Wales* only confirmed it. To understand the decision better, it is necessary to look at it first from the perspective of Admiral Phillips and then from the perspective of Winston Churchill and the Admiralty.

To understand the decision from Admiral Phillips's perspective, it is necessary to examine in more detail the signals that were exchanged between the Admiralty and Admiral Phillips prior to his sailing. As we have seen, on 1 and 3 December, the Admiralty suggested that Phillips might get his ships away from Singapore, but he was not ordered to do so.[1] After the Japanese convoys had been sighted in the South China Sea, the Admiralty then changed course, and on 7 December sent this signal to Admiral Phillips:

> No decision has yet been taken by H.M. Government but on the assumption that it may be decided that if a Japanese expedition is located in the South China Sea in such a position that its course indicates that it is proceeding towards Thailand, Malaya, Borneo or Netherlands East Indies, report what action it would be possible to take with naval or air forces.[2]

Although the signal seems to be a mere inquiry, there is reason to think there was more to it than that. According to Paymaster Captain Dougal Doig, Admiral Layton's secretary, 'The enquiry must have carried for Admiral Phillips a strong implication that something positive in the way of interference with the enemy was expected, and was the deciding factor which made Phillips decide he *must* act, however hazardous the enterprise might be.'[3]

The signal has also been referred to as a 'prodding' signal.[4] The signal is stated to be from 'the Admiralty', not Churchill, but it bears his stamp. The Prime Minister was known to have a propensity for sending prodding signals, a habit he began in his first stint as First Lord of the Admiralty, from 1911 to 1915, to the great annoyance of the First Sea Lord, Admiral 'Jackie' Fisher.[5] In the Second World War, Churchill's habit of sending prodding signals also annoyed Admiral Andrew Cunningham, the C-in-C of the Mediterranean Fleet.[6] It is likely to be no coincidence that the prodding signal to Phillips had the same ring as a signal Churchill himself sent to Admiral Cunningham only two weeks before the one to Phillips, on 23 November 1941, regarding two Italian tankers with fuel that was vital to General Rommel and to the outcome of the battle in North Africa: 'I shall be glad to hear through [the] Admiralty what action you propose to take.'[7] Doubtless he needed no prodding, but Cunningham saw to it the tankers were sunk.

Phillips evidently understood the signal from the Admiralty as a prodding signal, and at 1601Z or 2331 Singapore time on the 7th, he replied:

If the relative strength of the enemy and our forces permit endeavour would be made to attack expedition by day or night.

If we are in inferior strength raid will be attempted and the Air Force will attack with bombs and torpedoes in conjunction with our naval forces within limit of aircraft radius of action.[8]

The beginning of the signal, Phillips's 'endeavour' signal, states 'Your 1329A 7th', the prodding signal, and in his 25 January 1942 report to the Prime Minister, Admiral Pound referred to the two signals in a sequence that suggests that the Admiralty inquiry prompted Admiral Phillips's reply.[9] There is no record of any Admiralty reply to Phillips's signal.

After the Japanese landings had begun, Admiral Phillips sent off another signal to the Admiralty, this one at 0934 Singapore time on 8 December:

(1) (corrupt group: (?) Provided that) as I hope I can make 4 destroyers available intended to proceed with *Prince of Wales* and *Repulse* dusk tonight 8/12 to attack enemy force off Kota Bharu daylight Wednesday 10th.

(2) Endeavours will be made to estimate strength of enemy naval forces by air R/C [reconnaissance], but large proportion of aircraft are naturally required for attack.[10]

The key word in this signal is 'intended'. According to the British naval historian Captain Stephen Roskill, 'Every British naval officer of those days was familiar with the convention whereby the originator of a signal using the word "intend" neither demanded nor expected an answer *unless the addressee disapproved of the intention expressed.*'[11]

The Admiralty did not reply to the 'intend' signal either, positively or negatively, and there is no evidence that the signal went astray or that it did not reach the Admiralty in time.[12] Accordingly, Admiral Phillips would have been justified in assuming the Admiralty agreed with his stated intention; he had stated his intention, and had received no disapproval from the Admiralty. Furthermore, having stated his intention, Phillips would have been hard pressed to change his mind and cancel the operation even if he still harboured doubts about it. The die was effectively cast.

In making his decision, Admiral Phillips had received some advice from Admiral Palliser, who is said to have advised him to go,[13] and Admiral Layton, who wrote to Dudley Pound just a week later:

I talked to Phillips twice about the operation and told him that if I were in his shoes I should do the same as he was going to do, but that I should not start on it unless the Air Force could guarantee me Reconnaissance and fighter protection and he entirely agreed – the last time was just before lunch the day he sailed and he as [sic] then going off to see Pulford the Air Vice-Marshal, and I did not see him again.[14]

Since the RAF could not guarantee fighter protection, the advice from Layton was probably not very helpful, particularly coming from someone who had requested in October that one or two battleships be sent to Singapore. Of course, whatever advice he received, Phillips was no doubt a man who would make up his own mind.

While the Admiralty had sent Admiral Phillips a 'prodding signal', that is not to say that he needed any prodding. Even before Phillips received the prodding signal, he told Admiral Hart when he left the Philippines that he would collect such ships as he could and would put to sea to meet the enemy.[15] Phillips's decision to sail Force Z to attack the Japanese was still a courageous decision. Even though he could not know exactly how seriously the odds were stacked against him, he knew the Japanese had bombers in Indo-China, that the chances of fighter protection were slim, that his screen would consist of no cruisers and only four destroyers, and that the Japanese had substantial surface forces and a number of submarines waiting for him.[16] Admiral Phillips knew he was running great risks, but accepted them.

Still, there is a point where a decision ceases to be courageous and becomes rash, and Phillips's decision came close to that point, even allowing for the fact that he thought he faced one capital ship instead of two. Phillips actually planned to leave his destroyers behind just before attacking the Japanese because of their low fuel, and to rendezvous with them before heading back to Singapore.[17] Phillips himself came to realize how dangerous a situation he had put Force Z in; after turning back on the evening of the 9th, a tired Admiral Phillips told the *Prince of Wales*'s Engineer Officer, Commander L.J. Goudy, that he would 'never again put capital ships in the position we are now in'.[18]

In spite of the risks incurred, or perhaps because of them, Admiral Phillips's decision was one that was fully in accord with Royal Navy traditions of attacking the enemy, no matter what the odds, and of going to the assistance of the Army. The Royal Navy had not built its magnificent reputation over the centuries by avoiding battle. As one historian had said of Admiral Christopher Cradock before the Battle of

Coronel in 1914, when he put his cruiser squadron against a superior German one commanded by Admiral von Spee,

> Avoiding action with the enemy was no more within Cradock's conception than it had been in Sir Richard Grenville's 'at Flores in the Azores' or was to be in Captain Warburton-Lee's at Narvik in 1940. Flight is the antithesis of the British naval tradition; there have been so many occasions when a numerically inferior British force has not hesitated to engage a stronger enemy.[19]

Unfortunately, like Tom Phillips, Admiral Cradock and Captain Warburton-Lee also lost their lives.

Given that the Admiralty had sent the prodding signal and that Phillips had indicated that he was planning to sail against the Japanese, the only thing that would have stopped him from sailing to attack the Japanese would have been a direct order from London to take his ships out of harm's way; to do otherwise would have seemed like running away.[20] Indeed, Phillips had realized before the war that such an order would be necessary. According to Captain S.E. Norfolk, who had been under Admiral Phillips when he was Director of Plans before the war, he and Phillips had a conversation in which Phillips agreed that [by implication, withdrawing from Singapore] was the 'correct course' but said that 'the decision to carry it out could not be left to the man on the spot as it would look like cowardice. . . . He little knew that when the time came he would be the man-on-the-spot and that the order would not be given by the man responsible.'[21]

Indeed, it would also have taken a different kind of courage to have not attacked and to have borne the criticism that would undoubtedly have come. The Royal Navy had not shot an admiral for not attacking the enemy since Admiral John Byng in 1757, *pour encourager les autres*,[22] but there were more recent reminders of what happened to those who did not show the proper offensive spirit. In 1914, Rear Admiral Ernest Troubridge had been court-martialled but acquitted for not engaging the German battlecruiser *Goeben* with his armoured cruisers; in November 1940, the Admiralty had set up a short-lived board of inquiry to investigate Admiral Somerville's supposed failure to pursue a fleeing Italian force at the Battle of Spartivento;[23] and, even closer to home, in May 1941, Mr Churchill and the First Sea Lord had wanted Captain Leach and Admiral Wake-Walker of the cruiser *Norfolk* court-martialled for their supposed failure to continue engaging the

Bismarck after the *Hood* had been sunk. An ill-informed Churchill even said that the *Prince of Wales* not pressing home her attack was the 'worst thing since Troubridge turned away from the *Goeben* in 1914'.[24] Fortunately, the idea of the court martial died when the C-in-C of the Home Fleet, Admiral Sir John Tovey, said he would strike his flag and testify as prisoners' friend.[25] There is no evidence that such a worry affected Tom Phillips's decision to go on the attack, and perhaps it would do him a disservice to suggest it did. If it did, he would only have been human; after all, it may have affected Admiral Cradock, who wrote before the Battle of Coronel, 'I will take care not to suffer the fate of poor Troubridge.'[26]

In the end, Churchill and the Admiralty had prodded Tom Phillips into an operation his aggressive nature may have welcomed, but his intellect must have told him was very risky, an operation that only the Admiralty could have ordered him out of. To some extent, the First Sea Lord appreciated the position into which his friend had been put; a few months after the battle, Pound told Admiral Layton that he was glad that Phillips had decided to take the action he did, but added, 'I am only sorry that a set of circumstances arose which placed him in such a difficult position.'[27] Indeed.

Having looked at the decision from Admiral Phillips's perspective, it is time to look at the decision from the perspective of Winston Churchill and the Admiralty, specifically the First Sea Lord, Dudley Pound. Was it really the intention of Churchill and the Admiralty that Force Z sail against the Japanese? As we shall see, answering that question is no easy task. We shall first look again at the exchange of signals, then at what Dudley Pound wrote, and, finally, at what Winston Churchill said and wrote about the matter.

As for the exchange of signals, on the face of it, the 'prodding' signal, which implied that some action was expected of Phillips, and the lack of a reply to the 'endeavour' signal or the 'intend' signal would mean that at least the Admiralty, if not also Churchill, believed that Phillips should take some action against the Japanese. The matter could be left there, but for several reasons it is unsatisfying to rely on silence alone as an indication of agreement. For one thing, we do not know for sure that we have all the pertinent signals that passed between the Admiralty and Admiral Phillips; for instance, we know that the Admiralty sent Phillips a signal at 0950Z on 7 December,[28] but we do not know what it said. For another thing, the circumstances were not conducive to the Admiralty or Churchill being able to consider Phillips's 'intend' signal for very long before he sailed. Finally, while neither Churchill nor Pound ever wrote anything about the prodding signal or about Phillips's signal about his intentions, each did write something about the matter that is worth considering.

Under the circumstances, neither Pound nor Churchill would have had much time to consider whether they agreed with Phillips's 'intend' signal or not, given the time difference between London and Singapore, the short period of time between the dispatch of Phillips's signal and the time he sailed, the time of day involved, and the distracting impact of the Japanese attack on the United States and Great Britain. There was a 7½-hour difference between GMT (Zone Z) and Singapore time (GH), but in December 1941 the real difference was 6½ hours, since London was on British Summer Time (Zone A), one hour ahead of GMT. Phillips's 'intend' signal was sent at 0934 Singapore time, or 0304A, on 8 December, and would have taken time to be transmitted and then decoded (and the corrupt code group in the signal could have delayed decoding) before it could be passed to Pound and then to Churchill. Churchill and Pound would have had only from sometime after 0304A to 1100A on the 8th, when Force Z sailed, to inform Phillips if they disagreed with his intention to take the ships out against the Japanese. Since the 'endeavour' signal was received in London three hours after transmission, and it had a corrupt group, it is reasonable to assume the 'intend' signal was received in London about 0604A on 8 December.

To make matters worse, Phillips's 'intend' signal would have arrived in London very early in the morning on 8 December. Pound was probably in London, since he sent a signal to Admiral Stark at 2300A on 7 December[29] and one to Phillips at 0114A on 8 December.[30] Churchill was at the Prime Minister's country residence, Chequers, when he learned the news of the attack on Pearl Harbor just after 9.00 p.m., or 2100A, on 7 December.[31] He immediately called President Roosevelt to confirm the news of the Japanese attack, and then received a call from the Admiralty that confirmed the news.[32] After arranging for Parliament to meet the next day, and contacting the Foreign Office to arrange a declaration of war on Japan, he slept 'the sleep of the saved and thankful'.[33] At some point the next morning, he had to rise and leave for London, though we do not know if he adhered to his strict rule of not being awoken before 8 a.m. unless Britain itself had been invaded.[34] He then travelled from Chequers to London to be in time for a War Cabinet meeting at 12.30

p.m. (Z or A) on 8 December (at which there was no mention of the *Prince of Wales* and *Repulse*, at least according to the minutes),[35] but by then Force Z had already sailed. Presumably Churchill and Pound spoke at some point during the night of the 7th or the morning of the 8th, but apart from the call we know Churchill received from 'the Admiralty', there is no record of any communication between them. Even assuming he was informed of Phillips's signal, these circumstances would have at least made it more difficult for Churchill to carefully consider it.

While we do not know what consideration Mr Churchill or the First Sea Lord was able to give Phillips's 'intend' signal before he sailed, we do have some record of what Dudley Pound wrote about the matter before his death in 1943. While Pound never wrote about receiving Phillips's 'intend' signal, he firmly supported Phillips's decision to go on the attack in his letters to Admiral Layton,[36] to Phillips's friend Mildred Barker[37] and to Lady Phillips.[38] To Lady Phillips, he wrote that members of the Board of Admiralty were of the unanimous opinion that he had done the right thing in embarking on the operation, and added, perhaps revealingly, 'It might well have been a brilliant success.'

Pound was also supportive of Tom Phillips in his January 1942 report to the Prime Minister on the loss of the ships. One of the main conclusions was that 'the risks he took were fair and reasonable in the light of the knowledge he had of the enemy when compared to the very urgent and vital issues at stake and on which the whole safety of Malaya may have depended', although he added that 'in the light of after events it would have been better if he had asked for fighter protection at least when the attack was known to be developing'.[39]

Perhaps most importantly, we have the signal that Pound sent at 2300A on 7 December, or 0530 Singapore time, to the US Navy's Chief of Naval Operations, Admiral Harold R. 'Betty' Stark. In reference to discussions between Admiral Phillips and Admiral Hart, Pound said, '[A]s long as you are happy about it, I have complete confidence in anything Admiral Phillips agreed to, and I am sure we can rely on our representatives on the spot to acquit themselves forcefully.'[40]

By that, Pound must have expected his representative on the spot – Tom Phillips – to acquit himself 'forcefully' by attacking the Japanese.

Pound's message to Admiral Stark also shows Pound's willingness to rely on Phillips's judgement. The same theme was sounded by Admiral Henry Moore, Phillips's successor as Vice-Chief of the Naval Staff, who later recalled:

I remember clearly that I tried to persuade Dudley Pound to send Phillips a signal during his passage out to the effect that it would be wise, after refuelling at Singapore, to get himself 'lost' in the Pacific, thereby offering a dangerous and highly mobile threat to any operations the Japanese might contemplate. However, no such signal was sent for it was Pound's assessment that Phillips, with his very recent Admiralty experience, was sufficiently within the picture to have a clear idea of the problems.[41]

Admiral Pound was notorious for being a 'back-seat driver' – that is, for interfering with the decisions of commanders at sea[42] – but in this case he may have tempered his instinct to interfere with Phillips, whose judgement he trusted so much.

In contrast to what Dudley Pound wrote on the subject, what Mr Churchill said and wrote about Tom Phillips and the operation is much more complicated, if not baffling. Starting with his best-known writing about the battle, in Chapter 12 of *The Grand Alliance*, Churchill first gave a fairly straightforward account of the operation, which even mentioned that Phillips 'reported his intentions to the Admiralty'.[43] That passage was no doubt drafted by Mr Churchill's naval assistant, Captain G.R.G. Allen, whose draft of the account was modified after discussions with Commander Goodenough to make it more favourable to Admiral Phillips.[44]

Then Mr Churchill wrote this famous passage:

I convened a meeting, mostly Admiralty, in the Cabinet War Room at ten o'clock on the night of the 9th to review the naval position. We were about a dozen. We tried to measure the consequences of this fundamental change in our war position against Japan. We had lost the command of every ocean except the Atlantic. Australia and New Zealand and all the vital islands in their sphere were open to attack. We had only one key weapon in our hands. The *Prince of Wales* and the *Repulse* had arrived at Singapore. They had been sent to these waters to exercise that kind of vague menace which capital ships of the highest quality whose whereabouts is unknown can impose upon all hostile naval calculations. How should we use them now? Obviously they must go to sea and vanish among the innumerable islands. There was general agreement on that.

I thought myself they should go across the Pacific to join what was left of the American Fleet. It would be a proud gesture at this moment, and would knit the English-speaking world together. We had already cordially agreed to the American Navy Department withdrawing their capital ships from the Atlantic. Thus in a few months there might be a fleet in being on the west coast of America capable of fighting a decisive sea battle if need be. The existence of such a fleet and of such a fact would be the best possible shield to our brothers in Australasia. We were all much attracted by this line of thought. But as the hour was late we decided to sleep on it, and settle the next morning what to do with the *Prince of Wales* and the *Repulse*.

Within a couple of hours they were at the bottom of the sea.[45]

As the saying goes, 'What's wrong with this picture?' As one famous naval historian has commented, 'It is an extraordinary fact that 48 hours after the Japanese attack on Pearl Harbor, the authorities in London seemed to be discussing in a leisurely way what the operational role of Force Z should be, and deciding to sleep on it, when that Force was already committed to a hazardous enterprise.'[46]

But was that in fact the way the meeting went? Unfortunately, we do not know exactly what was said at the meeting, since by 1948, when Churchill was working on that chapter of his memoirs, there was no longer a verbatim record of what had been said, as Mr Churchill well knew.[47] There were official minutes of the meeting, which was a Chiefs of Staff Committee meeting, which stated in part:

> The Prime Minister discussed with the First Lord of the Admiralty and the Chiefs of Staff possible naval dispositions and other measures to redress the balance of naval power in the Pacific.
>
> . . .
>
> The Admiralty were invited to give careful attention to the following alternative plans: – (a) A plan to restore the command of the Pacific by concentrating a superior Anglo-American battle fleet at Hawaii, with a view to offensive action against the Japanese mainland, and (b) A plan to employ 'Prince of Wales', 'Repulse' and 'Centurion'[48] as rogue elephants.[49]

Like Mr Churchill's account, the minutes evidence no awareness that the ships had already gone to sea to attack the Japanese.

Mr Churchill's account of the meeting and the minutes have been criticized by Sir Andrew Gilchrist, who in December 1941 was a junior diplomat in Bangkok. Sir Andrew has suggested that it was 'highly misleading' for Churchill to suggest that the ships 'must go to sea', since he should have known they were already at sea, and criticized the minutes as 'remarkably uninformative' and 'no doubt tailored after the event to take account of the fate of Force Z'. He continued:

> A fuller account could well have contained some reference to a warning by the First Sea Lord that at the very moment they were sitting down to their meeting about Force Z, then – if Phillips had adhered to the plan he had signalled to London – he and his ships must be within an hour of doing battle with the Japanese navy. To await the outcome of that battle would have been a very reasonable ground for deferring any decision on the future of Force Z. To defer a decision 'because the hour was late' was lame and uncharacteristic, given what Churchill regarded as normal working hours!'[50]

Sir Andrew may well be right, but it is impossible to prove that the meeting actually went the way he suggests. Indeed, the recollections of two men who attended the meeting are not so different from Mr Churchill's account or from the minutes. General Alan Brooke was present, and he wrote in his diary:

> We were summoned to a C.O.S. [Chiefs of Staff Committee] meeting under the P.M. for 11.00 p.m.[51] The P.M. was mainly concerned about naval situation in the Pacific due to Japanese action on U.S.A. fleet in Honolulu in which three battleships were sunk and three badly damaged out of eight. This has entirely upset the balance in the Pacific and leaves Japs master of the ocean until we can assemble some forces there. We therefore examined the possibility of sending British battleships to restore situation. Finally left matters to be thought over and broke up at midnight.[52]

Unfortunately, this account is maddeningly susceptible to several interpretations: sending British battleships to restore which situation, the one in northern Malaya or the one in the Pacific? The context would seem to make the latter more likely than the former.

Churchill's Chief of Staff, General Hastings Ismay, was also present at the meeting, and later recalled:

> [Colonel Leslie] Hollis and I clearly remember the meeting to which you refer, but I think you must have summoned it unexpectedly and,

for some reason or another, there is no record of what was said. On the other hand, Hollis and I distinctly remember that the movements of the *Prince of Wales* and the *Repulse* were the main subject of discussion, and that you put forward two alternatives, namely:-

(a) That they should either vanish into the ocean wastes and exercise a vague menace. Your description of them was that they should be 'rogue elephants': or

(b) That they should go across the Pacific and join the remnants of the American fleet.

Hollis and I also agree that no decision was taken and that you proposed to re-consider the problem in the morning light.

From the above, it will be seen that both Hollis and I agree with your account on page 6: but unfortunately we are unable to confirm it from our records.[53]

Unfortunately, we do not know which draft of the passage on the meeting Ismay and Hollis had reviewed, so it is not exactly clear what they were agreeing with. Strangely, in the same letter, General Ismay also suggested that Mr Churchill should not call the meeting a 'naval meeting', but for some reason Churchill insisted on referring those attending as 'mostly Admiralty', which they were not: the minutes of the meeting listed ten participants or observers, only four of whom were 'Admiralty', even if you count the First Lord of the Admiralty, A.V. Alexander.[54]

While we cannot know for sure what transpired in the meeting, we can examine the unstated assumptions in Mr Churchill's account of the meeting: namely, that (a) Churchill and the Chiefs of Staff did not know that Tom Phillips had already taken his ships to sea and thought that they were still in Singapore, and (b) using Force Z to attack the Japanese was not the course of action they wanted at that time.

With respect to the first assumption, did Churchill and the Admiralty really not know that Phillips had gone off to attack the Japanese? It seems inconceivable that, by the evening of 9 December, Churchill and the Admiralty did not know the whereabouts of the *Prince of Wales* and *Repulse*. Admiral Phillips's signal about his intentions had been sent almost thirty-one hours before. There is no reason to believe it did not reach the Admiralty, even though one of Phillips's signals from the Philippines was delayed,[55] and Phillips sent another signal to the Admiralty just 47 minutes later that referenced the signal stating his intentions ('My 0204').[56] According to General

Ismay, Churchill knew 'where every cruiser is';[57] how could he not have known where the *Prince of Wales* and *Repulse* were, especially if he thought they were his 'one key weapon'? And how could Dudley Pound not know the whereabouts of Tom Phillips and the Royal Navy's only capital ships in the Far East? If Pound knew, how could he have failed to inform Churchill? It is true that there is no record of a message from London that references Phillips's 'intend' signal ('Your 0204') or that specifically evidences knowledge that the ships had sailed. Nor is there any record that London was informed that the ships had actually sailed, apart from the rather cryptic suggestion in a situation report sent by Brooke-Popham to the War Office at 1300GH (0630A) on 9 December that stated, 'Naval. Our forces are operating in the South China Sea,'[58] but since Admiral Phillips had already signalled his intentions to the Admiralty, an additional signal should have been unnecessary.

Regarding whether at least Churchill and Pound knew the ships were at sea, there are two admittedly strange pieces to the puzzle. First, there is evidence that the First Lord, A.V. Alexander, may not have known where the ships were. Years later, Lord Alexander's secretary, Sir Clifford Jarrett, recalled that the First Lord's reaction to the news of the disaster was 'one of shock and almost unbelief. The news, so far as I can remember, came right out of the blue and no one could understand why Tom Phillips should have decided to venture his ships up a coast virtually controlled by the Japs and devoid of air cover.'[59]

Indeed, there is nothing about the ships' sailing in the daily operations reports for the First Lord leading up to 10 December.[60] For whatever reason, perhaps because he was a member of the Labour Party, Lord Alexander was not trusted with knowledge of the 'Ultra secret',[61] the breaking of German codes by the British, and he may not have been trusted with other sensitive information, such as knowledge of Admiral Phillips's operation, far-fetched as that may seem.

There is also the riddle of the message sent by the First Sea Lord to Tom Phillips on 9 December referring to defence against torpedo attack in harbour. Why would Pound send such a message if he knew that Phillips was not in harbour, but at sea? The most likely explanation is that Pound simply wanted Phillips to have the information before his return to Singapore; if Pound really thought the ships were in harbour and that an attack on them was imminent, he would have marked the signal 'Immediate' or 'Most Immediate', instead of just 'Important'. Another possible explanation is that Admiral Pound had access to intercepts of Japanese signals about the ships still being in Singapore on 9 December and about the Japanese plan to attack them there on the morning of the 10th, assumed the ships were in harbour, and wanted to warn Phillips. That explanation assumes the British could decode Japanese naval signals[62] *and* that Pound would rely on Japanese signals for information on the location of his own capital ships, but that hardly seems very likely. The signal must remain a mystery, though the first explanation is still the most probable explanation.

While the evidence is not conclusive, in the end the unstated assumption in Churchill's account that he did not know the ships had gone to sea is too inconsistent with the available evidence, which indicates that at least Pound and Churchill must have known. Whether the rest of the Chiefs of Staff Committee knew is another matter. If they didn't know before the meeting, there may well have been some discussion at the meeting about the operation the ships had embarked upon, but for some reason it did not find its way into the minutes; this may have been an example of where 'official minutes of high-level meetings are often as notable for what they omit as for what they record'.[63] It is also possible, however, incredible as it may seem, that Churchill and Pound were the only ones in attendance who knew the ships had gone to sea to attack the Japanese, and neglected to reveal it to the others.

The second unstated assumption in Churchill's account of the 9 December meeting was that Phillips's operation was not at all what he and the Chiefs of Staff Committee had in mind. We have two contemporaneous indications of what the Prime Minister thought of the idea of going out against the Japanese.

The first, on 7 December, presumably before he learned that the Japanese had actually attacked, is that he had General Ismay dictate a minute to the Chiefs of Staff and Foreign Secretary Anthony Eden. Referring to a telegram from Lord Halifax in Washington after a meeting with President Roosevelt, Mr Churchill stated:

This removes all political difficulty from initiating naval or air action, and I agree with the President that 'we should obviously attack Japanese transports' in conditions prescribed. . . . Attack is therefore solely one of naval opportunity and expediency. Admiral Phillips should be made fully aware of all these telegrams from the United States, including the President's proposed programme of warnings to Japan, culminating Wednesday the 10th.[64]

By then, Mr Churchill obviously had no problem with Tom Phillips attacking the Japanese convoys while they were at sea, subject, however, to 'opportunity and expediency'.

The second, and perhaps better, indication of what Mr Churchill really thought is to be found in a speech he made to the House of Commons at 3.00 p.m. (1500A) on 8 December, a few hours after Tom Phillips had sailed, on the subject of the war with Japan. In the speech, he said,

> . . . the House and the Empire[65] will notice that some of the finest ships of the Royal Navy have reached their stations in the Far East at a very convenient moment. Every preparation in our power has been made, and I do not doubt that we shall give a good account of ourselves.[66]

That was not the part of the speech quoted by Churchill in *The Grand Alliance*,[67] and is hardly the sort of thing one would say about ships that were about to vanish among the islands or undertake a long voyage to Pearl Harbor. Mr Churchill's statement did not go unnoticed: one Member, Mr Hore Belisha, said that Mr Churchill, 'in an act which recalls what he did as First Lord of the Admiralty in 1914, is to be congratulated on having a British fleet ready in the Pacific. That was a decision of great foresight, for which the nation – and more than one nation – has cause to be grateful.'[68] As for what Churchill did in 1914, Hore Belisha was probably referring to the decision in November 1914 to dispatch the battlecruisers *Invincible* and *Inflexible* to the Falklands, just in time for them to annihilate Admiral von Spee's cruiser force on another 8 December, twenty-seven years earlier.

Shortly after the battle, Churchill was very supportive of Phillips and his foray. In a speech to the House of Commons on 11 December, he said that

> Admiral Phillips was undertaking a thoroughly sound, well-considered offensive operation, not indeed free from risk, but not different in principle from many similar operations we have repeatedly carried out in the North Sea and the Mediterranean.[69]

When questioned after the speech, Mr Churchill stated, 'My opinion, on expert authority, is that what was done was rightly and wisely done and risked in the circumstances.'[70] If the Prime Minister had thought

Admiral Phillips had erred, he presumably would have chosen his words a bit differently.

A few days later, on his way to the United States in HMS *Duke of York*, the recently completed sister ship of the *Prince of Wales*, the Prime Minister confided to the American envoy Averell Harriman,

> It is a sad business, the *Prince of Wales* and *Repulse*. They could have harassed the enemy, always a threat, playing the second role to your big fleet. We made great sacrifices to send them [to the Far East]. They came in time. It is a cruel thing. Perhaps it was bad judgement. But I will never criticize a man who aims his arrows at the enemy. I will defend him.[71]

In this, we see echoes of the 'vague menace' Churchill says he spoke of at the 9 December meeting; the question is whether he had thought in such terms prior to the meeting on 9 December. Evidently by the time of the conversation in the *Duke of York*, Mr Churchill was already having doubts about Tom Phillips's judgement – presumably he was not referring to his own bad judgement – but still vowed to defend him; whether he did so later is quite another question.

Then, on 23 April 1942, Mr Churchill gave a speech at a secret session of the House of Commons. According to his notes, he said:

> The *Prince of Wales* and *Repulse* arrived at Singapore on 2 December. This seemed to be a timely moment. It was hoped that their presence there might be a deterrent upon the war party in Japan, and it was intended that they should vanish as soon as possible into the blue. I have already explained to the House how they became involved in a local operation against Japanese transports in the Gulf of Siam which led to their destruction. On the night of 9 December, in view of the news we had received about the heavy losses of the American fleet at Pearl Harbor, I proposed to the Chiefs of Staff that the *Prince of Wales* and *Repulse* should join the undamaged portion of the American fleet in order to sustain the position in the Pacific. The matter was to be considered next day, but in the morning arrived the news of the loss of both these great ships.[72]

The speech takes much the same line on the 9 December meeting as Mr Churchill's memoirs, and was delivered shortly after the fall of Singapore, when Mr Churchill was under fire for his government's handling of the situation in the Far East. Interestingly, the speech ties the meeting on the night of 9 December to the receipt of the news of American losses at Pearl Harbor.

Mr Churchill's later writings were not so supportive of Tom Phillips or of the operation he undertook. In a letter relating to the account of the battle in Captain Roskill's *War at Sea* series, Churchill blamed Tom Phillips, stating, 'The last thing in the world that the Defence Committee wished was that anything like the movement which Admiral Phillips thought it right to make to intercept a Japanese invasion force should have been made by his two vessels without even air cover.'[73] In the same letter, Churchill claimed that it was always his intention that the ships should show themselves at Singapore and then disappear, but Captain Roskill searched the documentation and found nothing to support Churchill's assertion, finally declaring it to be 'wisdom after the event'.[74] Not that Captain Roskill had reason to be a member of Churchill's fan club; according to Roskill, he had got in Churchill's bad books early in the war and had not got out,[75] and he could not have been happy about Churchill's holding up the publication of the first volume of *The War at Sea*. Still, there is no reason to doubt Roskill's conclusion.

Even Captain Allen would not help Mr Churchill show that he had always been in favour of sending the ships away. During the dispute with Captain Roskill, Captain Allen reminded Mr Churchill that the documents showed that the purpose of the ships was to be a deterrent, and the idea of their disappearing does not appear until 1 December.[76] When Captain Allen was helping him with his memoirs, he reminded Mr Churchill that he had asked him

> to find out whether action was taken by you or whether discussions took place between you and others regarding the possible withdrawal of the 'Prince of Wales' from Singapore at this time. I could find no trace of anything in the minutes either of the Chiefs-of-Staff or the Defence Committee.[77]

To be fair to Mr Churchill, at one time he had urged caution, telling Dudley Pound on 11 November, 'I do not quite see what all this haste is to arrive at Singapore for a pow-wow. This is one of those cases where I am for "Safety First".'[78] He may even have had a hand in the signals of 1 and 3 December that suggested that Phillips get away from Singapore, but after that the record is bare of any such cautionary notes, and instead there was the 'prodding signal' of 7 December. Mr

Churchill's file on the subject is completely and conspicuously empty after 4 December.[79]

Perhaps this is what really happened. The First Sea Lord, at Churchill's insistence or with his concurrence, sent the prodding signal asking Phillips what action he could take, and Phillips's reply showed that he understood that action was what they wanted. Phillips then sent the signal that he intended to attack the Japanese with the *Prince of Wales* and *Repulse* and four destroyers. In the precious little time they had to consider the matter, Churchill and the Admiralty sent no reply to the signal because they agreed with the decision to attack, perhaps in part because they believed the *Prince of Wales* and *Repulse* would face only the *Kongo*. It is also possible that there was a misunderstanding, and that Pound and Churchill went along with what Phillips proposed because they trusted his judgement, and Phillips had merely proposed what he was prodded into proposing; however, it is more likely that they understood each other perfectly. After the ships had sailed, Churchill learned the extent of the disaster suffered by the Americans at Pearl Harbor, and began to get cold feet about Phillips's operation. When Churchill had lunch with the King on 9 December, the King came away from the lunch very concerned about the *Prince of Wales* and *Repulse*, and Churchill may well have come away with the same feeling. Realizing that the Japanese were not pushovers after all, and that the two most important British warships in the Far East were in danger, Churchill called a Chiefs of Staff meeting for that night to discuss what could be done. Nothing was decided at the meeting because the participants realized it was too late to do anything; though the minutes do not say so, the participants knew that the ships had gone to sea and, as far as they knew, were just hours away from attacking the Japanese, and could hardly be recalled. Vanishing among the islands and sailing to Pearl Harbor may well have been discussed as potential options *once the ships had returned to Singapore*. The shock and unbelief expressed by First Lord A.V. Alexander as to why Tom Phillips would have gone up the east coast of Malaya does not establish that he did not learn about the operation until he learned they were sunk, but is more likely an indication that he did not know that Phillips had been prodded into the operation by Pound and Churchill. Alan Brooke's reaction to the loss of the ships in his diary entry for 10 December shows no surprise that the ships had gone into harm's way.[80] The alternative explanation, that Mr Churchill called the meeting and then he and Pound did not reveal to the others there that the ships had already gone to sea, would mean that the meeting was no more than a charade, and would assume an unbelievable level of duplicity on the part of Churchill.

If that is what actually happened, how do we explain Mr Churchill's later writings on the *Prince of Wales* and *Repulse*, especially his account of the 9 December meeting? In part, it may have been his way of coping with what was for him a very painful and emotional issue.[81] After a stroke in 1953, he had a disturbing dream about the loss of the ships, but could not bring himself to discuss it with his physician, Lord Moran.[82] As time passed, Mr Churchill seems to have persuaded himself that he had always been in favour of sending the ships away from Singapore and was never in favour of Phillips's operation, and his later writings reflected that.

Whatever he thought at the time of writing, his account of the 9 December meeting seems to be an ideal way of subtly criticizing Phillips's decision to attack the Japanese with Force Z and of avoiding responsibility and blame. In at least one case, that is exactly how it worked: one historian cited Churchill's account of the meeting of 9 December in support of the rather remarkable statement, 'Churchill had no responsibility for the tragic fate of those two battleships.'[83] Churchill's insistence on mischaracterizing the attendance of the meeting as 'naval' and then as 'mostly naval' is difficult to explain except as a way of diverting enquiry into what really transpired at the meeting.

In several other instances, Mr Churchill was not above finding ways in his writings to distance himself from the worst naval disasters that occurred on his watch. For example, in July 1942, the Arctic convoy PQ-17 was destroyed by German bombers and U-boats on its way to the Soviet Union after being ordered to scatter by First Sea Lord Dudley Pound, who feared that the battleship *Tirpitz* was about to descend on the convoy. According to naval historian Stephen Roskill, Churchill's recollection that he never discussed the matter with Pound and that 'so strictly was the secret of these orders being sent on the First Sea Lord's authority [to the convoy escort] guarded by the Admiralty it was not until after the war that I learned the facts'[84] seemed to show 'a lapse in the Prime Minister's memory'.[85] Not that Mr Churchill was responsible for the disaster that befell PQ-17; however, he seems to have gone to inordinate lengths to distance himself from that disaster.

A second, and even more pertinent, example is from Churchill's history of the First World War, *The World Crisis*. One of the worst British naval disasters of the war occurred at the Battle of Coronel in November 1914, when two British armoured cruisers commanded by Admiral

Christopher Cradock, the *Good Hope* and *Monmouth*, were sunk with very heavy loss of life off the coast of Chile by Admiral von Spee's cruiser squadron, which was centred around the armoured cruisers *Gneisenau* and *Scharnhorst*. The Admiralty had denied Cradock the more powerful armoured cruiser *Defence*, and Cradock had more or less informed the Admiralty that the old battleship *Canopus* was too slow to accompany him into battle. The Admiralty nevertheless let Cradock seek out von Spee's far superior squadron.

Churchill, who was First Lord of the Admiralty at the time of the battle, wrote of the defeat at Coronel in *The World Crisis*: 'I cannot therefore accept for the Admiralty any share in the responsibility for what followed.'[86] Churchill's statement 'could have only one interpretation; that the whole responsibility was Cradock's.'[87] One noted naval historian has written that Churchill's statement of disavowal was 'far too sweeping',[88] and another naval historian has described Churchill's verdict on the battle and his argument in support of it as 'specious'.[89] While Admiral Cradock may have been partly to blame for sending signals that were not perfectly clear, the Admiralty certainly was far from blameless, and, more importantly, 'to Churchill belongs a considerable measure of personal responsibility for the disaster'.[90] While Churchill's treatment of Tom Phillips in *The Grand Alliance* is not as clear a disavowal as his treatment of Admiral Cradock in *The World Crisis*, it is perhaps because Churchill, who had been taken to task for 'attacking the memory of a heroic martyr to his duty and his orders',[91] had learned to be more subtle.

There are a number of almost eerie parallels between the stories of Battle of Coronel and the loss of the *Prince of Wales* and *Repulse*. Admiral Cradock was given the task of destroying the German cruisers with a force insufficient for the task, and Phillips was prodded into an operation to forestall the Japanese invasion with a force much too unbalanced for the task. Cradock, when informed he could not have the powerful armoured cruiser *Defence*, said, 'All right; we'll do without,'[92] and Phillips, when informed he would have no fighter protection on 10 December, said, 'Well, we must get on without it.'[93]

Mr Churchill, on the other hand, may have been thinking in terms of the seeming parallels with another battle. In a glorious moment for Churchill and his new First Sea Lord, Jackie Fisher, the defeat at Coronel was avenged just weeks later, on 8 December 1914, at the Battle of the Falklands, when a force including the battlecruisers *Invincible* and *Inflexible* virtually annihilated Admiral von Spee's cruiser squadron. The victor at the Falklands was Vice-Admiral Doveton Sturdee, who, just like Tom Phillips, had just come from the top staff job at the Admiralty (Sturdee had been Chief of the War Staff, and Phillips had been Vice-Chief of the Naval Staff), was of small stature and was no extrovert.[94]

One naval historian has suggested that 'Churchill may have recalled this choice [Sturdee] and hoped that the despatch of two capital ships even further afield in 1941, under the command of a flag officer plucked from the same desk at the Admiralty, would produce a comparable result.'[95] Perhaps thinking along the same lines, the Admiralty gave Phillips's force a cover plan with the Falklands as its destination, and for dummy radio traffic it was allocated the vacant delivery groups (a form of call sign) of Sturdee's long-gone *Invincible* and *Inflexible*.[96] If that were not enough, the *Prince of Wales* and *Repulse* even sailed from Singapore on 8 December, the anniversary of the Battle of the Falklands. There, unfortunately, the parallels ended: instead of a Falklands-like victory, Mr Churchill would reap a Coronel-like defeat. Unlike the situation in 1914, the situation in 1941 could not be restored within a few weeks by sending out a few more ships.

Notes

1   See Appendix, Nos 10 and 11.

2   See Appendix, No. 19.

3   Marder, *Old Friends, New Enemies*, at 406, quoting 'Misfortune Off Malaya', at 38, an attachment to a letter from Doig to Marder of 8 September 1978. Marder Papers.

4   Gilchrist, *Malaya 1941*, at 121–2.

5   Roskill, *Churchill and the Admirals*, at 293 and 49n.

6   Admiral of the Fleet Viscount Cunningham of Hyndhope, *A Sailor's Odyssey*, New York, E.P. Dutton & Co., 1951, at 231.

7   Churchill Papers, 20/36, quoted in Martin Gilbert, *Winston S. Churchill, Vol. 6: Finest Hour 1939–1941*, Boston, Houghton Mifflin Co., 1983, at 1244. Reproduced with permission of Curtis Brown Ltd, London, on behalf of C&T Publications.

8   TNA Cab 121/114. For the full text of the signal, see Appendix, No. 22.

9   TNA Prem 3/163/2, at 11.

10 See Appendix, No. 36.

11 Roskill, *Churchill and the Admirals*, at 100 (emphasis in original). The passage was written in connection with Captain Warburton-Lee and the First Battle of Narvik in April 1940.

12 The Admiralty replied to a later signal sent by Phillips at 1021GH on the 8th that referenced the 'intend' signal ('My 0204Z/8'), so it should have been aware of the existence of the earlier signal. See Appendix, No. 37.

13 Unpublished memoirs of Rear Admiral O.W. Phillips, at 337. Papers of Rear Admiral O.W. Phillips. Imperial War Museum, Department of Documents.

14 Letter from Layton to Dudley Pound of 18 December 1941. Layton Papers, British Library. Layton told his secretary, Paymaster Captain Dougal Doig, that he had given Phillips the same advice. Attachment to letter from Doig to Arthur Marder of 20 September 1978. Marder Papers.

15 Leutze, *A Different Kind of Victory*, at 226.

16 Admiral Phillips's decision to sail with such an unbalanced force can be compared to the decision made by Admiral William 'Bull' Halsey to send Admiral Willis Lee with the battleships *Washington* and *South Dakota* and four destroyers to seek a night battle with the Japanese off Guadalcanal in November 1942. Lee was one of the most skilful of the admirals of the US Navy, whose admirals had so far shown little skill in the battles off Guadalcanal, and that night he won a great victory, sinking the battleship *Kirishima* and stopping the Japanese effort to resupply its men on Guadalcanal, against the loss of three of his four destroyers and considerable damage to the *South Dakota*. It was nevertheless a great gamble; if even one of the many Japanese 'Long Lance' torpedoes launched that night had found its mark, Admiral Lee and his ships might have shared the sad fate of Tom Phillips.

17 See Appendix, No. 48, para. 9.

18 Letters from L.J. Goudy to A.J. Marder of 17 December 1975 and 15 January 1976. Marder Papers.

19 Geoffrey Bennett, *Coronel and the Falklands*, New York, MacMillan Co., 1962, at 27.

20 Admiral Layton's secretary, Captain Doig, later wrote that the ships should have kept out the way and gone to Darwin, but that that 'would have been running away from the enemy, and the officer on the spot would need imperative authority from above to do it. That authority he clearly did not receive.' Doig, 'Misfortune off Malaya', at 39, attachment to letter from Doig to Arthur Marder of 6 September 1978. Marder Papers.

21 Letter from Captain S.E. Norfolk to T.V.G. Phillips of 2 December 1977. T.S.V. Phillips Papers.

22 John Winton, *An Illustrated History of the Royal Navy*, San Diego, Calif., Thunder Bay Books, 2000, at 51–2, quoting Voltaire's line in *Candide*, which translates as 'to encourage the others'.

23 Roskill, *Churchill and the Admirals*, at 169–71.

24 Gilbert, *Winston S. Churchill: Finest Hour 1939–1941*, at 1095. Reproduced with permission of Curtis Brown Ltd, London, on behalf of C&T Publications.

25 Ludovic Kennedy, *Pursuit: The Chase and Sinking of the Battleship Bismarck*, New York, Viking Press, 1974, at 226. Years later Admiral Tovey recounted the same story to Lieutenant-Commander Colin McMullen. Transcript of interview with McMullen in 1989, at 18. Accession No. 10975/5, Imperial War Museum.

26 Marder, *From the Dreadnought to Scapa Flow, Vol. 2: The War Years: To the Eve of Jutland 1914–1916*, London, Oxford University Press, 1965, at 111.

27 Pound to Layton of 12 February 1942. Layton Papers, British Library.

28 See Appendix, No. 20, a signal from Phillips to the Admiralty that refers to 'Your 0950 7th December'.

29 See Appendix, No. 32.

30 See Appendix, No. 35.

31 Churchill, *The Grand Alliance*, at 604–5.

32 W. Averell Harriman and Elie Abel, *Special Envoy to Churchill and Stalin 1941–1946*, New York, Random House, 1975, at 112.

33 *The Grand Alliance*, at 605–8.

34 Gilbert, *Winston S. Churchill: The Finest Hour 1939–1941*, at 1119. Reproduced with permission of Curtis Brown Ltd, London, on behalf of C&T Publications.

35 TNA Cab 65/20, at 106.

36 Letter of 12 February 1942. Layton Papers, British Library.

37 Letter of 25 February 1943. Roskill Papers.

38 Letter of 25 January 1942. Roskill Papers.

39 'Loss of H.M.S. Prince of Wales & H.M.S. Repulse', 25 January 1942. TNA Prem 3/163/2, at 22.

40 TNA Cab 105/20; see Appendix, No. 32.

41 Attachment to letter from Admiral Moore to Professor Marder of 23 June 1976, Marder Papers.

42 Roskill, *Churchill and the Admirals*, at 116–17.

43 Churchill, *The Grand Alliance*, at 617.

44 Letter from Captain G.R.G. Allen to Mr Churchill via General Lord Hastings Ismay of 23 November 1948. Ismay Papers, Liddell-Hart Centre for Military Archives, King's College London.

45 Churchill, *The Grand Alliance*, at 615–16. The earlier drafts of this passage in Churchill's papers are not very enlightening. Some of the earlier drafts state incorrectly that 'They [the ships] were already at the bottom of the sea.' Churchill Papers 4/233, Churchill Archive Centre, Churchill College, Cambridge.

46 Marder, *Old Friends, New Enemies*, at 405, quoting, without attribution, the attachment to a letter from Paymaster Captain Dougal Doig to Arthur Marder of 9 July 1979. Marder Papers.

47 Ismay wrote to Churchill, 'Hollis and I clearly remember the meeting to which you refer, but I think you must have summoned it unexpectedly and, for some reason or another, there is no record of what was said.' Attachment to letter from Ismay to Churchill of 3 December 1948. Ismay Papers.

48 The *Centurion* was an old battleship disguised as HMS *Anson*, a sister ship of the *Prince of Wales*.

49 TNA Cab 79/55, at 329–31.

50 Gilchrist, *Malaya 1941*, at 137–8.

51 The minutes say the meeting started at 10.00 p.m. Presumably Brooke's watch was on BST and the official minutes used GMT, one hour earlier.

52 Alanbrooke Papers, Liddell-Hart Centre for Military Archives, King's College, London.

53 Attachment to letter from Ismay to Churchill of 3 December 1948. Ismay Papers. To the same effect is the passage describing the meeting in General Ismay's memoirs. General Lord Hastings Ismay, *The Memoirs of General Lord Ismay*, New York, Viking Press, 1960, at 242.

54 TNA Cab 79/55, at 329–31.

55 The Admiralty Battle Summary on the battle points out that another message, sent on 7 December from Phillips to the Admiralty about his meeting with Admiral Hart, was not received until 11 December, but it says nothing about any other messages being delayed. Admiralty Battle Summary No. 14, at 6 n.2.

56 See Appendix, No. 37.

57 Bradley F. Smith, *The Ultra–Magic Deals: And the Most Secret Special Relationship 1940–1946*, Novato, Calif., Presidio Press, 1993, at 12, quoting the memoirs of Admiral John Godfrey. Godrey Papers, Churchill Archive Centre, Churchill College, Cambridge.

58 TNA Cab 105/20 and TNA WO 172/15.

59 Letter from Sir Clifford Jarrett to Marder of 15 February, 1976. Marder Papers.

60 TNA Adm 199/1943.

61 Patrick Beesly, *Very Special Intelligence*, Garden City, NY, Doubleday & Co., 1978, at 103.

62 It is a hotly debated matter, but at the time the British may have had a limited ability to read Japanese naval signals. In 1945, HMS *Anderson* claimed that 'Intelligence that the "Prince of Wales" and "Repulse" had been spotted and would be attacked from the air, four hours before the attack was launched. By the time the Japanese signals had been decoded and got to FECB and then transmitted to the "Prince of Wales" the disaster had occurred.' TNA Adm 223/297. The same report boasts that it deduced that the Japanese aircraft carriers that attacked Ceylon in 1942 were not accompanied by battleships; in fact, the Japanese aircraft carriers *were* accompanied by battleships.

63 Roskill, *Churchill and the Admirals*, at 283.

64 TNA Cab 121/114, at 482.

65 One might ask whether he meant the British Empire or the Japanese Empire!

66 *Winston S. Churchill: His Complete Speeches 1897–1963, Vol. 6: 1935–1942*, at 6525.

67 Churchill, *The Grand Alliance*, at 611.

68 Statement of Mr Hore Belisha, Parliamentary Debates, Commons, 5th ser. vol. 376 (1941–42), col. 1363.

69 *Winston S. Churchill: His Complete Speeches, Vol. 6: 1867–1963*, at 6532.

70 Parliamentary Debates, Commons, 5th ser. vol. 376 (1941–42), col. 1698.

71 Harriman and Abel, *Special Envoy to Churchill and Stalin 1941–1946*, at 113–14.

72 Charles Eade, ed., *Winston Churchill's Secret Session Speeches*, New York, Simon & Schuster, 1946, at 57.

73 Letter from W.S. Churchill to G.R.G. Allen of 2 August 1953. Roskill Papers.

74 Letter from Roskill to Butler of 22 August 1953. Roskill Papers.

75 Roskill, *Churchill and the Admirals*, at 296. Churchill was not a member of the Roskill fan club either. Presumably referring to Captain Roskill, after the war he wrote to his wife Clementine, 'Speaking of War historians, I have an overwhelming case against the Admiralty historian. He belongs to the type of retired Naval Officers who think that politicians should be in the Admiralty in time of war to take the blame for naval failures and provide the Naval Officers with rewards in the cases of their successes, if any.' Martin Gilbert, *Winston Churchill, Vol. 8: Never Despair 1945–1965*, Boston, Houghton Mifflin Co., 1988, at 979. Reproduced with permission of Curtis Brown Ltd, London, on behalf of C&T Publications.

76 Letter from G.R.G. Allen to Winston S. Churchill of 24 August 1953. Roskill Papers.
77 Letter from Captain Allen to Mr Churchill via General Ismay of 23 November 1948. Ismay Papers.
78 TNA Adm 205/10.
79 TNA Prem 3/163/3.
80 Alanbrooke Papers.
81 Letter from J.R.M. Butler to Stephen Roskill of 20 August 1953. Roskill Papers.
82 See also *Churchill Taken from the Diaries of Lord Moran: The Struggle for Survival 1940–1965*, Boston, Houghton Mifflin Co., 1966, at 107–8.
83 Richard Lamb, *Churchill as War Leader*, New York, Carroll & Graf Publishers, 1991, at 181.
84 Winston S. Churchill, *The Second World War, Vol. 4: Hinge of Fate*, Boston, Houghton Mifflin Co., 1950, at 264.
85 Roskill, *The War at Sea, Vol. 2: The Period of Balance*, at 144.
86 Winston S. Churchill, *The World Crisis, Vol. 1: 1911–1914*, New York, Charles Scribner's Sons, 1923, 1951, at 451.
87 Geoffrey Bennett, *Coronel and the Falklands*, at 94.
88 Admiral Sir Peter Gretton, *Winston Churchill and the Royal Navy*, New York, Coward McCann, Inc., 1968, at 181.
89 Bennett, *Coronel and the Falklands*, at 98.
90 *Ibid.* at 101.
91 Geoffrey Bennett, *Naval Battles of the First World War*, New York, Charles Scribner's Sons, 1968, at 102.
92 *Ibid.* at 92.
93 Grenfell, *Main Fleet to Singapore*, at 114.
94 Sturdee was 'physically on the small side', and 'lacked the extrovert personality which made Cradock so well liked'. Bennett, *Coronel and the Falklands*, at 121. Not that Phillips was chosen to get him away from Churchill, but Sturdee *was* chosen by Churchill to get him away from Admiral Fisher, whose wrath Sturdee had incurred. *Ibid.* at 120.
95 Geoffrey Bennett, *The Loss of the Prince of Wales and Repulse*, Annapolis, Naval Institute Press, 1973, at 33.
96 *Ibid.*

Part III

Decisions at Sea – Where to Go and Whom to Tell

CHAPTER NINE

The Opposing Forces

Before the operation began, Captain Leach told his son Henry, a midshipman in the cruiser *Mauritius*, 'I don't think you have any idea of the enormity of the odds we are up against.'[1] And enormous they were indeed. As he began the operation, Phillips had some intelligence information about the Japanese forces he would face, some of it perhaps from the oddly named 'Far East Combined Bureau', or FECB, in Singapore, but he certainly did not have the full picture of what he would have to face.

With respect to Japanese warships, Phillips believed he would face the battlecruiser *Kongo*, seven cruisers and twenty destroyers in the area; in fact, he faced two Japanese forces. In overall command of the Southern Force was Vice-Admiral Kondo Nobutake, with two battlecruisers, the *Kongo* and the *Haruna*, two cruisers, and ten destroyers. Under Admiral Kondo, and in command of the 'Malay Force', was Vice-Admiral Ozawa Jisaburo with eight cruisers, fourteen destroyers and twelve submarines.[2] Kondo's flagship was the *Kongo* and Ozawa's was the heavy cruiser *Chokai*.

As to Japanese aircraft, British intelligence had informed Phillips that the Japanese had bombers near Saigon, but it is not clear if he had the latest information on how many. The British rated Japanese air power as equivalent to that of the Italians, not intending it as a compliment, but they were in for a rude surprise. In fact, the Japanese 22nd Air Flotilla alone had a well-trained, powerful force of ninety-nine bombers, six reconnaissance planes and thirty-nine fighters under Rear Admiral Matsunaga Sadaichi.[3] The bombers, however, were supplied with only one torpedo each.[4] In contrast, at the beginning of the war there were only 182 Allied aircraft in Singapore and Malaya, including Lockheed

Hudson patrol bombers, Blenheim medium bombers, grotesquely obsolete Vildebeest light bombers and Brewster Buffalo fighters.[5] There would soon be far fewer of them. No. 453 Squadron, which was equipped with twelve Buffaloes, was stationed at Sembawang airfield near Singapore to provide fleet defence.

Admiral Phillips's force was centred around his capital ships, the *Prince of Wales* and *Repulse*, since no aircraft carrier was available. The *Prince of Wales* and the *Repulse* seemed to have little in common, except that they were both relatively fast ships and had excellent captains, John Leach of the *Prince of Wales*[6] and William Tennant of the *Repulse*. The two men were also very good friends,[7] and were very popular with the crews of their ships.

Captain Leach was a very fine man and an excellent captain.[8] When he returned to the *Prince of Wales* after an operation following the *Bismarck* action, the crew turned out to cheer him as he boarded the ship.[9] The night before his ship sailed from Singapore, he wrote letters in his own hand to the parents of the midshipmen on board to let them know how their sons were getting along.[10] According to Vice-Admiral Ronald Brockman, who had been an assistant to First Sea Lord Dudley Pound, Captain Leach was

one of the outstanding officers I have ever met . . . a very fine games player; Navy standard at lawn tennis, and indeed he could hit any ball that moved, let alone being a fine shot. Immensely popular with both officers and ratings, and always ran a very happy ship in spite of being a firm disciplinarian. He also had a good brain and there was no question he would have gone right to the top in the Navy.[11]

One of the Captain's sons, later Admiral of the Fleet Sir Henry Leach, *did* go to the top of the Royal Navy, and was the First Sea Lord during the Falklands War in 1982.

The *Prince of Wales* also had a fine executive officer, Commander H.F. Lawson, who had an unusual nickname. Sub-Lieutenant Stuart Paddon, the ship's Canadian radar officer, later recalled Lawson. After Paddon and another officer had performed some acrobatics with chairs in the anteroom to the wardroom, Lawson

stood up, walked over, took off his monkey-jacket, arranged these two chairs in such a way that they were both in their normal position about four to six feet apart. He then went to the end of the anteroom.

He made a flip in the air off the first one and landed seated in the second, picked up his jacket, walked out of the anteroom saying, 'They used to call me Tarzan.' Needless to say, the Executive Officer sold himself completely to us on his first testing. . . . [H]e was one of the finest naval officers I have ever had the pleasure of serving with, because he did everything in just the right proportions.[12]

'Tarzan' Lawson it was!

Captain Tennant, a true British officer and gentleman,[13] was an extraordinary man in his own way. One of his officers, Lieutenant (later Vice-Admiral) J.O.C. Hayes, said that Captain Tennant was 'the finest sea captain I have ever known', and that the crew's 'awe of him became an undisguised affection and respect for someone in whom they saw a power of discernment and command, someone who would meet in war whatever was asked of *Repulse*'.[14] Lieutenant-Commander V.C.F. Clark, the officer of the watch on the bridge of the *Repulse* on 10 December, recalled Captain Tennant as 'a tall, upright, fine looking man, tending to be reserved until you got to know him. . . . He was a most efficient Captain, greatly respected by his crew.'[15]

The flagship of Force Z and the British Eastern Fleet was the battleship *Prince of Wales*. The *Prince of Wales* was a very new ship, having been launched in 1939 and completed only in March of 1941. More powerful than graceful in appearance, she displaced 36,730 tons in standard condition, and had a length of 745ft overall, a beam of 103ft, and a maximum speed of about 28¼ knots.[16]

By December 1941, the *Prince of Wales* had already seen considerable action. Just weeks after her completion and after a very brief period to work up, she and the battlecruiser *Hood* engaged the German battleship *Bismarck* on 24 May 1941, in the Battle of the Denmark Strait. In that action, the *Bismarck* sank the *Hood*, but the *Prince of Wales* hit the *Bismarck* three times[17] – not the one hit reported in C.S. Forester's book *Sink the Bismarck!* and the movie of the same name. It was these hits, which among other things damaged fuel tanks and flooded a boiler room, that forced the *Bismarck* to break off her convoy raiding mission and head for the port of Brest in occupied France. The *Prince of Wales* was herself damaged in the action, taking three hits from the 15in guns of the *Bismarck* and four from the 8in guns of the heavy cruiser *Prinz Eugen*. A shell from the *Bismarck* passed through the bridge and killed or wounded everyone there except Captain Leach, who was injured when flung across the bridge by the blast,[18] and the yeoman of signals.

Nevertheless, the ship's damage control officer, Lieutenant D.B.H. Wildish, and her crew coped well with the damage.

After undergoing repairs, in August 1941 the *Prince of Wales* was chosen to carry Winston Churchill and a delegation across the Atlantic to meet President Roosevelt at the Atlantic Charter Conference in Placentia Bay. In September, the *Prince of Wales* sailed to the Mediterranean to help escort a convoy bound for Malta in Operation Halberd. On 27 September, when the convoy and its escort was attacked by Italian torpedo-bombers, the *Prince of Wales* shared credit for shooting down four of them,[19] and the British force narrowly missed bringing the Italian fleet to battle.

For her main armament, the *Prince of Wales* carried ten 14in guns in three turrets, a quadruple ('A') and a twin ('B') forward and another quadruple ('Y') aft. For her secondary armament, she was equipped with sixteen of the vaunted new 5.25in guns in eight twin turrets, four on the port side (P.1 and P.2 forward of the catapult amidships, and P.3 and P.4 aft of the catapult) and four on the starboard side (S.1 and S.2 forward, and S.3 and S.4 aft). The 5.25in gun was designed as a dual-purpose weapon for use against both ships and aircraft. They were powerful guns, but the design of the twin turrets made their rate of fire disappointingly slow, and their training speed was not considered adequate.[20] For use against aircraft, the 5.25in gun compared unfavourably with the US Navy's 5in dual-purpose gun (known as the 5in/38), which was not as powerful but had a higher rate of fire and great reliability.

The *Prince of Wales* was also equipped with a number of light anti-aircraft guns. Most numerous were her forty-four 2-pounders, or 'pom-poms', in five 8-barrelled mounts, two on each side of her fore funnel and one on B 14in turret, and a 4-barrelled mount on Y turret.[21] The pom-poms dated from 1928, and their short barrels resulted in a low muzzle velocity and insufficient range. By December 1941, the *Prince of Wales* also carried seven 20mm Oerlikon guns, two on each side of the forward superstructure and three on the quarterdeck; they were good guns, but had insufficient range and hitting power to deal with the Japanese bombers dropping torpedoes at long range. Finally, on her quarterdeck the *Prince of Wales* carried a single 40mm Bofors gun,[22] one of the most effective light anti-aircraft guns in the world at the time. The 40mm and 20mm guns had been ordered by the British in 1939 as a result of competitive trials carried out at the Eastney range and at sea in 1938,[23] but they were still far too few in number.

In the matter of radar, the *Prince of Wales* was, for the day, very well equipped. The first ship in the Royal Navy to have a multiple suite of radar, she carried one Type 281 set to search for aircraft, one Type 273 set for surface search, one Type 284 gunnery radar set for her main guns, four Type 285 sets for the directors for her 5.25in guns and, finally, four Type 282 sets for the directors for her pom-poms. Shortly after arriving on board, Admiral Phillips told the ship's Canadian radar officer, Sub-Lieutenant Stuart Paddon, that he wanted to visit every radar office in the ship, sit in the operator's chair and have explained to him what the operator had to do in each set aboard, and that is what he did. Unfortunately, not all of the ship's radars would be operable at the beginning of the battle on 10 December.[24]

Fire control is as important as the guns they control, but the four directors that controlled the *Prince of Wales*'s 5.25in guns were not of the best possible design. Although they were of a relatively new model, the directors were not fully stabilized, or 'tachymetric', and did little better than guess at the location of the aircraft they targeted.[25] According to *Prince of Wales* survivor Geoffrey Brooke, the control arrangements for the 5.25in guns were 'dreadfully antiquated'.[26] They were certainly less effective than the tachymetric directors developed by the Germans and the Americans, whose Mk 37 director was being fitted to the newest ships of the US Navy.

In stark contrast to the very new *Prince of Wales*, the venerable *Repulse* had been launched and completed in 1916 during the First World War. She was a classic battlecruiser, whose original design emphasized speed over armour protection. More graceful than powerful in appearance, she displaced 32,000 tons in standard condition, with a length of 794ft overall, a beam of 90ft, and a maximum speed in 1941 of about 28½ knots.[27]

In her long career, she fought against units of the German High Seas Fleet at the Battle of the Heligoland Bight on 17 November 1917, when she hit and seriously damaged the light cruiser *Königsberg*.[28] The *Repulse* had been refitted and somewhat modernized several times between the wars, most recently from 1933 to 1937, with thicker side and deck armour, new anti-torpedo bulges, additional anti-aircraft guns, and hangars and a catapult for aircraft. She had been chosen to take the royal family to Canada in 1939, but with war approaching, the liner *Empress of Australia* was chosen instead. Up to December 1941, she had had an active yet largely uneventful war, having seen no combat other than being present when HMS *Barham* was torpedoed by a U-boat in 1939[29] and being the target of an unsuccessful attack by three German bombers off Norway in April 1940.[30] Nevertheless, the *Repulse* was a very happy and proud ship.

For her main armament, the *Repulse* mounted six powerful and reliable 15in guns in three twin turrets, A and B forward and Y aft, and for her secondary armament she carried nine Mark IX low-angle 4in guns in three triple mountings and six single Mark V 4in anti-aircraft guns. The *Repulse* had a reputation as a ship poorly equipped to fight off aircraft, but that was really only true of her heavy anti-aircraft armament. Her triple 4in guns were nearly useless for anti-aircraft fire, and her single 4in guns were too few and of a design that dated back to 1914.[31] It was of little comfort that the barrels of the 4in guns were relatively new.[32]

The *Repulse* was actually well equipped with short-range anti-aircraft guns for the time, having three eight-barrelled 2-pounder pom-poms, six 20mm guns[33] and four obsolescent four-barrelled 0.5in Vickers machine-guns. In this area, she was actually better off than any ship in the US Navy or in the Imperial Japanese Navy in December 1941, the former having only the unreliable 1.1in gun and the puny 0.50 cal. machine-gun, and the latter having a rather inadequate 25mm gun and a 13.2mm machine-gun.[34]

As for radar, the *Repulse* carried one Type 284 gunnery radar for her 15in guns and one Type 286P air search radar. She also had one Type 273 surface search radar that was still packed in crates.[35] To control her 4in anti-aircraft guns, she carried only two older-model directors that were not equipped with radar.

It had been planned to give the *Repulse* a major refit in which her old 4in guns were to be replaced by a much-improved secondary armament of fourteen more modern Mk XVI 4in guns in seven twin mountings, and to fit an additional director,[36] but there had not been time. The *Repulse*'s sister ship, the *Renown*, had been completely reconstructed between 1936 and 1939, and had received, among other things, a very modern and effective dual-purpose secondary armament of twenty 4.5in guns in a new type of twin mount. Incredibly, two prototypes of that mount with twin 4in guns had been fitted to the *Repulse* during her 1933–7 refit, but the mountings were removed in 1939 when she was being prepared to take the royal family to Canada. When it was decided not to use her for the voyage, the two modern mountings were not replaced, and two old single 4in guns were put in their place, giving her a total of only six 4in anti-aircraft guns. If the planned refit had taken place, the *Repulse* would have been a much more battleworthy ship, but it is impossible to say if the refit would have made a difference to her survival on 10 December 1941.

The *Prince of Wales* and *Repulse* had either more (ten v. eight) or heavier (15in v. 14in) main guns and heavier armour than the Japanese battlecruisers that they might face, the *Kongo* and *Haruna*. The Japanese ships had been launched in 1912 and 1913, respectively, but had been considerably modernized. Even so, they carried eight 14in guns and had armour belts just under 8 inches thick.[37] The *Prince of Wales* had an armour belt up to 14.71 inches thick[38] and the *Repulse* had a belt 9 inches thick. The *Kongo* alone would not have been much of a match for the *Prince of Wales* and *Repulse*, but the *Kongo* and *Haruna* together would have been tough enough opponents, and superior gunnery would have been more important than differences between individual ships in guns and thickness of armour.

It is important, however, to understand that the armour belts of the *Prince of Wales* and *Repulse* were designed to defeat enemy shells, not torpedoes; like all other capital ships of the day, protection against torpedoes was designed to come from a structure built onto the outside of the hull, in the case of the bulges added to the *Repulse*, or a structure built into the hull, in the case of the multiple layers of air and liquids in the *Prince of Wales*, to absorb the explosion of a torpedo's warhead rather than to defeat it with armour at the outer edge of the hull.[39]

Not a single modern cruiser was available to join Force Z, and the destroyers of Force Z were most notable for their scarcity. Tom Phillips had to settle for the only four that were available, the *Express*, *Electra*, *Vampire*, and *Tenedos*. The *Jupiter* and *Encounter*, which had accompanied the *Prince of Wales* and *Repulse* from Ceylon, were undergoing repairs, and the *Isis* was already undergoing repairs in Singapore. The four destroyers of Force Z were not exactly the latest design; although the *Express* and *Electra* were fairly new, both launched in 1934, the *Vampire* and *Tenedos*, launched in 1917 and 1918, respectively,[40] became part of Force Z because no other destroyers were available.

The destroyers were only marginally well armed for surface combat, with no more than four low-angle 4.7in (*Express* and *Electra*) or 4in guns (*Vampire* and *Tenedos*) and 21in torpedo tubes. Unfortunately, none of the four destroyers was well equipped for shooting down aircraft, the first two having only a 3in (12-pounder) anti-aircraft gun, a few 20mm Oerlikon guns, and perhaps two quadruple 0.5in Vickers machine-guns.[41] The *Vampire* and *Tenedos* were even worse off, with only machine-guns.

With two capital ships, no aircraft carrier, no cruisers, and just four destroyers, Force Z was a powerful yet unbalanced and vulnerable force that set off to do battle with the Imperial Japanese Navy.

Notes

1 Admiral of the Fleet Sir Henry Leach, *Endure No Makeshifts: Some Naval Recollections*, London, Leo Cooper 1993, at 7.
2 Admiralty Battle Summary No. 14, at 7 and 7n.; *Japanese Monograph No. 107*, at 3–4.
3 Admiralty Battle Summary No. 14, at 9.
4 Okumiya, Horikoshi, and Caidin, *Zero!*, New York, E.P. Dutton & Co., 1956, at 104.
5 Admiralty Battle Summary No. 14, Appendix C, at 23.
6 John Leach was actually the second captain of the *Prince of Wales*. The first was Captain L.H.K. 'Turtle' Hamilton, who was appointed while she was building. When Hamilton was promoted to rear admiral, he left the ship and Leach was appointed captain. Letter from L.J. Goudy to Arthur Marder of 28 May 1975. Marder Papers. As a result of Captain Leach's appointment to the *Prince of Wales*, his son Henry, a midshipman, had to leave the ship. Leach, *Endure No Makeshifts*, at 3.
7 Attachment to letter from Admiral of the Fleet Sir Henry Leach to Arthur Marder of 21 April 1975. Marder Papers.
8 The tributes to Captain Leach are well summarized in Marder, *Old Friends, New Enemies*, at 374–5.
9 Brooke, *Alarm Starboard!*, at 76.
10 Letter from Admiral Sir Peter Anson to the author of 16 August 1999.
11 Admiral Sir Ronald Brockman, in an attachment to a letter to A.J. Marder of 31 December 1975. Marder Papers.
12 Stuart Paddon, 'HMS Prince of Wales – Radar Officer', in Mack Lynch, ed., *Salty Dips*, vol. 1, Ottawa, Naval Officers' Association of Canada, Ottawa Branch, 1983, at 66.
13 Letter from Admiral John Litchfield to Arthur Marder of 28 February 1978. Marder Papers. Captain Tennant's fine qualities are described in greater detail in Marder, *Old Friends, New Enemies*, at 376–8.
14 Hayes, *Face the Music*, at 127.
15 Letter from Commander V.C.F. Clark to the author of 5 August 1999.
16 H.T. Lenton, *British and Empire Warships of the Second World War*, London, Greenhill Books, 1998, at 27, 29.
17 William H. Garzke, Jr, and Robert O. Dulin, Jr, *Battleships: Axis and Neutral Battleships in World War II*, Annapolis, Naval Institute Press, 1985, at 224, 226.
18 Leach, *Endure No Makeshifts*, at 5.
19 Letter from David Brown, Naval Historical Branch, to Arthur Marder of 6 March 1979. Marder Papers.
20 Alan Raven and John Roberts, *British Battleships of World War Two*, Annapolis, Naval Institute Press, 1976, at 286.

21 Published sources state that the *Prince of Wales* had either two eight-barrelled pom-poms or two four-barrelled pom-poms on B and Y turrets, but photographs seem to show one of each. See Brooke, *Alarm Starboard!* at 101, 102.

22 The 2-pounder pom-poms were also of 40mm bore diameter, but were totally different guns. The Bofors had a longer barrel (56 calibres in length, 56 × 40mm) than the pom-pom (40 calibers in length, 40 × 40mm). John Campbell, *Naval Weapons of World War Two*, London, Conway Maritime Press, 1985, at 67, 71.

23 Stephen W. Roskill, *Naval Policy between the Wars, Vol. 2, The Period of Reluctant Rearmament 1930–1939*, Annapolis, Naval Institute Press 1976, at 421 and nn. 2, 3.

24 Derek Howse, *Radar at Sea: The Royal Navy in World War 2*, Annapolis, Naval Institute Press, 1993, at 89, 122–5, and S.E. Paddon, 'HMS Prince of Wales – Radar Officer', in *Salty Dips*, vol. 1, at 71.

25 Roskill, *Churchill and the Admirals*, at 180–1. For more on this, see Stephen Roskill, *Naval Policy Between the Wars*, vol. 2, at 333–4.

26 Letter from Geoffrey Brooke to the author of 30 November 1997.

27 Lenton, *British and Empire Warships of the Second World War*, at 20.

28 Marder, *From the Dreadnought to Scapa Flow, Vol. 4, 1917: Year of Crisis*, London, Oxford University Press, 1969, at 304.

29 Raven and Roberts, *British Battleships of World War Two*, at 343.

30 Alan Matthews, *Sailors' Tales*, Wrexham, Wales, 1997, at 43.

31 *Ibid.* at 58.

32 Four of the six had been mounted in Rosyth in August 1941, and the other two were practically new. A.E. Jacobs, 'The Loss of the Repulse and Prince of Wales, December 10, 1941: A Participant's Account', *Warship International* 23, No. 1 (1986), at 26.

33 This figure is based on a letter from Admiral J.O.C. Hayes to Marder of 17 August 1979, Marder Papers, and on Jacobs, 'The Loss of the Repulse and Prince of Wales, December 10, 1941: A Participant's Account', at 12, 28. Some sources claim four, eight, or even eleven 20mm guns.

34 Both guns were based on the French Hotchkiss design. Campbell, *Naval Weapons of World War Two*, at 200–1.

35 Letters from Kenneth Armstrong, the radar officer of the *Repulse*, to the author, 4 July 1998, 22 July 1998.

36 R.A. Burt, *British Battleships 1919–1939*, London, Arms and Armour Press, 1993, at 215.

37 A.J. Watts, *Japanese Warships of World War II*, London, Ian Allen, 1966, at 10.

38 Garzke and Dulin, *Allied Battleships of World War II*, at 231.

39 Norman Friedman, *Battleship Design and Development 1905–1945*, New York, Mayflower Books, 1978, at 75.

40 Lenton, *British and Empire Warships of the Second World War*, at 137, 141, 157.

41 See Cain and Sellwood, *H.M.S. Electra*, at 113.

CHAPTER TEN

Off to Look for Trouble

At 1730 on 8 December Force Z sailed from Singapore, embarking on an operation without a codename, much less a striking one such as 'Tiger', 'Pedestal' or 'Halberd'. As the ships cast off and left the naval base, Captain O.W. Phillips, the fleet engineer officer, 'had a deep sense of foreboding come over me. I felt this situation was too much like that existing just before the Battle of Coronel in World War I.'[1]

After the ships had sailed, Admiral Phillips made a signal to be addressed to the men of the ships, and concluded, 'Whatever we meet, I want to finish quickly and to get well clear to the eastward before the Japanese can mass too formidable a scale of air attack against us. So, shoot to sink.'[2] Addressing the crew of the *Repulse*, Captain Tennant began, 'We are off to look for trouble. I expect we shall find it. . . .'[3]

Before sailing, Phillips had asked the Royal Air Force for (a) reconnaissance ahead of his force on 9 December, (b) reconnaissance off Singora the morning of the 10th, and (c) fighter protection off Singora on 10 December.[4] Shortly after sailing, however, he received a visual signal from the Changi signal station from Air Vice-Marshal Pulford, 'Regret fighter protection impossible.' At that, Admiral Phillips is said to have shrugged his shoulders and said, 'Well, we must get on without it.'[5] Later that night, he received a more detailed signal from Admiral Palliser, informing him that the RAF could provide the reconnaissance ahead of his force, that it hoped to provide the reconnaissance requested off Singora on the 10th, but that, 'Fighter protection on Wednesday 10th will not, repeat not, be possible.'[6] Phillips decided to continue the operation, but because of the lack of fighter protection on the 10th, he decided to head for Kota Bharu rather than Singora, which was 120 miles farther north, and then only if surprise was achieved.[7]

With the receipt of the signal from Admiral Palliser that fighter protection would not be available on the 10th, at the very start of the operation Phillips had to decide whether to continue the operation at all. Since the two requirements for the operation were fighter protection and surprise, it could be argued that Admiral Phillips should have turned back as soon as he was informed that the first requirement could not be met. At that stage, Force Z would surely have made it back to Singapore without loss, but it would also have been very difficult to turn back so early in an operation, at least pyschologically.

Phillips no doubt regretted the lack of fighter protection, but probably hoped that with surprise and bad weather the danger of air attack would be lessened, and that the importance of the operation to the campaign in Malaya made the risk acceptable. Tom Phillips may have recalled Mr Churchill's words to the House of Commons in June 1941 after the Battle of Crete, when the Royal Navy had had hardly any air cover and had suffered frightful losses while supporting the British Army:

> There are some who say we should never fight without superior or at least ample air support, and ask when this lesson will be learned. But suppose you cannot have it. The questions which have to be settled are not always questions between what is good and bad; very often it is a choice between two very terrible alternatives. Must you, if you cannot have this essential and desirable air support, yield important key points one after the other?[8]

The Prime Minister had a point, but the point could be carried too far; there are no doubt times when the objective is not worth the danger from air attack. This may have been such a time; although the information available to Phillips gave him no reason to foresee the full extent of the threat from Japanese aircraft, there was clearly *some* danger from air attack, and his decision to continue on and to hazard two very valuable capital ships, rather than returning to Singapore or sailing elsewhere, was a very risky one.

Shortly after receiving the signal that no fighter protection would be possible on 10 December, Admiral Phillips received another signal from Admiral Palliser, this one informing him that the Japanese had large bomber forces in Indo-China and that Brooke-Popham had asked

General MacArthur to bomb their airfields with his long-range bombers as soon as possible.[9] Unbeknown to Admiral Palliser, by that time most of General MacArthur's B-17 bombers were permanently unavailable for operations against the Japanese, having been destroyed on the ground at Clark Field in the Philippines just hours after the attack on Pearl Harbor.

Regardless of the impossibility of fighter protection on the 10th, Force Z sailed on towards Kota Bharu. At first, fortune seemed to favour Force Z. Steering a course to avoid the mines that had been laid for it, and sailing in overcast weather, it was not immediately detected by Japanese aircraft or submarines. A solitary aircraft was briefly sighted on the morning of the 9th by a single lookout in the *Vampire*, but the report was disregarded, and the aircraft does not seem to have been Japanese. As the RAF had promised, a Catalina flying-boat from No. 205 Squadron appeared out of the fog just before 1300, and signalled that the Japanese were landing at Singora.[10] It would be the last friendly aircraft Force Z would see for some time.

Force Z would not remain undetected for long. At 1345 on 9 December, it was sighted by the Japanese submarine *I-65*, running at the time at periscope depth. While still submerged, *I-65* raised its shortwave radio mast and reported two enemy battleships on a course of 340° at a speed of 14 knots. The submarine surfaced, but lost the ships in a squall at 1550. Contact was re-established at 1652, but was quickly lost when a float plane – a Japanese one, as it turned out – appeared and made threatening moves, forcing the submarine to submerge. At 1710, *I-65* signalled that it had lost sight of the British battleships.[11]

For some reason, the initial sighting report of *I-65* did not get into the right hands, such as Admiral Ozawa's, until 1540, a delay of almost two hours.[12] Until then, the Japanese had thought that Force Z was still in harbour, as a Japanese reconnaissance plane sent to Singapore had reported at 0950 that day and Ozawa had received at 1250.[13] Ozawa quickly ordered his cruisers to send out search planes and made dispositions to counter Force Z, but, because of the delay in receiving the contact reports from *I-65*, the Japanese air and naval units could not bring Force Z to battle that day. The Japanese did order their transports, which had not yet finished unloading supplies for the invasion forces, to quickly sail north into the Gulf of Siam.[14] Meanwhile, Force Z sailed on, blissfully unaware that it had been sighted.

On the quarterdeck of HMS *Prince of Wales* in August 1941: from right to left, Prime Minister Winston Churchill, First Sea Lord Admiral Sir Dudley Pound and Captain John Leach. *(Imperial War Museum A4859)*

Admiral Sir T.S.V. Phillips. *(Courtesy of Mrs T.V.G. Phillips)*

Captain William Tennant, shown after promotion to Admiral. *(Imperial War Museum A29072)*

Captain John Leach in his cabin in the *Prince of Wales. (Imperial War Museum A3894)*

The battlecruiser HMS *Repulse* at speed on her voyage to the Far East. *(Imperial War Museum A6792)*

The battleship HMS *Prince of Wales* after departing Scapa Flow for Cape Town. *(National Maritime Museum via Steve Kirby)*

The destroyer HMS *Electra* in wartime. *(Australian War Memorial 302365 and Author's Collection)*

The destroyer HMS *Express*, with wartime modifications. *(Imperial War Museum A17867)*

The aircraft carrier HMS *Indomitable* as completed. *(Fleet Air Arm Museum CARS I/218)*

The *Prince of Wales* arriving at Cape Town. *(South African Museum of Military History 1197)*

The rum ration in HMS *Prince of Wales*. (*South African Museum of Military History 1203*)

The aircraft carrier HMS *Hermes* after her last refit. (*Fleet Air Arm Museum CARS H/130*)

The *Prince of Wales* in heavy seas in the Indian Ocean. *(Courtesy of P.F.C. Satow)*

The light cruiser HMAS *Sydney*, lost before she could join Force Z. *(Australian War Memorial 301407)*

HMS *Prince of Wales* nearing Singapore. *(Imperial War Museum Film Archive)*

Watching the *Prince of Wales* arrive at Singapore: from left, Rear Admiral Arthur Palliser, Admiral Phillips and Commander Michael Goodenough. *(Imperial War Museum Film Archive)*

The light cruiser HMS *Mauritius*, which was at Singapore but could not be part of Force Z. *(Courtesy of Admiral of the Fleet Sir Henry Leach)*

The heavy cruiser HMS *Exeter*, which arrived too late to join Force Z. *(Author's Collection)*

The *Prince of Wales* prepares to leave Singapore. *(Imperial War Museum A29068)*

The *Repulse* leaving Singapore. *(Imperial War Museum A29069)*

The Australian member of Force Z: the destroyer HMAS *Vampire*. (*Australian War Memorial 106665*)

The oldest and smallest member of Force Z: the destroyer HMS *Tenedos*. (*Australian War Memorial 302488 and Author's Collection*)

Japanese G3M Type 96 ('Nell') medium bombers. *(Imperial War Museum HU3514)*

Japanese G4M Type 1 ('Betty') medium bombers. *(Maru Magazine)*

Lieutenant Iki Haruki, IJN, of the Kanoya Air Group. *(Courtesy of Alan Matthews and Iki Haruki)*

Inside the bridge of the *Prince of Wales*. *(South African Museum of Military History 1200)*

The best anti-aircraft gun in Force Z: the 40mm Bofors gun on the fantail of the *Prince of Wales,* here manned by Royal Marines. *(Imperial War Museum A3915)*

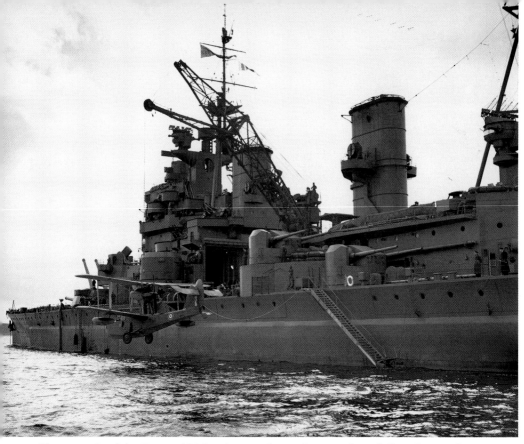

The port side of the *Prince of Wales*, showing her Walrus seaplane (left) and P.3 and P.4 5.25in turrets (right), where one of the first torpedoes hit. *(Imperial War Museum A3868)*

The stern of the *Prince of Wales*. Some of the most damaging hits were on the port side aft and later on the starboard side aft. *(South African Museum of Military History 1298)*

The port side of HMS *Repulse*, which absorbed four of the five torpedoes that hit her. *(Imperial War Museum FL12334)*

The *Prince of Wales* listing to port and about to capsize, as seen from HMS *Express*. *(Imperial War Museum HU2675, photo by P.F.C. Satow)*

Last to arrive: a squadron of RAF Brewster Buffalo fighters. *(Imperial War Museum K1221)*

Then, at about 1700 on the 9th, the weather cleared,[15] and Force Z was sighted again – and this time was well aware it had been sighted – initially by a search plane launched from the cruiser *Kinu*, which began sending sighting reports at 1705, and then by search planes from the cruisers *Suzuya* and *Kumano*.[16] Admiral Ozawa received the first report at 1600, and began making new dispositions. Eventually, however, he had to give up the idea of trying to bring Force Z to battle that night.

For the time being, Force Z continued on its course, except for the destroyer *Tenedos*, which was low on fuel and was detached to return to Singapore at 1835. Before going on her way, she was ordered to transmit a message to Singapore the next day at 0800.[17]

Meanwhile, in London Winston Churchill was having lunch with King George VI. Afterwards, the King wrote in his diary:

> The Prime Minister came to lunch. He gave me the latest news from America which was dreadful. In Pearl Harbour 3 U.S. Battleships were sunk and 3 seriously damaged.[18] There are now only 2 effective U.S. ships in the Pacific, which means that U.S.A. has already lost command of the sea in the Pacific. A very serious situation for our ships the P of W & Repulse who are out there.[19]

One might well suppose that Mr Churchill left the lunch just as concerned about the *Prince of Wales* and *Repulse* as the King.

Back in the South China Sea, Tom Phillips, realizing that he had lost the element of surprise, reluctantly decided to call off the operation. The only voice in favour of continuing on was Phillips's secretary, Paymaster Captain S.T. Beardsworth, who said it was a pity not to try their luck since they had come so near the objective.[20] At 2015, after darkness had fallen and his shadowers could no longer see him, Admiral Phillips began to change course for Singapore. Captain Tennant sent Admiral Phillips a signal sympathizing with the difficulty of the decision. Many aboard the ships of Force Z were keenly disappointed at losing the chance to have a go at the Japanese, while others probably felt at least as much relief as disappointment. Admiral Phillips continued to maintain radio silence, and did not inform Admiral Palliser of the change in plans.

When Force Z turned back, it was but a few miles away from the force of Japanese cruisers and destroyers that was desperately searching for it. At about 2000 the same night, bombers of the 22nd Air Flotilla that had been sent out to search for Force Z instead found the heavy cruiser *Chokai*, Admiral Ozawa's flagship, and mistook it for a British ship. When one of the planes dropped a flare over the *Chokai*, it took repeated and frantic signals from the *Chokai*, and even from Admiral Matsunaga in Saigon, to prevent the bomber pilots, who were a bit slow on the uptake, from attacking the *Chokai*, thus averting a disaster for the Japanese.[21] The flare was evidently close enough to be sighted by the *Electra*,[22] but was not seen by the other ships of Force Z. In any event, for better or worse there would be no battle that night.

No one seems to have questioned Admiral Phillips's decision to abandon the operation when Force Z was sighted by Japanese aircraft the evening of the 9th, since surprise had clearly been lost.[23] Indeed, had Admiral Phillips decided to maintain his course and continue the operation, Force Z would have received the undivided attention of every Japanese surface ship, submarine, and bomber in the area. While the decision to turn back was undoubtedly correct, there have been questions about the time it took Admiral Phillips to abandon the operation and the circumstances of the change of course.

First, Admiral Phillips has been criticized for taking so long to turn back after being sighted. However, again according to Captain Bell, Admiral Phillips 'would not have turned back *before* he knew these reconnaissance aircraft were out of touch with us and could not report our final course'.[24] Although sunset was at 1800, the last report from the reconnaissance planes was not sent until some time after 1846,[25] and the moon did not rise until 2238.[26] Given that, Admiral Phillips's decision to hold his course until 2015, until after the last report from a Japanese plane and before the moon rose, seems reasonable enough.

Secondly, it has been written that Force Z turned away upon sighting a flare,[27] presumably relying on the after-action report of HMS *Electra*, which states, 'At 1909 what appeared to be a surface flare was dropped about 5 miles ahead of the Fleet. This was avoided by an emergency turn to port. . . .'[28] However, Captain L.H. Bell, Admiral Phillips's Chief of Staff while at sea, vehemently disagreed with this idea, and stated categorically that 'NO emergency turn was ordered to pass well clear of *any* flare.'[29] That night Lieutenant John Hayes was perched in the foretop of the *Repulse*, his eyes straining into the darkness, but he and his men saw no flare.[30] Indeed, no one in the other ships seems to have sighted the flare either.[31]

There is a possible explanation for this mystery. The *Electra* had been on the starboard side of the formation before the departure of the *Tenedos*,[32] and probably still was after the *Tenedos* left; if so, she would have been the closest ship to the flare dropped by a Japanese aircraft near the *Chokai*. That is most likely the flare sighted by the *Electra*, but she sighted it shortly after 2000,[33] not at 1909. Force Z made alterations in course to 320° at about 1850 and to 280° at about 1930,[34] and when the men of the *Electra* prepared her report a few days later, they took one of those course changes as an emergency turn to avoid the flare they saw at about the same time.

The *Prince of Wales*'s Type 281 air warning radar had been shut down that night as part of a policy of 'radar silence' (to keep the Japanese from detecting its transmissions);[35] if it had been turned on, it might have detected the Japanese aircraft that dropped the flare near the *Chokai*, a fact that would have been of some interest to Admiral Phillips. The *Prince of Wales* did have at least one radar set on, probably her Type 273 surface search set, since later that night her radar detected 'a small vessel',[36] but the distance was too great for the set to have detected the *Chokai*.

At any rate, whatever the men on the *Electra* saw, Admiral Phillips's decision to turn back is not open to serious question, and was not a panic move prompted by the flare dropped on the *Chokai* by Japanese aircraft. Before the night was over, however, Tom Phillips was to have more difficult decisions to make.

Notes

1 Memoirs of Rear Admiral O.W. Phillips, at 337. Papers of Rear Admiral O.W. Phillips, Imperial War Museum, Department of Documents. In Chapter 8 we heard much about the Battle of Coronel, which was fought on 1 November 1914.
2 O'Dowd Gallagher, *Action in the East*, New York, Doubleday, Doran & Co., 1942, at 51–2.
3 *Ibid.* at 40.
4 'Loss of P of W & Repulse', Appendix A. TNA Air 23/4745.
5 Grenfell, *Main Fleet to Singapore*, at 114. Middlebrook and Mahoney quote the admiral's reaction a bit differently, as saying 'it was best to get on with it'. *Battleship*, at 117.
6 See Appendix, No. 44.
7 Letter from L.H. Bell to Marder of 14 July 1978. Marder Papers.
8 *Winston S. Churchill: His Complete Speeches 1897–1963, Vol. 6: 1935–1942*, at 6413–14.
9 TNA Adm 199/1149, at 51.
10 Shores, Cull and Izawa, *Bloody Shambles*, Vol. 1, at 110. American war correspondent Cecil Brown reported that the Catalina was seen at 1245. Cecil Brown, *Suez to Singapore*, New York, Random House, 1942, at 304. Strangely, the

sighting of Force Z does not appear in Squadron Leader Jardine's report of the flight. TNA Air 23/4745, Appendix E.

11 Official Japanese History, at 431–3, 435.

12 *Ibid.*, at 431–3.

13 *Ibid.* at 429, 434.

14 *Ibid.* at 434, 438.

15 Statement of Captain L.H. Bell of 10 December 1941. TNA Adm 199/1149, at 35.

16 Official Japanese History, at 442–3.

17 See Appendix, No. 56.

18 The Admiralty had learned details of the attack from 'Spenavo', the US Navy's Special Naval Observer in London, Admiral Ghormley, at 0322Z on 8 December. See Appendix, No. 39. In *The Grand Alliance*, however, Mr Churchill wrote, 'We were not told for some time any details of what had happened at Pearl Harbour. . . .' At 613.

19 John W. Wheeler-Bennett, *King George VI: His Life and Reign*, New York, St Martin's Press, 1958, at 532, with the gracious permission of Her Majesty the Queen.

20 Grenfell, *Main Fleet to Singapore*, at 116.

21 Official Japanese History, at 445.

22 Report of HMS *Electra* of 12 December 1941. TNA Adm 199/1149, at 172. For more on the mysterious flare and the *Electra*, see *infra*.

23 There is another possibility. That evening the Japanese ships in the South China Sea were observing the opposite of radio silence; indeed, they had been ordered to attract the British force. Official Japanese History, at 437. The Japanese signals should have been picked up in Singapore, and, even if they were not decrypted, the use of direction finding should have disclosed that Japanese naval forces were in the South China Sea in Admiral Phillips's path. There is no evidence, however, that the unusual amount of Japanese radio traffic was detected or that there was any attempt to warn Admiral Phillips of this.

24 Letter from L.H. Bell to Arthur Marder of 2 August 1978 (emphasis in original). Marder Papers.

25 Official Japanese History, at 443. The next-to-last report was at 1846, but no time is given for the last report.

26 Official Japanese History, at 450.

27 Middlebrook and Mahoney, *Battleship*, at 137.

28 Report of HMS *Electra*, 12 December 1941. TNA Adm 199/1149, at 172.

29 Letter from Captain L.H. Bell to Marder of 2 August 1978 (emphasis in original). Marder Papers.

30 Hayes, *Face the Music*, at 133.

31 Long after the war, Phillips's assistant secretary, Lieutenant Kenneth Farnhill, first wrote that he had forgotten about the flare, but later wrote that Captain Bell was right in saying that no report of the incident was received in the *Prince of Wales*. Letters to Arthur Marder of 7 August 1978, and 20 September 1978. Marder Papers.

32 This is shown in a diagram drawn by Lieutenant Dyer of the *Tenedos* in a letter to Professor Marder of 7 August 1978. Marder Papers.

33 Official Japanese History, at 445.

34 Report of HMAS *Vampire*, 12 December 1941. TNA Adm 199/1149, at 151. For some reason, these changes in course appear only in the *Vampire*'s report.

35 Howse, *Radar at Sea: The Royal Navy in World War 2*, at 124, quoting the *Prince of Wales*'s radar officer, Sub-Lieutenant Stuart Paddon, RCNVR, in S.E. Paddon, 'HMS Prince of Wales – Radar Officer', in Mack Lynch, ed., *Salty Dips*, vol. 1, Ottawa, Ontario, Naval Officers' Association of Canada, 1983.

36 *Ibid.*

CHAPTER ELEVEN

Finding Trouble

Shortly before midnight on 9 December, the peaceful homeward voyage of Force Z was interrupted. At 2238, the moon rose and it stopped raining,[1] a harbinger of unwelcome finer weather the next day. Then Admiral Phillips received two important signals from Admiral Palliser.[2]

The first signal, received at 2302, informed him that enemy bombers were in force and undisturbed, and could attack him five hours after sighting. The signal also stated that the situation with the airfields in northern Malaya was becoming untenable and that Brooke-Popham was hinting that he would concentrate all air efforts on Singapore.[3]

Then, at 2355, Admiral Phillips received a second signal from Admiral Palliser, 'Enemy reported landing Kuantan, latitude 03° 50' North.'[4] At 2210, 22 Brigade had reported to Singapore that a landing was taking place near Kuantan, and the brigadier in command had requested RAF and naval help.[5] Kuantan was located much farther down the Malay peninsula from where the Japanese had landed at Kota Bharu, and was much closer to Singapore. After considering the situation, at 0052 Admiral Phillips ordered a change in course to the south-west for Kuantan. Once again, he kept radio silence and did not inform Palliser of his decision.

Some believe the decision to divert to Kuantan was a mistaken one and a cause of the disaster the next day, but it would have been very difficult for Phillips not to divert there. A Japanese landing at Kuantan, located well down the east coast of Malaya, would have threatened to cut off all of the British Army units in northern Malaya. The risk of diverting to Kuantan must not have seemed very great, because Phillips believed he was beyond the range at which the Japanese could mount a really effective air attack against him.[6] It is true that Phillips acted on a report that was not graded as to reliability[7] and could have been false, but for him to have asked for confirmation of the report would have meant breaking radio silence, giving away his location and costing him surprise at Kuantan if the report had been correct. Phillips probably thought that the danger of a landing at Kuantan was too great for him to ignore just because it was not absolutely confirmed. Given the information available to him, he was justified in diverting to Kuantan.

Phillips had sufficient reason to divert to Kuantan, but he could be forgiven if there was another reason. The diversion would have also given him and Force Z a golden opportunity to have another go at the Japanese after having to turn back from the planned attack on the Japanese off Kota Bharu or Singora: the prospect of returning to Singapore without having done battle with the Japanese must have been galling.

Some of the blame for the diversion to Kuantan and the subsequent disaster has been directed at Tom Phillips's Chief of Staff at Singapore, Admiral A.F.E. Palliser, for sending an ungraded report, for not sending a follow-up signal about the report being false, and for not sending air cover to Kuantan to meet Phillips. However, while Palliser's signal did not 'grade' the reliability of the report, most reports at the time were not graded, and Palliser had done his best to confirm that the report was accurate before sending the signal.[8] The alternative was not to inform Phillips of the report of the landing, which was surely not an option. Again, while Palliser does not seem to have sent a follow-up signal about the report being false, we do not know when it became absolutely certain in Singapore that there was no landing at Kuantan. Even as late as 0800, the situation at Kunatan was reported quiet but 'with occasional shelling from two ships close in',[9] something less than a clean bill of health.[10] A later report that there was no landing would have done Phillips no good, since by 0845 he knew himself that there was no landing. Finally, as regards not sending air cover, we have seen that RAF aircraft *were* sent to Kuantan, not because Force Z was expected to come calling, but to attack an expected Japanese landing force. Unfortunately, all but one of them missed Force Z when it did arrive, and that one evidently did not realize it had seen Force Z. As for not keeping aircraft over Kuantan until Force Z showed up, Palliser had no reason to believe that Phillips would divert to Kuantan, since he did not know that Phillips had turned back on the night of the 9th. Palliser must have assumed that Phillips was still on his mission to attack the

Japanese transports off Singora, as shown by the signal he sent Phillips at 0911 on the 10th[11] about transports and an aircraft carrier off Singora. If Palliser had any inkling that Phillips was heading for Kuantan, the signal from Phillips that the *Tenedos* relayed at 0800 that morning[12] would have dispelled it. Even if Phillips actually expected Palliser to provide air cover off Kuantan, a debatable point, 'One cannot but feel that Admiral Phillips's belief that air cover would meet him off Kuantan, when he had given Singapore no hint that he was proceeding there, demanded too high a degree of insight from the officers at the base.'[13] Admiral Palliser certainly did not have an easy job trying to assist an admiral who was maintaining very strict radio silence.

While it has been suggested that if Phillips had ignored Palliser's report of the landings at Kuantan and continued to sail for Singapore, the ships would have evaded the Japanese aircraft and arrived safely back in Singapore,[14] that is highly debatable. Indeed, the Japanese attack force took off and set its course based on a submarine report that had Force Z heading for Singapore, not Kuantan, so it would have been unlikely to miss Force Z if it had stayed on its course for Singapore. The Japanese attack force actually flew almost to Singapore itself before it received the sighting report, and it actually had to turn back to search for Force Z. Force Z would probably have been caught on its return to Singapore even if it had not diverted to Kuantan. Indeed, if it had, the Japanese airmen would have been fresher and the squadrons more concentrated if they had found Force Z sooner rather than later, and the result would have been no different.

Under the circumstances, Admiral Phillips's decision to change course for Kuantan was a reasonable one. Almost immediately, however, things began to go awry. At 2352, almost exactly the moment that Admiral Phillips received the signal about the landing at Kuantan, Force Z was sighted again by the Japanese, this time by the submarine *I-58*,[15] which was running on the surface only 600 metres from the ships and may have been the 'small vessel' detected by the *Prince of Wales*'s radar that night. *I-58* promptly submerged, but a change in course by Force Z gave the submarine a favourable attacking position. The attack was delayed by a faulty torpedo tube hatch, and when *I-58* finally got around to launching five torpedoes at the *Repulse*, they all missed.

I-58 sent off four sighting reports, the first one at 2352 and the last one at 0445, reporting that it had lost contact with the British ships. Two of the sighting reports did not reach any of the Japanese admirals that night; they were the first one and the third one, sent at 0255 and reporting Force Z's change of course toward Kuantan.[16] After receiving the report sent by *I-58* at 0211, which reported the enemy ships' course as 180°, the Japanese admirals realized that their surface forces were now too far away to bring the British to battle, but ordered the 22nd Air Flotilla to attack the ships the next day.

The men of the 22nd Air Flotilla must have been exhausted from their night mission just hours before, but there would be no respite for them. Beginning at 0455 on the morning of the 10th, a force of eleven search planes, nine Mitsubishi G3M2 'Nells' and two C5M 'Babs' reconnaissance planes, took off to search for Force Z.[17]

The search planes were soon followed by eighty-five bombers from the Genzan, Kanoya, and Mihoro Air Groups. The Genzan Group left from Saigon at 0625, the Kanoya Group from Thu Dau Mot at 0644, and the Mihoro Group from Thu Dau Mot between 0650 and 0800.[18] This élite force was equipped with modern twin-engined bombers, fifty-nine more Nells and twenty-six Mitsubishi G4M1 bombers, codenamed 'Bettys'. The bombers were organized in ten squadrons, or more accurately, divisions (*chutai*), of eight or nine aircraft, each of which was organized into sections (*shotai*) of three aircraft.[19] The aircrews were very well trained in attacking ships with bombs or torpedoes, and on this mission thirty-four bombers had been armed with two 550lb bombs or one 1,100lb bomb, and fifty-one were armed with torpedoes. The bombers were to have no fighter escort on this mission, even though the 22nd Air Flotilla had twenty-five very formidable Mitsubishi A6M Zero fighters in the Saigon area,[20] as even they would not have had the range for the mission.

Early on the morning of 10 December, Admiral Phillips received a message marked 'Important' and 'Personal from First Sea Lord'. It stated:

As torpedo aircraft attack on ships at anchor in Johore Strait [located between Singapore and Malaya] cannot be ruled out, I am sure you have in mind M/LD. 02033/41, dated 22 April 1941, paragraph 18-(14), which you took so much interest in.

T.O.O. 1829A/9
T.O.R. 2210Z/9/12/41[21]

The document to which Pound referred, 'M/LD.02033/41', has finally been found: it was a secret memorandum entitled 'Defence of Harbours

Against Special Craft', and it was prompted by the attack on the cruiser HMS *York* in Suda Bay, Crete, on 26 March 1941, by Italian explosive motor boats. The paragraph referred to in the First Sea Lord's signal reads as follows:

Measures that can be taken locally . . .

(14) When circumstances permit, vessels should be berthed in docks (afloat) or in basins in preference to lying in the stream.[22]

According to one account, Phillips could not understand the relevance of the signal and 'said something about "the [F]irst Sea Lord going off at half-cock".'[23] While we now know what the First Sea Lord was referring to in his signal, why he was referring to it when Force Z was at sea and just hours from the Japanese is still something of a mystery.

As Force Z neared Kuantan, in London Winston Churchill was convening a meeting deep underground in the Cabinet War Rooms at 10.00 p.m. (2200Z or 2300A/BST) on 9 December. According to Mr Churchill's account in *The Grand Alliance*, the meeting consisted of 'mostly Admiralty', and the discussion concerned what to do with the *Prince of Wales* and *Repulse*. He recalled that some of those present favoured withdrawing the ships to Colombo, but that he thought it would be a grand gesture to send the ships to join the Americans after their defeat at Pearl Harbor. According to Mr Churchill, no decision was made, and they decided to sleep on it. According to one participant, the meeting broke up about midnight BST (0000A), or about 0630 off Kuantan.[24]

Back in Singapore, before dawn on the morning of the 10th, the RAF sent a strike of three Hudsons and six old Vildebeest bombers to Kuantan, but they found nothing to attack. Two Buffaloes from No. 243 Squadron were also sent to Kuantan that morning, but they saw nothing and evidently were not seen by Force Z.[25] As late as 0800 on the 10th, the war diary for Brooke-Popham's headquarters noted that the situation at Kuantan was reported quiet, but 'with occasional shelling from two ships close in'.[26] After that, little attention seems to have been paid to the situation at Kuantan, and it is not clear when anyone finally concluded that the report of a landing had been false. In any event, Admiral Palliser did not send a message to Admiral Phillips informing him that the report was false, and most likely assumed that Phillips was still steering for Singora or Kota Bharu.

Dawn on Wednesday 10 December brought a beautiful day, with sunshine and few clouds. As the ships of Force Z neared Kuantan, a solitary aeroplane was sighted from the *Repulse* at about 0630. The aircraft was assumed to be Japanese, but there is no reason now to believe it was, and its identity has remained a mystery. It may have been a British Blenheim bomber that took off from Kuantan at 0448 and reported that at 0637 it had sighted, among other things, six stationary merchant vessels not exceeding 10,000 tons, and at 0649 an aircraft carrier or battleship steaming at 20–25 knots. The Blenheim did not make its report until after it had landed because its radio was useless within fifteen minutes of takeoff.[27] If it miscounted by one, the six vessels could well have been the five ships of Force Z, and the 'aircraft carrier or battleship' steaming at 20–25 knots could well have been the *Repulse* or *Prince of Wales*. The Blenheim did not make a report until 1013, and it does not seem to have aroused any suspicion that the aircraft had sighted Force Z. In any event, Force Z maintained its course for Kuantan and continued to maintain radio silence.

When it finally arrived off Kuantan, Force Z found neither a Japanese invasion force nor friendly air cover. At 0720, the *Prince of Wales* launched a seaplane,[28] a Supermarine Walrus piloted by Lieutenant C.R. 'Dick' Bateman, to carry out a reconnaissance and then return to Singapore, all the while keeping radio silence.[29] Later the *Repulse* launched a Walrus piloted by Petty Officer Pilot W.T.J. Crozer for anti-submarine patrol.[30] The destroyer *Express* was sent ahead to Kuantan, and upon its return at 0845 it reported, 'Complete peace.'[31] As the ships sailed along the coast, a wag on the flag deck of the *Repulse* parodied a travel talk, 'On the starboard beam, dear listeners, you see some of the beauty spots of Malaya.'[32] At Captain Tennant's suggestion, Admiral Phillips then proceeded to investigate some barges and other small craft in the area. At 0952, the *Prince of Wales* received a signal from Admiral Palliser reporting fifteen Japanese transports and an aircraft carrier off Singora,[33] further reinforcing the obvious, that no one in Singapore had expected Force Z to arrive off Kuantan that morning.

Also at 0952, while on her solitary way back to Singapore, the *Tenedos* was sighted and attacked by one of the Japanese reconnaissance planes, but its two bombs missed,[34] and at 0955 the *Tenedos* sent off a signal reporting the attack.[35] She soon sighted more Japanese aircraft, part of the massive force sent to find and sink Force Z, and sent off signals at 1005 and 1020 reporting what she had seen. At 1030, she skilfully evaded the nine 1,100lb bombs dropped by Lieutenant Nikaido's squadron of the Genzan Group, and sent off the signal, 'Enemy aircraft are dropping bombs.'[36] The *Tenedos* proceeded unscathed, her captain having found the whole incident 'exciting rather than frightening',[37] and reached the Singapore naval base at 1610 that day.[38]

The *Tenedos*'s signals were taken in by Force Z,[39] and by the *Electra* at 1005 and 1030,[40] but it is unclear whether any of them were received by the British command in Singapore,[41] though at least one of them was taken in by the British cruiser *Danae* in the Indian Ocean. An earlier signal, the one that Phillips had ordered the *Tenedos* to send at 0800,[42] was in fact received at Singapore on the forenoon of the 10th, but there it was only inferred that the Admiral's plan had changed and that he could not have gone as far north as Singora.[43]

At about 1015, a Nell search plane piloted by Ensign Hoashi Masane sighted Force Z, and sent off a contact report.[44] At about the same time, the *Repulse* detected Ensign Hoashi's plane on its radar,[45] and at 1020 his plane was visually sighted by Force Z.[46] At 1030, Admiral Phillips ordered first-degree readiness for air attack,[47] increased speed to 25 knots, and set a course for Singapore. He did not, however, break radio silence to notify Admiral Palliser of his position or to ask for air cover.

Because Ensign Hoashi's reports were not being received clearly by the Japanese aircraft already in the air, he was eventually ordered to transmit his reports in clear.[48] In one of the bombers, Flight Petty Officer First Class Katsumi Ogawa recalled, 'We had come more than 600 nautical miles. Seeing only clouds and water, we were depressed, and started thinking, "Hopeless today." Then we received the report, "Enemy sighted at 75 degrees, 40 nautical miles off Kuantan." Everyone jumped up.' The Japanese bombers that had not attacked the *Tenedos* began to head for the reported location of Force Z.

As it turned out, Ensign Hoashi's reports unwittingly enjoyed a very wide audience: he was overheard by the Americans on Corregidor Island in the Philippines[49] and in Chungking, China,[50] by the Nationalist Chinese, who reported them to the British ambassador,[51] and (at least as far as some of Hoashi's later reports were concerned) by the British in Singapore.[52]

In Singapore, Admiral Palliser had still heard nothing from Admiral Phillips. At some point, perhaps after receiving the signals from the *Tenedos*, Palliser sent Phillips a signal informing him that he had two aircraft and asking for instructions on where to send them.[53] Admiral Palliser received no reply, and sent the aircraft off based on what he thought Phillips would do; unfortunately, his guess was not correct, and the aircraft went to the wrong location.[54]

As the first Japanese bombers neared Force Z, a lone Australian Hudson happened upon the scene, at least according to its pilot, Flight Lieutenant Herb Plenty.[55] The Hudson was returning from a reconnaissance mission that day, and Plenty has described how he and his crew then watched as the entire battle played out before them. On what became something of a sightseeing trip, the Hudson circled Force Z for more than two hours, yet had enough fuel to return to Singapore. Plenty did not radio a report of the battle to Singapore, as it had not occurred to him that the ships had not done so, but he says he made a report upon his arrival back in Singapore. Making no secret of what he had seen, Plenty told his girlfriend about the battle that afternoon, and that night he told inquiring British naval officers at the Adelphi Hotel about it. Nevertheless, the incident is not mentioned in the Japanese, British, or Australian official histories, in the war diary of the Far East Headquarters,[56] or in the RAF Far East War Room Narrative for that day.[57] Nor was the lone Hudson noticed that day by any of the British seamen or Japanese airmen, who were soon to have much more pressing things on their minds.

Notes

1 Official Japanese History, at 450.

2 TNA Adm 199/1149, at 74, 76.

3 See Appendix, No. 51.

4 See Appendix, No. 53.

5 War Diary, General Headquarters Far East, December 1941. TNA WO 172/15.

6 Letter from Michael Goodenough to Lady Phillips of 6 June 1947. T.S.V. Phillips Papers.

7 The system of grading a report as to the reliability of its source and its contents is described in Patrick Beesly, *Very Special Intelligence*, at 79.

8 Grenfell, *Main Fleet to Singapore*, at 118.

9 War Diary, General Headquarters Far East, entry for 0800GH on 10 December 1941. TNA WO 172/15.

10 Palliser evidently told Captain Grenfell that he did not learn the falsity of the report until after the ships had been sunk. Grenfell, *Main Fleet to Singapore*, at 118 n. 1.

11 See Appendix, No. 57.

12 See Appendix, No. 56.

13 Roskill, *War at Sea, Vol. 1: The Defensive*, at 565. Captain Roskill later said he spoke to Palliser, who denied Goodenough's account, and that what he wrote in *The War at Sea* was a 'judicious compromise' between two irreconcilable views. Letter from Roskill to Marder of 20 January 1979. Marder Papers. Interestingly, the *Prince of Wales*'s Yeoman of Signals, E.A. Randall, told Professor Marder that Phillips assumed Palliser would send air cover at Kuantan. Letter from Randall to Marder of

15 September 1978. Marder Papers. One might wonder if Randall actually recalled that or whether he had read it in *The War at Sea*.

14 Martin Stephen, *The Fighting Admirals*, Annapolis, Naval Institute Press, 1991, at 130.

15 It is sometimes written that *I-58* did not sight Force Z until 0211 on the 10th, but, according to the Official Japanese History, *I-58* had sent off her first sighting report by 2352 on the 9th. This was one of the two reports from *I-58* that did not reach Ozawa or Matsuanaga. Official Japanese History, at 452.

16 Official Japanese History, at 451–2.

17 Official Japanese History, at 455; Shores, Cull and Izawa, *Bloody Shambles*, vol. 1, at 113.

18 Official Japanese History, at 455–7.

19 Hata, Ikuhiko and Izawa, Yazuho, *Japanese Naval Aces and Fighter Units in World War II*, Annapolis, Naval Institute Press 1989, at xiv.

20 *Ibid.* at 143. The remainder of the 22nd Air Flotilla's fighters were older Mitsubishi A5M 'Claudes'.

21 See Appendix, No. 54, and TNA Adm 199/1149, at 85.

22 TNA Adm 199/1950. The author is indebted to the late Mr J.D. Brown, then head of the Naval Historical Branch, who suggested that the letters 'LD' in the document designation might mean 'Local Defence'. He was right!

23 Middlebrook and Mahoney, *Battleship*, at 124, quoting an unidentified staff officer. Paymaster Lieutenant Kenneth Farnhill, Phillips's assistant secretary, claims to have brought what sounds like the signal to Phillips, though he first said he brought it to him shortly after their arrival in Singapore. Letter to Professor Marder of 16 October 1975, Marder Papers, but he was not listed among those consulted by Middlebrook and Mahoney. The Time of Origin and the Time of Receipt listed in the signal cannot both be correct, since there is less than a 6½hr time difference between Zone A and Zone GH; as a result, we cannot know for sure exactly when the signal was sent and when it was received.

24 Diary of General Sir Alan Brooke. Alanbrooke Papers, Liddell Hart Centre for Military Archives, King's College, London. Brooke's diary states the meeting started at 11.00 p.m. (2300), but his watch was probably on BST, while the official minutes, which say the meeting started at 10.00 p.m. (2200), were probably using GMT, one hour earlier.

25 Shores, Cull and Izawa, *Bloody Shambles*, vol. 1, at 112.

26 War Diary, General Headquarters Far East, entry for 0800GH on 10 December 1941. TNA WO 172/15.

27 RAF Far East War Room Narrative, December 1941, Air 23/3577, at 39. A second observer from another Blenheim that was in the area suggested that this was a large merchant ship that he had seen and strafed, and the two observers agreed the aircraft carrier or battleship seen by the first observer was really the merchant ship seen by the second one. Air 23/3577, at 40. Still, the first Blenheim could have been the mysterious aircraft.

28 Letter from L.J. Goudy to Professor Marder of 21 May 1980. Marder Papers.

29 Letter from C.R. Bateman to Brian Cull of 6 August 1985. Courtesy of Mr Cull.

30 After witnessing much of the battle, this Walrus later headed for Singapore. After running out of fuel and landing on the water, it was towed back to Singapore by the destroyer HMS *Stronghold*. Letter from Crozer to the author of 20 April 1998, and Imperial War Museum Sound Archives Interview.

31 Report of Captain L.H. Bell, TNA Adm 199/1149, at 36.

32 Gallagher, *Action in the East*, at 59.

33 See Appendix, No. 57.

34 Report of HMS *Tenedos* to Rear Admiral Malaya, 10 December 1941. TNA Adm 199/1149.

35 For this and other signals from the *Tenedos*, see Appendix, Nos 58–61.

36 This information is from the *Tenedos's* after-action report and the attached signals. TNA Adm 199/1149, at 161. The times given by the Japanese are 0922 for the first attack and 1044 for the second one. Official Japanese History, at 461–2.

37 Letter from Lieutenant Richard Dyer to Richard Hough of 11 September 1963. Marder Papers.

38 Log of HMS *Exeter* for 10 December 1941. TNA Adm 53/114260.

39 Admiralty Battle Summary No. 14, at 13.

40 Report of HMS *Electra* of 12 December 1941. TNA Adm 199/1149, at 173.

41 Admiral Layton's personal war diary has this entry for 10 December: '1046 Tenedos reported bombed.' TNA Adm 199/1473. It is not clear if the entry was made contemporaneously or later.

42 See Appendix, No. 56.

43 'Loss of PoW & Repulse', Appendix J. TNA Air 23/4745.

44 Official Japanese History, at 462.

45 Letter from Lieutenant Kenneth Armstrong, who was then the radar officer of the *Repulse*, to the author of 14 June 1998.

46 Report of HMS *Electra*, 12 December 1941, TNA Adm 199/1149, at 173, and Gallagher, *Action in the East*, at 59.

47 Report of HMAS *Vampire*, 12 December 1941. TNA Adm 199/1149, at 151.

48 Statement of Iki Haruki for Arthur J. Marder, October 1977, at 3. Marder Papers.

49 Letter from Duane Whitlock to Graydon A. Lewis, 25 April 1997, provided by Mr Lewis to the author.

50 John Winton, *Ultra in the Pacific*, Annapolis, Naval Institute Press, 1993, at 17.

51 Maochun Yu, 'Chinese Codebreakers, 1927–45', in David Alvarez, ed., *Allied and Axis Signals Intelligence in World War II*, London, Frank Cass & Co., 1999, at 209.

52 At 1252, the British wireless station at Kranji intercepted the message, 'A number of torpedoes hit. One ship sunk. One ship listing but not sunk.' At 1441, the message, 'Let me know the condition of the other ship', was intercepted. Layton Papers, British Library.

53 These could have been Buffaloes of No. 243 Squadron flown by Geoff Fisken and Mowbray Garden, which later came upon Force Z, or what was left of it. Shores, Cull and Izawa, *Bloody Shambles*, vol. 1, at 122–3.

54 A Knowledgeable Confidential Source. Marder Papers. The RAF Far East War Room Narrative states that at 1312 Admiral Palliser asked for fighter cover for a ship in

trouble off Kuantan, and at 1555 he relayed a request for a destroyer steaming south for fighter protection until dark. TNA Air 23/3577, at 41, 44.

55 H.C. Plenty, 'The End of Force Z', *Sabretache* 27 (July/September 1986), 29–32, and Herb Plenty, *Singapore Slip*, Canberra, LEN Pty Publishing, 1990, at 79–89, 97–100.

56 According to this war diary, an Air Headquarters Intelligence Summary at 2030 on the 10th noted that a Hudson 'carried out a recce up East Coast to a point North of Kuantan, but saw nothing'. TNA WO 172/15. In his book, Plenty wrote that another Hudson had searched before his and had not seen anything of note. *Singapore Slip*, at 80.

57 TNA Air 23/3577.

CHAPTER TWELVE

Repel Aircraft!

As the Japanese bombers approached, bugles on the ships of Force Z sounded 'Repel aircraft!' Scattered, tired, and low on fuel, the bomber squadrons of the 22nd Air Flotilla were converging on Force Z, drawn by the beacon of Ensign Hoashi's lone plane. As squadron after squadron arrived on the scene, they began to execute wave after wave of attacks against the *Prince of Wales* and *Repulse*.

The first bombers to arrive on the scene were Lieutenant Shirai's squadron of eight Nells from the Mihoro Group. As they neared, the anti-aircraft guns of the ships opened fire with deafening effect. Admiral Phillips attempted to manoeuvre his ships together, but a turn he ordered had the unintended effect of masking the anti-aircraft guns of the ships at a crucial moment. When this was pointed out to him by the Fleet Gunnery Officer, Commander H.N.S. Brown, Admiral Phillips left the ships free to manoeuvre as each ship's captain chose.[1]

Directing their attention to the *Repulse*, at 1115 each Nell dropped one 550lb bomb from about 10,000 feet. The *Repulse* disappeared in a deluge of water, along with British illusions about the lack of skill of Japanese aviators. Fortunately, the vessel was hit by only a single bomb, which went through the port hangar and burst in the after boiler room uptakes[2] and fractured steam pipes in E and F boiler rooms.[3] Thanks to the deck armour added in one of her many refits, the bomb did little real damage, but the release of superheated steam caused many painful burns. Several of the attacking aircraft were damaged, two of them seriously enough to return to base,[4] while the others circled around to make another pass.

Meanwhile, at 1129 the *Prince of Wales*'s Walrus landed at Seletar in Singapore.[5] Lieutenant Bateman, who had left Force Z before it was sighted, made a report, and his arrival in Singapore was noted by the Far East Headquarters at 1129[6] and by the RAF Far East War Room at 1130,[7] but surprisingly no one seemed to take much notice.[8] Bateman had left his papers in the *Prince of Wales*, and had difficulty getting out of Seletar; by the time he was taken to see Air Chief Marshal Brooke-Popham, the disaster was already unfolding.[9]

At 1132, Force Z was sighted by sixteen Nells of the Genzan Air Group, and the first attack was directed against the *Prince of Wales* by nine Nells of Lieutenant Ishihara's squadron.[10] As the aircraft crossed the bows of the *Prince of Wales* from starboard to port and then approached her from the port bow, the destroyer *Express* signalled to the *Prince of Wales*, 'Planes approaching have torpedoes.'[11] An officer on the bridge of the *Prince of Wales*, Lieutenant-Commander R.F. Harland, watched the aircraft approach and remarked, 'I think they're going to do a torpedo attack.' Admiral Phillips heard the remark and said something like, 'No, they're not. There are no torpedo aircraft about.'[12]

The nine Nells were indeed making a torpedo attack, and a skilful one it was. The anti-aircraft guns of the *Prince of Wales* opened fire, but the bombers, flying at a faster speed and greater height than the British thought possible for a torpedo attack, were very difficult to hit.[13] Captain Leach ordered the ship to turn hard to port, causing one of the nine Nells to lose its launching point and make the *Repulse* its target instead,[14] but the other eight Nells dropped their torpedoes on the *Prince of Wales*. One Nell was shot down after dropping its torpedo, but, in the meantime, eight torpedoes raced toward the *Prince of Wales*.

It was impossible to avoid all the torpedoes, and at 1144, as the *Prince of Wales* was still turning,[15] she was rocked by a massive explosion aft on the port side. Royal Marine Captain Claude Aylwin commanded the pom-pom mount atop Y turret, and he recalled a vast column of water and smoke that rose to a height of 200 feet, a vast shudder that shook the ship, and a jolt to the ship that was 'just as though the ship had encountered a rock below the surface, and though hitting the ship, the latter's momentum was sufficient to clear it'.[16] Lieutenant-Commander Harland recalled hearing 'expensive noises' after the hit,[17] and after the initial reverberating explosion, Sub-Lieutenant Geoffrey Brooke heard another noise, the percolating noise of water pouring into the ship, transmitted up the ship's pipes with chilling clarity.[18]

At the time, most men in the *Prince of Wales* thought that only one torpedo had hit her, but in fact there had been at least two. One torpedo exploded on the port side near the after pair of 5.25in turrets (P.3 and P.4) and forward of the after (Y) 14in gun turret. The second one hit the stern aft of Y turret. Unlike the first, the second one did not throw up a noticeable plume of water, although some water welled up over the quarterdeck.[19] The second torpedo, which hit very far aft and at an angle of about 40° to the ship as it swung to port,[20] must have come within just a few feet of missing completely. Another torpedo passed down the starboard side of the ship and just missed hitting the starboard quarter.[21]

The second torpedo tore a hole in the ship's plating about 12 feet in diameter, but, far worse, it destroyed the bracket securing the port outboard propeller shaft to the hull.[22] Without its bracket, the shaft, 17½ inches in diameter, began to vibrate appallingly and tore apart the shaft alley leading back to B engine room,[23] flooding compartments along the alley and allowing thousands of tons of water to enter the ship as if through a 'back door'. Lieutenant D.B.H. Wildish, who was in charge of the power unit that included 'B' engine room, saw water pouring into the compartment and ordered it to be evacuated after ordering the engine to be rigged to run while submerged.[24] At that time, the propeller shaft was intact and the propeller was still attached, but at some later time the propeller came off completely.[25]

The damage inflicted by the two torpedoes on the *Prince of Wales* was nothing less than catastrophic. The inrush of water caused the ship to take a list of 11½ degrees to port.[26] Progressive flooding and mechanical breakdowns wreaked further havoc with the ship's machinery spaces, and by 1202 both port shafts had stopped.[27] With only the two starboard shafts in operation, the ship slowed from 25 to 16 knots. Flooding also caused massive damage to the ship's dynamos and electrical system, which, with the list and shock damage, put much of the ship's anti-aircraft armament, her radar sets, and her steering out of action. As lights went out, dim emergency lights came on. Deep in the ship, as Paymaster Sub-Lieutenant G.L. Kipling later recalled, 'Everyone had the same expression on their faces – wide-eyed and wondering what was going to happen next as the ship began to take a heavy list to port.'[28]

Damage control efforts began at once on the *Prince of Wales*, but they were hampered by damage to communications and lighting and by the horrific heat below decks in a ship that was already rather hot in the tropics. Captain Leach ordered the counter-flooding of empty spaces on the starboard side of the ship, which reduced the ship's list to about 9 degrees.[29] Efforts were also made to rig emergency electrical leads, to establish a flooding boundary and to repair the steering gear. At 1210, still unable to regain control of her steering, the *Prince of Wales* hoisted two black balls from a yardarm, the signal that she was 'not under control'.

As the *Prince of Wales* tended her wounds, the *Repulse* received the attention of the seven Nells from the Genzan Group led by Lieutenant Takai. At first, Takai hesitated, fearing that the ship he was to attack was really the Japanese battlecruiser *Kongo*. As he began the attack, Lieutenant Takai recalled, 'The fleet opened up with a tremendous barrage of shells. . . . The sky was filled with bursting shells which made my plane reel and shake.'[30] Skilfully manoeuvred by Captain Tennant, the *Repulse* evaded the seven torpedoes aimed at her between 1145 and 1152. The last torpedo was dropped by Lieutenant Takai himself in a solo attack after his torpedo release failed on the first try,[31] but it too missed.

The *Repulse* also bore the brunt of the next two attacks. At 1148, she evaded the six 550lb bombs dropped by the remaining aircraft of Lieutenant Shirai's squadron of the Mihoro Group, which this time prudently chose to attack from 12,000 feet, instead of their earlier attack altitude of 10,000 feet.

Then, at 1157, the *Repulse* was attacked by the eight Nells of Lieutenant Takahashi's squadron, also of the Mihoro Group.[32] A crewmember of one of Takahashi's planes, Flight Seaman First Class Susumo Uno, later recalled his observations and emotions during the attack on the *Repulse*:

> The order to charge was given. As we rushed towards the enemy second after second, the defensive fire intensified, and explosions were closer to us. We closed from 4,000 to 3,000 metres, and I released the safety mechanism. The enemy seems to be turning away from us. If we go on like this, our course may fall off from the target. I kept shouting, 'Turning away, turning away', and almost wanted to take the control stick for myself.
>
> The thing I was thinking was, 'I have got to have this torpedo hit the target even if I have to give up my life. I've got to have this one hit the enemy.' The distance was 2,000 metres, and then 1,000 metres. I kept staring at the enemy bridge, holding the release handle, waiting for the order to shoot.

At a distance of 1,000 metres, I said, 'Get ready', and repeated the order in a raised voice. 'Fire!' I released the handle with all my might. 'Please, go hit the target!' I could not control my exploding emotions.

A crewman was raking the bridge with his face flushed. The plane was turning to port gradually in an evading motion. Fretting, I felt as if something was in pursuit and catching up to us. At an altitude of 30 metres, our plane continued turning to port as if it was watching the ship. We could not see any sign that the target had been hit. My feeling was inexpressible. 'We and our aeroplane attack the enemy as if we were a fireball, and still we failed.' I was in a daze, while tears rolled down my cheeks.[33]

All seven torpedoes missed the *Repulse*. As for the eighth, Lieutenant Takahashi twice tried to drop his own torpedo, then gave it up as a bad idea.[34]

During the Japanese torpedo attacks on the *Repulse*, Captain Tennant strolled from side to side of the bridge, saying nothing, but indicating with circular movements of his hand the direction in which the wheel was to be put to the navigating officer at the voice pipe, Lieutenant-Commander Gill, who relayed the commands to the chief quartermaster manning the helm below.[35]

After Lieutenant Takahashi's abortive attack, there was a lull in the battle. Captain Tennant was heard to say, 'We must close the *Prince of Wales* and give her some protection',[36] and the *Repulse* turned toward the *Prince of Wales*. It was then that Captain Tennant learned that Admiral Phillips had made no report,[37] and at 1158[38] he sent the signal 'OEAB', the code letters for 'Enemy Aircraft Bombing' – also known as 'Help!' – and gave his position.[39] The signal was received in Singapore at 1204, and eleven Buffalo fighters of No. 453 Squadron, under the command of Flight-Lieutenant Tim Vigors, a veteran of the Battle of Britain, were scrambled by 1225 to go the assistance of Force Z.

Before the Buffaloes could begin to arrive, new attacks developed from twenty-six Bettys of the Kanoya Group, which were low on fuel and had almost missed Force Z entirely. The Bettys first sighted a seaplane, most likely the *Repulse*'s Walrus, through the clouds, and then sighted the ships themselves at 1218, and divided their efforts between the *Prince of Wales* and the *Repulse*. For Force Z, the moment of reckoning had arrived.

Six Bettys from the squadrons of Lieutenants Nabeta and Higashi attacked the *Prince of Wales*, launching their torpedoes from the starboard side. She could not take any evasive action, and had difficulty firing at her attackers due to her list to port. As the torpedoes approached, men watched fascinated, but helpless,[40] and at about 1223[41] four torpedoes began hitting her starboard side, literally from stem to stern. One torpedo hit abreast the bridge, and threw up a vast column of water that drenched everyone in an exposed position, 'its noise like all the rainstorms ever invented'.[42] As a torpedo hit the stern, Sub-Lieutenant Geoffrey Brooke thought to himself, 'There goes my cabin.'[43] The damage to the ship's starboard side had the effect of reducing her list to 3 degrees,[44] at least temporarily, but it also reduced her speed, as one of the torpedoes damaged the starboard outer shaft,[45] leaving her able to steam at only 8 knots on the remaining engine room and the starboard inboard shaft and propeller. The torpedo that hit right aft was probably 'the decisive hit in the loss of ship buoyancy. It negated all the damage-control efforts in this section of the ship, and the intact buoyancy of the ship was so substantially reduced by stern flooding that the ship began a slow plunge by the stern.'[46]

Then the remainder of the Kanoya Group's Bettys concentrated on the *Repulse*. First came eleven bombers, again from the squadrons of Lieutenants Nabeta and Higashi. The *Repulse* was attacked by one group of torpedo-bombers, and after it had turned to avoid its torpedoes, by another group that had broken off its attack on the *Prince of Wales* at the last moment. Already committed to a turn to avoid the first torpedoes, the *Repulse* suffered one torpedo hit, on the port side amidships.[47] The old girl shook off the hit, and steamed on at 25 knots.

After these attacks, the *Prince of Wales* broke radio silence to send a signal to Singapore reporting four torpedo hits on the *Prince of Wales* and one on the *Repulse*, and asking first for destroyers and then for all available tugs.[48]

Notes

1   Letters from Brown to Arthur Marder of 5 and 31 January 1979. Marder Papers.
2   K.R.B. [Kenneth R. Buckley], 'A Personal Account of the Sinking of H.M.S. Repulse', *Naval Review* 30, No. 3 (August 1942), at 198.
3   Statement of Commander R.J.R. Dendy. TNA Adm 199/1149, at 20.
4   Official Japanese History, at 465.
5   For some reason, General Kirby reported that the Walrus had landed at Penang, at the opposite end of the Malay Peninsula. S. Woodburn Kirby, *Singapore: The Chain of Disaster*, New York, MacMillan Co., 1971, at 139, and Kirby, *The War against Japan, Vol. 1: The Loss of Singapore*, at 198. Lieutenant Bateman later confirmed to author

Brian Cull that he was never in Penang. Attachment to letter from Bateman to Brian Cull of 6 August 1985, by courtesy of Mr Cull.

6   TNA WO 172/15.

7   TNA Air 23/3577.

8   This incident may account for the belief held by Flight-Lieutenant Tim Vigors that there was a 50-minute delay in scrambling his fighters, rather than a 15-minute delay. Middlebrook and Mahoney, *Battleship*, at 281.

9   Letter from Bateman to Brian Cull of 6 August 1985. Copy courtesy of Brian Cull.

10 Official Japanese History, at 466.

11 TNA Adm 199/1149, at 159.

12 Middlebrook and Mahoney, *Battleship*, at 181.

13 The same Japanese tactics gave US Navy gunners fits when B5N2 'Kate' torpedo-bombers attacked the aircraft carrier USS *Yorktown* at the Battle of Midway on 4 June 1942. Pat Frank and Joseph D. Harrington, *Rendezvous at Midway: U.S.S. Yorktown and the Japanese Carrier Fleet*, New York, John Day Co., 1967, at 206.

14 Official Japanese History, at 467.

15 Testimony of Lieutenant-Commander R.F. Harland before the Bucknill Committee. TNA Adm 116/4554, at 158.

16 Memoirs of Captain C.D.L. Aylwin, RM, at 15. Papers of Captain C.D.L. Aylwin. Imperial War Museum, Department of Documents. With the kind permission of the copyright holder on Captain Aylwin's papers.

17 Interview, 'Battleships at War 1941/42', Naval Video Time Capsules.

18 Brooke, *Alarm Starboard!*, at 97.

19 Testimony of Lieutenant-Commander A. Terry, Report of Second Bucknill Committee. TNA Adm 116/4554, at 36.

20 Testimony of Commander Goodenough before the Second Bucknill Committee. TNA Adm 116/4554, at 154. Goodenough estimated the angle of the torpedo track he saw, which may have been the one to hit near P.3 and P.4 turrets; the one that hit further aft may have hit at a slightly different angle. Goodneough also testified that he thought at the time they had turned a little late, but that the tracks were not exactly parallel and that it may have been some tracks he did not see that affected the Captain's decision when to turn. *Ibid.* at 155.

21 Testimony of Lieutenant-Commander Harland before the Second Bucknill Committee. TNA Adm 116/4554, at 158.

22 Lieutenant-Commander D.P.R. Lermitte, RN, 'With All Flags Flying – 200 Feet Down', in Kendall McDonald, ed., *The Second Underwater Book*, London: Pelham Books, 1970, at 58–9.

23 The *Prince of Wales*'s machinery was organized in four separate units, A, B, X and Y, each with a boiler room containing two boilers, an engine room with a set of steam turbines, and an action machinery room. Each engine room drove a shaft capped by a propeller. 'A' unit drove the starboard outer shaft, 'B' unit drove the port outer shaft, 'X' unit drove the starboard inner shaft, and 'Y' unit drove the port inner shaft.

24 Letter from Vice-Admiral D.B.H. Wildish to the author of 28 October 1999, and Unpublished Memoirs of Admiral D.B.H. Wildish, at 139.

25 Notes of the author's discussion with Vice-Admiral Wildish on 19 March 2003.

26 Post-Action Statement of Lieutenant-Commander A.G. Skipwith of 12 December 1941. TNA Adm 199/1149, at 89.

27 Power Control Room Narrative, Appendix A to Report of the Second Bucknill Committee. TNA Adm 239/349.

28 'An Account of the Loss of H.M.S. Prince of Wales', at 6, enclosure to letter from G.L. Kipling to the author of 9 July 1998.

29 Technical Report on Damage to and Loss of H.M.S. 'Prince of Wales', at 7. TNA Adm 239/349.

30 Okumiya, Horikoshi and Caidin, Zero!, at 112, 113–14.

31 Ibid. at 112–15; Official Japanese History, at 467.

32 Official Japanese History, at 468.

33 Ibid. at 475.

34 Marder, Old Friends, New Enemies, at 507.

35 Lieutenant-Commander Gill's account is quoted in Brooke, Alarm Starboard!, at 113.

36 Attachment to letter from Lieutenant-Commander O.M.B. de las Casas to Arthur Marder of 1 July 1976. Marder Papers. De las Casas was then a midshipman assigned to Captain Tennant as his 'doggie'. Letter from de las Casas to Arthur Marder of 17 September 1975. Marder Papers.

37 According to then-Lieutenant John Hayes, the signal officer of the Repulse, when the guns began firing, in the main wireless office the questions and pithy epithets of his telegraphists 'conveyed their disbelief that no enemy report had yet been transmitted by the Flagship'. John Hayes, Face the Music, Edinburgh, Penland Press Ltd, 1991, at 139.

38 According to the note handed to Air Chief Marshal Brooke-Popham, the signal was sent at 1150. Brooke-Popham Papers, King's College, London.

39 See Appendix, No. 62. Captain Tennant's signal did give his position, contrary to General Woodburn Kirby's account. Kirby, Singapore: The Chain of Disaster, at 139.

40 Brooke, Alarm Starboard!, at 100.

41 Paymaster Lieutenant W.T. Blunt, Compass Platform Narrative. TNA Adm 199/1149.

42 Brooke, Alarm Starboard!, at 100.

43 Ibid.

44 Appendix 1 to Report of Captain L.H. Bell of 10 December 1941. TNA Adm 199/1149, at 39.

45 Personal statement of Lieutenant-Commander D.P.R. Lermitte, RN, Far East Fleet Clearance Diving Team, Appendix 6 to Middlebrook and Mahoney, Battleship, at 348–9.

46 William H. Garzke, Jr, and Robert O. Dulin, Jr, Battleships: Allied Battleships in World War II, Annapolis, Naval Institute Press, 1980, at 206.

47 Further Report by Captain W.G. Tennant, attachment to Admiral Sir Geoffrey Layton, 'Loss of H.M. Ships Prince of Wales and Repulse', 17 December 1941, Supplement to the London Gazette of 20 February 1948. TNA Adm 1/2006.

48 See Appendix, Nos 63, 64.

CHAPTER THIRTEEN

The End of the Line

A t about 1220, the *Repulse* was set upon by the remaining squadron of nine Bettys from the Kanoya Group, led by Lieutenant Iki Haruki, who had first intended to attack the *Prince of Wales*.[1] One of Iki's pilots later told him, 'As we dived for the attack, I didn't want to launch my torpedo. It was such a beautiful ship, such a beautiful ship.'[2]

Beauty was not to be enough; the Bettys of Iki's squadron dropped their torpedoes on the *Repulse* in a pincer attack from both port and starboard sides. Lieutenant Iki had not planned a pincer attack, but one developed when he changed sides due to the movements of the *Repulse*.[3] She could not evade them all. After the first one had hit, on the port side abreast the gunroom, her rudder jammed. Unable to take further avoiding action, she was quickly hit by three more torpedoes, two on the port side, one aft abreast the wardroom bathroom and the other abreast the port engine room, and one on the starboard side, abreast E boiler room.[4]

During the last attack the anti-aircraft fire from the *Repulse* was intense, and two Bettys were shot down, both by the *Repulse*'s portside 8-barrelled pom-pom, which was commanded by Sub-Lieutenant R.A.W. 'Dicky' Pool.[5] Lieutenant Iki later recalled, 'I saw my second plane flying next to mine set ablaze and plunging into the water close to the starboard bow of the *Repulse*, followed by my third plane falling on the point to the left of my second plane. . . . My plane got seventeen holes [in] the fuselage and wings.'[6]

Captain Tennant harboured no illusions about his ship's fate, and promptly ordered 'Away and man Carley floats', and then, 'Save yourselves and good luck.'[7] After the battle, the First Lieutenant of the

Repulse, Lieutenant-Commander Kenneth Buckley, wrote, 'There is not the slightest doubt that the opportune decision of the captain to pass the order and the sturdiness of the loud-speaker installation saved the lives of hundreds of men.'

Continuing, Lieutenant-Commander Buckley described the last moments of the *Repulse* and his escape. After putting some air into his Gieves' life-saving waistcoat, he looked around, and saw:

It was a glorious day with the bluest of blue seas. The port side of the ship, usually about 20 feet above the water, was just awash, and the starboard side correspondingly higher. Forward the boatswain was chucking wooden planks over the side, and aft of me an Australian midshipman was still madly firing his Oerlikon gun at an aircraft and blaspheming anyone who dared to foul the sight. The group of men with me, some blinking in the unaccustomed sunshine, showed no sign of fear; in fact, considering that they were still grappling with death, one might have described their attitude as jocular. I looked over the starboard, or high, side and saw we were still doing a good 16 knots. The propellers, still covered, were churning up a huge race which was brown with the oil fuel that was pouring from a forward tank. As I watched, a stoker whom I knew well went in, and was quickly chewed up in that ugly race.

It's a hell of a job getting out of a ship moving fast. The boatswain, cool as a cucumber, was urging the men to go forward on the high side, ahead of all the turmoil, and most people followed him over the guard-rails. I hung my tin hat tidily on a clip and was tempted to take the low side as I had seen two men do it successfully. In a second I was toboganning at high speed on my pants across the ship, and I met the water when the top guard-rail was about a foot below water. As I entered the water a strong backwash, which was flooding the port hangar, swept me back on board; I held on to the side of the hangar like grim death; but it was hard work and, as every second's delay lessened my chance of escape, I let go and was swept under the door into the darkness within. I was travelling fast, all underwater, and bumping occasionally; at least one other was there, too, as I was kicked by a boot from above. I was in a very bad temper at this turn of fate, and was just beginning to wonder what it would be like when I had to open my mouth, when the top of the hangar rolltop-desk door split open and I was spewed out into blue sea again. The ship was still moving fast and I saw the mainmast rigging cutting through the water towards me: I slipped inside the main shrouds and, as I passed aft, resisted a second backwash which was filling a hole from which an H.A. gun had presumably just fallen out.

What joy it was to be in still water again! I blew up my waistcoat some more and found myself with a crowd of about a hundred men, none of them in any difficulty and all shouting and singing. I swam on my back and watched the *Repulse* as she turned over with her forefoot high in the air. Someone led 'three cheers'; but her clean red hull seemed to hold the position indefinitely, and we had swum another hundred yards and cheered twice more before she finally dipped. It was a sad end to a very happy and efficient commission; but it was also a clean and honourable end to the gallant and beautiful old lady.[8]

Many years later, Sub-Lieutenant Paul Satow of the *Express* still recalled the horror of seeing the capsized hull of the *Repulse* immediately prior to her sinking.[9] The end of the *Repulse* was astonishingly sudden, within five minutes of the last hit, at about 1233. Admiral Phillips ordered the *Electra* and *Vampire* to begin picking up her survivors. While waiting to be picked up, the men of the *Repulse* gave three cheers for their captain and their ship, the 'Old Girl', and those who could sang 'Roll out the Barrel'.[10]

The Australian midshipman noticed by Commander Buckley was no doubt Midshipman R.I. Davies, who manned a 20mm Oerlikon gun on the starboard side aft. During the action he had manned his gun with gusto. When Lieutenant A.E. Jacob asked him how he was situated for ammunition, Davies said, 'All right so far, but if you can get us any more we'll get rid of it,' and Jacob recalled that Davies 'seemed as happy as a sand-boy and went on loading a magazine'.[11] Davies went down with his gun, but his courage did not go unnoticed, even by the Japanese: Lieutenant Iki recalled that the *Repulse* 'fought gallantly against us indeed', and did not cease firing her anti-aircraft guns 'until her last moment'.[12] Davies was honoured with a posthumous Mention in Dispatches, but at least one *Repulse* survivor later wondered what the difference was between his conduct and that of the famous Jackie Cornwall, who posthumously won a Victoria Cross for staying at his gun in HMS *Chester* during the Battle of Jutland.[13]

The next-to-last Japanese attack of the day was a flop, a rare Japanese mistake on a day when they made very few. At 1233, nine Nells of the Mihoro Group dropped their 1,100lb bombs into the empty sea about

4 miles from the *Prince of Wales*.[14] The Official Japanese History says their target was the escorting destroyers,[15] but more likely the squadron leader, Lieutenant Ohira, accidentally dropped his bomb and the rest of his squadron followed suit.[16]

The final attack of the day was, unfortunately, no flop. At about 1243, Lieutenant Takeda's squadron of eight Nells of the Mihoro Group, each carrying a 1,100lb bomb, attacked the *Prince of Wales*. The gallant ship fought to the last, and managed to damage five of her attackers, even though only three of her 5.25in turrets were operating and could be brought to bear.[17] One bomber could not release its bomb, and six bombs were near misses, but a single bomb hit, bursting in the cinema flat under the catapult deck, causing dreadful casualties among the exhausted and wounded men gathered there. The bomb also damaged the uptakes and downtakes to the last operating boiler room, and, when flash and fumes penetrated to X boiler room, it had to be evacuated.[18] The *Prince of Wales* stopped, dead in the water.[19]

Splinters from near-misses in the last attack may have caused more flooding. By then, to make matters worse, a commissioned gunner had needlessly and without orders decided to flood several magazines, presumably to prevent an explosion.[20] Stopped by the ship's engineer officer, Commander L.J. Goudy, this nevertheless caused yet more water to enter the ship and would have put her stern even lower in the water.

At this point, the destroyer *Express* came alongside the *Prince of Wales*'s starboard quarter. Captain Leach came aft to the quarterdeck, where he told some of the men there to evacuate to the *Express* and appealed to other men whose guns were still in action to remain by him and fight the ship, before he returned to the bridge.[21] Lines were passed, and a number of wounded and unnecessary personnel were then transferred to the *Express*. The last stretcher case to make it across was Able Seaman Christopher Rhodes, who had been taken from the working chamber under P.4 5.25in turret to the cinema flat, and was burned and knocked unconscious when the bomb exploded.

By this time, the *Prince of Wales* had an astonishing 18,000 tons of water aboard,[22] and progressive flooding was causing her to take on even more water. With her quarterdeck already awash, the ship's list to port began to increase, and the *Prince of Wales* finally began to capsize. Whether it emanated from the Captain on the compass platform or not, word was passed to abandon ship. In S.3 turret, the sight checker, Boy Seaman First Class Ken Byrne, was told by a voice from the High Angle Control Position below, 'We are evacuating the position. Good luck, mates.'

Waiting until the last possible moment, the men on the *Express* cut all lines to the *Prince of Wales* when their captain, Lieutenant-Commander F.J. Cartwright, yelled 'Slip!' and then 'Starboard ten, full astern together.'[23] Before the *Express* could get away, the starboard bilge keel of the *Prince of Wales* gave the *Express* a heavy bump and caused her to heel violently before she swung back and surged clear.[24]

Those men remaining on board the *Prince of Wales* had to make the best of it. As Lieutenant Kenneth Townsend-Green left the 20mm Oerlikon gun he had manned on the starboard side of the bridge, Captain Leach spied him and said, 'Tiggy, you should have gone long ago.'[25] Lieutenant W.M. Graham recalled that,

> when the time came to abandon ship, it was done quietly and almost as if hands had been piped to bathe! I suppose that many felt, like me, that this just could not be happening to them as it seemed like a bad dream – a long swim brought one back to reality![26]

Leading Baker F.L. 'Bim' Hardy's escape topside was blocked, and he had to climb out of a porthole and jump into the sea.[27] The ship's gunnery officer, Lieutenant-Commander Colin McMullen, managed to survive by climbing from his director up the foremast, clinging to it as the ship capsized, and then setting down comfortably in the water at a safe distance as the ship turned over onto her side.[28] McMullen then climbed into a Carley float with four sailors who were singing the Volga Boat Song.[29] Captain L.H. Bell, after coming up for the second time, started swimming 'like hell for the most beautiful biscuit tin that I have ever seen floating about', and when he reached it he said, 'You and I are going to be great friends for a long time.'[30]

The *Prince of Wales* finally sank at 1320. Just as she sank, two Buffaloes flown by Mowbray Garden and Geoff Fisken of No. 243 Squadron arrived on the scene;[31] perhaps they were the Buffaloes that had been dispatched by Admiral Palliser. Then the Buffaloes of No. 453 Squadron arrived, led by Flight Lieutenant Tim Vigors. The survivors of the *Prince of Wales* and *Repulse* greeted the Buffaloes with either cheers (so the pilots thought) or jeers (so said some of the survivors). At the appearance of the Buffaloes, Ensign Hoashi quickly made himself scarce and radioed his good news to Admiral Matsunaga in Saigon.

Tragically, Admiral Phillips and Captain Leach were among those lost. According to Captain Bell, as the *Prince of Wales* started to capsize he and Captain Leach tried hard to persuade the Admiral to go down to the upper deck where chances of escape would be better, but although he gave orders for all personnel to blow up their life-saving belts and set the example himself, he refused to leave the bridge himself until the last possible moment.[32]

Finally, as it became obvious the ship was about to go, Phillips leaned over to where the staff on the admiral's bridge could see him, and smiled and waved them to go on and abandon ship.[33] According to Paymaster Lieutenant W.T. Blunt, Captain Leach's secretary,

> There was never any talk, nor I think any thought, of leaving the compass platform until the rapidly increasing list showed that the ship was about to founder. It was only then that occurred what I can best describe as a spontaneous consensus that time was up and that it had become a matter of 'every man for himself'. It was then we all left the compass platform.[34]

When Admiral Phillips and Captain Leach finally left the bridge, Admiral Phillips, Lieutenant-Commander C.G. Lawson, and Blunt chose to move to a sponson off the admiral's bridge on the starboard side of the ship, while Captain Leach and Chief Yeoman Howell decided to go down one more level.[35] Blunt was the only one of the five to survive. Admiral Phillips had not tried to 'go down with the ship', although he may have been sorely tempted to do so; before the end, he had been heard to say, 'I cannot survive this.'[36]

Another tragic loss was the *Prince of Wales*'s fine executive officer, Commander Lawson. Commander Goodenough had urged him to leave the damage control headquarters in the lower conning tower of the ship as the ship was sinking, but Lawson refused.[37]

The *Electra* sent a signal to Singapore with the shocking news of the sinking of the *Repulse*, and then sent another with the even more shocking news of the *Prince of Wales*.[38] The three destroyers of Force Z were busy picking up survivors for hours. Thankfully, the weather was perfect for rescue, the sea was warm, the infamous local sharks were conspicuous by their absence, and, for whatever reason, the Japanese made absolutely no attempt to interfere. Satisfied that no one had been left alive, the destroyers then sped to Singapore,[39] with air cover from sections of two Buffaloes from No. 488 Squadron.[40] Loaded with about 2,000 survivors, they arrived at Singapore just before midnight, after passing the destroyer HMS *Stronghold* and the four American destroyers that had been sent by Admiral Hart to assist Admiral Phillips.

Upon landing in Singapore, the survivors were cared for and given food, drink, new clothing, medical care, and, in at least one case, a ride.

> One filthy survivor, walking gingerly barefoot over the gravel chippings of the quayside, was offered a lift by an officer. The survivor protested that the officer would ruin his spotless white uniform, but the officer replied, '—— the uniform. Get on my back.'[41]

After arriving at Singapore, correspondent Cecil Brown met up with Captain Tennant, and reported that he was 'smiling and cheerful, shaking hands with his surviving officers, but you could see, in his eyes, that his heart was breaking apart'.[42] Most survivors were sent to the Fleet Shore Accommodation or to HMS *Exeter*, and the wounded were sent to the Alexandra Military Hospital for treatment.

The destroyers were also met by Midshipman Henry Leach, the son of the captain of the *Prince of Wales*, who was in Singapore at the time with the cruiser *Mauritius*. After many fruitless enquiries, he finally learned of his father's death from the senior surviving officer of the ship's company, Lieutenant-Commander A.G. Skipwith, who ended the bad news with, 'He was . . . a fine man . . . and we all loved him.'[43]

The *Prince of Wales* and *Repulse* had shot down three Japanese aircraft – the former one and the latter two – in which all twenty-one crewmen were killed. Contrary to at least one Japanese account, the three did not crash themselves into the British ships.[44] In all, 837 officers and men did not survive. The *Prince of Wales* took 20 officers and 307 ratings with her, and 24 officers and 486 ratings were lost on the *Repulse*. Twenty-four men of the *Prince of Wales* and *Repulse* received a Mention in Dispatches for their bravery that day, twelve of them posthumously.[45] No doubt some, like Midshipman Davies, deserved better than that.

On 18 December, Lieutenant Iki flew back to the scene of the battle in his Betty and dropped bouquets of flowers, one over the *Repulse* and another over the *Prince of Wales*, to honour his fallen comrades and the British dead.[46]

Notes

1 Middlebrook and Mahoney, *Battleship*, at 234.

2 John Toland, *The Rising Sun I*, New York, Random House, 1970, at 304.

3 Letter from Kozo Sekiguchi to Marder of 15 February 1979, at 11, based on interviews with Lieutenant Iki. Marder Papers.

4 Vice-Admiral Geoffrey Layton, 'Loss of H.M. Ships Prince of Wales and Repulse, December 17, 1941', Supplement to the *London Gazette* of 20 February 1948, at 1239. TNA Adm 1/2006. For another account of the hits, see Jacobs, 'The Loss of the Repulse and Prince of Wales, December 10 1941: A Participant's Account', at 22.

5 Pool, *Course for Disaster*, at 65, and letter from R.A.W. Pool to Arthur Marder of 14 July 1979. Marder Papers.

6 Statement of Lieutenant Iki for Professor Marder of October 1977, at 5. Marder Papers.

7 Statement of Commander R.J.R. Dendy. TNA Adm 199/1149, at 20–1.

8 Buckley, 'A Personal Account of the Sinking of H.M.S. Repulse', at 200. Lieutenant-Commander Buckley was later awarded a Mention in Dispatches for his actions during the battle.

9 Letter to the author of 25 January 1997.

10 Pool, *Course for Disaster*, at 67.

11 Jacobs, 'The Loss of Repulse and Prince of Wales, December 10 1941: A Participant's Account', at 20.

12 Statement of Iki Haruki for Arthur J. Marder, October 1977, at 5. Marder Papers.

13 Letter from Hayes to Professor Marder of 17 August 1979. Marder Papers; also TNA Adm 1/12315.

14 Report of Lieutenant-Commander C.W. McMullen, attached to letter from McMullen to Marder of 3 March 1976. Marder Papers; also TNA Adm 239/349, at 94.

15 Official Japanese History, at 470.

16 Okumiya, Horikoshi and Caidin, *Zero!*, at 118.

17 These were P.2, S.1 and S.2. Report of Lieutenant-Commander C.W. McMullen, attachment to letter from McMullen to Marder of 3 March 1976. Marder Papers.

18 Technical Report on Damage to and Loss of H.M.S. 'Prince of Wales', at 9. TNA 239/349.

19 The last engine room, X, had been receiving steam from both A and X boiler rooms, Technical Report on Damage to and Loss of H.M.S. 'Prince of Wales', at 8, but evidently for some reason the turbines in X engine room stopped when X boiler room had to be abandoned.

20 The commissioned gunner, F. Luxton, was named in letters from Commander Goudy to Professor Marder. Marder Papers. In his after-action statement, Luxton stated that he was told that a pom-pom magazine had been flooded but that he could not find out who had ordered it. TNA Adm 239/349, at 32. Ordnance Lieutenant H. Lancaster said in his statement, 'Mr. Luxton said they were flooding the magazines.' TNA Adm 239/349, at 33.

21 Memoirs of Captain C.D.L. Aylwin, RM, at 17. Papers of Captain C.D.L. Aylwin, RM. Imperial War Museum, Department of Documents.

22 'Technical Report on Damage to and Loss of H.M.S. Prince of Wales', at 9. TNA Adm 239/349.

23 Brooke, *Alarm Starboard!*, at 108.

24 *Ibid.*

25 Letter from Sheila Townsend-Green to the author of 1 October 1998.

26 Middlebrook and Mahoney, *Battleship*, at 252.

27 Alex Dawson, 'Ghost of the Deep', *Leicester Mercury*, 1 December 1990, at 6.

28 Letter from W.T. Blunt to the author of 12 August 1999. In a 1989 interview, McMullen said he swam off the bridge, which is not nearly as interesting! Interview transcript, at 30. No. 10975/5, Imperial War Museum.

29 *Ibid.*

30 Letter of 17 December 1941 from Captain L.H. Bell to an unknown addressee. Imperial War Museum, Department of Documents.

31 Brian Cull with Paul Sortehaug and Mark Haselden, *Buffaloes over Singapore*, London, Grub Street, 2003, at 53.

32 Letter from Captain Bell to Lady Phillips of 12 December 1941. T.S.V. Phillips Papers.

33 Letter from Michael Goodenough to Lady Phillips of 22 December 1941. T.S.V. Phillips Papers.

34 Letter from W.T. Blunt to the author of 23 May 2003.

35 Letter from W.T. Blunt to the author of 12 August 1999, and conversation of 5 May 1999; Brooke, *Alarm Starboard!*, at 115.

36 Doig, 'Misfortune off Malaya', at 25, attachment to letter from Dougal Doig to Marder of 8 September 1978. Marder Papers. Doig thought he heard the remark from Captain L.H. Bell (although he first referred to him as 'T.I. Scott' Bell) when they were drawing up a narrative of the operation. Letter from Doig to Arthur Marder of 20 October 1978. Marder Papers.

37 Letter from Captain Roskill to Arthur Marder of 20 January 1979. Roskill Papers.

38 See Appendix, Nos 65, 70.

39 According to Paymaster Captain Doig, the *Electra* made a signal that they had 2,000 survivors and would reach Singapore from midnight onwards, that Captain Tennant was on board but that neither Admiral Phillips nor Captain Leach was among those rescued. 'Misfortune off Malaya', attachment to letter from Dougal Doig to Arthur Marder of 8 September 1978. Marder Papers. I have not been able to find any record of such a signal.

40 Squadron Leader J.M.S. Ross, *Royal New Zealand Air Force*, Nashville, Battery Press, 1955, 1993, at 84.

41 Middlebrook and Mahoney, *Battleship*, at 276.

42 Brown, *Suez to Singapore*, at 337.

43 Leach, *Endure No Makeshifts*, at 10.

44 Okumiya, Horikoshi and Caidin, *Zero!*, at 120.

45 Middlebrook and Mahoney, *Battleship*, Appendix 5, at 344–7, citing TNA Adm 1/12315.

46 Marder, *Old Friends, New Enemies*, at 508.

CHAPTER FOURTEEN

The Decision Not To Break Radio Silence

By far the most controversial decision of the story once Force Z had put to sea is Admiral Phillips's decision to maintain radio silence from the beginning of the operation until after the *Prince of Wales* had been hit and Captain Tennant had already broken radio silence. The decision has brought strong support from some,[1] mystified others[2] and elicited harsh criticism from yet others,[3] including a suggestion from one survivor that Phillips should have been court-martialled and disgraced.[4]

In examining Admiral Phillips's decision, we are handicapped by the lack of any evidence of actual discussions on the bridge of the *Prince of Wales* about breaking radio silence and calling for fighters, with one possible exception.[5] However, we do know something about Phillips's thinking from the recollections of members of his staff, Captain L.H. Bell, Commander Michael Goodenough, and Paymaster Lieutenant K.H. Farnhill, Phillips's assistant secretary. Unfortunately, years later Bell said he did not know why Phillips had not broken radio silence,[6] and Farnhill had less contact with Phillips during the voyage than Commander Goodenough. The most important evidence we have is two letters written by Goodenough to Captain S.W. Roskill[7] and to Lady Phillips;[8] most unfortunately, we do not have the letter Goodenough wrote to the Admiralty shortly after the event.[9] Even these letters have to be viewed with a little caution, since Goodenough, a staunch supporter of Tom Phillips and a detractor of Palliser, could not be expected to be completely objective about the incident.

Admiral Phillips could have broken radio silence at a number of points during the operation, i.e. when he was first sighted by aircraft on the evening of the 9th, when he called off the operation and turned back for Singapore at 2015 that night, when he changed course for Kuantan at 0052 on the 10th, when an unidentified aircraft was sighted at about 0630 on the 10th, when he received the bombing report from the *Tenedos* at about 1000 and when Ensign Hoashi's search plane was sighted at about 1020.[10] The appropriate signal would have been OEAS, which meant 'Enemy Aircraft Shadowing'.[11] Why did he not break radio silence at any of those points in the operation?[12]

The main reason for Phillips's decision not breaking radio silence was almost certainly the desire to keep the Japanese from using direction-finding equipment to determine his position. As a member of the Admiral's staff explained:

> Because the most accurate way of fixing the *exact* position of a ship at sea is by cross-bearings from two or more shore stations of the W/T signals made by the ship, the maintenance of strict W/T silence at sea was almost an article of faith in the Royal Navy at that time.[13]

That the Walrus launched from the *Prince of Wales* on 10 December was ordered not to break radio silence shows how important radio silence was to Phillips. As if he needed to be reminded, Phillips had been at the Admiralty in May 1941 when the *Bismarck*, unaware she had eluded her pursuers, broke radio silence to send a long message that was intercepted by the British. Although the message's bearings were incorrectly plotted and an opportunity to catch the *Bismarck* missed, the lesson would not have been lost on Phillips.

The danger of being located by Japanese direction finding alone explains and probably justifies Admiral Phillips's not calling for air cover at any point in the operation before Force Z was sighted by Ensign Hoashi. Breaking radio silence when he was sighted by aircraft or when he broke off the operation late on the 9th could well have given his location away to Japanese surface forces that were still very close by, even though doing so might have given the Japanese the false idea he was still heading for Kota Bharu or Singora. Breaking radio silence when he changed course for Kuantan would have given away his position at a time when he wanted to surprise the Japanese at Kuantan. Regarding the unidentified aircraft sighted early on 10 December, Phillips was justified in not breaking radio silence because it was not certain the aircraft was Japanese (and it was not), because it was evidently not heard to make a sighting report, and because Phillips still expected fighter cover to be provided at Kuantan. As we shall see shortly, there was another reason not to report a single aircraft. It also made some sense for Phillips to maintain radio silence when he heard the bombing reports from the *Tenedos*, since he hoped to elude the aircraft that were out looking for him and a signal would have given his position away.

However, the danger of giving away his location did not apply once Force Z was sighted by a lone search plane at about 1015 on 10 December. At that point, it is difficult to see any disadvantage to breaking radio silence; the enemy knew exactly where he was, since there was no reason to believe that Hoashi had not sent a sighting report. Even if it were true that, according to Captain Bell, 'Experience had shown that reports of enemy positions by S/M [submarines] or aircraft were often wildly inaccurate; as were indeed the Japanese reports in this operation,'[14] Force Z was not in the middle of the ocean; it was only 60 miles off the coast of Malaya, and surely there was little likelihood the one aircraft's sighting report would be so far off as to justify not breaking radio silence. So why did Admiral Phillips not break radio silence at that point? There are a number of reasons that have been advanced over the years, and there is a new reason to consider.

First, is it possible there was insufficient time to get off a contact report after Force Z had been sighted and before the attacks began? Captain Bell, in response to an Admiralty question, stated that he thought it was only a half an hour between the sighting of the Japanese aeroplane and the beginning of the attacks.[15] If, however, the search plane was sighted at 1020 and the first attack began at about 1115, Phillips surely had sufficient time to get off a message to Singapore if he had been so inclined.

Secondly, it has been suggested that Admiral Phillips might have ordered that a message be sent but that it was not sent off because of the damage to the communications equipment in the *Prince of Wales*.[16] True, the central communications office was flooded in the first torpedo attack, but there was another communications office in the ship, and it was evidently operable until almost the very end.[17] More importantly, there is absolutely no evidence that Phillips ordered that a message be sent until after the *Prince of Wales* was hit. Even if Phillips had ordered that a signal be sent even as late as, say, 1116, just after the *Repulse* was hit, it would not have taken until 1144, when the first torpedoes hit the *Prince of Wales*, to get a signal off.

Thirdly, it has also been suggested that Admiral Phillips did not break radio silence because he had been informed by Admiral Palliser that the Japanese could attack him five hours after he had been sighted, and that he knew time was on his side.[18] Admiral Palliser's signal would not have given him reason to maintain radio silence, or even to delay breaking radio silence, once he was sighted by Ensign Hoashi. Further, Phillips knew from the reports from the *Tenedos* starting at 0955[19] that a large number of Japanese bombers were much, much closer than five hours away, and that time was most certainly not on his side.

Fourthly, it has often been claimed that Admiral Phillips did not break radio silence and call for air cover because he did not take the threat from aircraft seriously enough, and believed that battleships and other warships were in little danger from aircraft. At one time, those were most definitely his views, at least through the Norwegian campaign, as Captain Roskill knew from bitter first-hand experience when he tried to persuade Phillips of the danger. The campaign in Norway lasted from April to June 1940, and German aircraft sank the anti-aircraft cruiser *Curlew*, the British destroyer *Afridi* and the Polish destroyer *Grom* and severely damaged the heavy cruiser *Suffolk*.

There is evidence, however, that Phillips's views on the danger aircraft posed to ships had changed to some degree by December 1941. In the first place, Admiral Phillips's son, Commander T.V.G. Phillips, told Captain Roskill that his father had changed his views by the time of the loss of the light cruiser *Southampton*,[20] which was sunk by German dive-bombers in January 1941 at the same time that the armoured aircraft carrier *Illustrious* was badly mauled. Years later, however, Captain Roskill wrote that if Phillips 'really had come to recognize the extent of the menace to ships without fighter cover by the time he reached Singapore the change must have come at a pretty late day'.[21] Secondly, Commander Goodenough told Lady Phillips that 'the Admiral most certainly did not believe that ships should be subjected to heavy air attack in 1941–2 without the assistance of fighter defence.'[22] Thirdly, even better evidence that Admiral Phillips took the threat from aircraft more seriously is that, almost on the eve of the battle, in a meeting with General MacArthur and Admiral Hart in Manila on 6 December, he stressed the need for long-range fighters to escort ships operating to break up an invasion, and said, 'With the Navy, what it really comes down to when you are within range, if you have the fighters you can do your job. And if you haven't it is, as at Crete – none too good.'[23] In the Battle for Crete in May 1941, the Royal Navy had lost three cruisers and six destroyers, with many other ships damaged, to German bombers in its efforts to forestall seaborne invasion of the island and to withdraw the Commonwealth troops once they were defeated by air-landed troops. Finally, there is the evidence of Phillips's actions. Just before sailing, he tried repeatedly to obtain air cover for the operation. Then on 10 December, once he received the report that the *Tenedos* was under air attack, he ordered an increase in speed and readiness for air attack. Indeed, he did everything but break radio silence. There is thus plenty of evidence that Admiral Phillips took the threat from the air much more seriously than he had before, but one may still wonder whether he took it seriously enough.

Fifthly, some have explained Admiral Phillips's decision not to call for air cover because he had been informed that, 'Fighter protection on Wednesday 10th will not, repeat not, be possible.'[24] This seemingly unequivocal message seems to provide an easy excuse: why ask for air cover if you have been told it would not be available? For several reasons, that may not be such an easy answer. After all, the message was sent in reply to Phillips's three-part request to the RAF for assistance, with the third part requesting air cover on 10 December *off Singora*, which was where he planned to be at dawn on the 10th. The reply to that request did not say 'off Singora', but when read in context with the request that is almost certainly what it meant. Then, Commander Goodenough has said that Phillips told him 'categorically, however, that fighter cover would be provided, and that his Chief of Staff . . . would arrange this'.[25] Goodenough told Lady Phillips, 'The Admiral continued to operate his ships to the Northward . . . partly because he had faith the fighters would still materialise. . . .'[26] If that is so, Admiral Phillips must not have interpreted the signal to mean that fighter protection would not be possible *anywhere* he might be on 10 December,[27] especially since Kuantan was much closer to air bases in Singapore than Singora was.

However, it may not have been as simple as that. In the same letter to Lady Phillips, Goodenough also wrote that Phillips

> thought his movements must be obvious to those on shore and that if there were any fighters they would come. If there were no fighters the Army must still be helped. He saw no point in crying for help [fighter protection] when he had already asked for it.[28]

In the letter to Captain Roskill, Goodenough wrote that

I am sure that Phillips's attitude was that he believed his Chief of Staff would arrange the provision of a fighter defence. It seemed incredible to him that his Chief of Staff would not appreciate that he had gone to Kuantan in answer to the signal reporting the landing. It was, therefore, quite unnecessary for him to give away his presence by a further signal asking for fighter support or bellyaching about his needs.[29]

Taken together, Goodenough seemed to be saying, first, that Admiral Phillips did not break radio silence to call for air cover on the 10th because he thought Admiral Palliser would provide fighter cover for him at Kuantan, and secondly, that he did not ask for fighters because he had already done so.

Goodenough's first point, that Phillips believed Palliser would provide air cover off Kuantan, would only explain not asking for air cover up to the time Force Z arrived off Kuantan and found no landing and no air cover; it does not explain why Phillips did not ask for air cover later that morning, especially once Force Z was sighted by Ensign Hoashi. Indeed, Captain Leach's secretary, Paymaster Lieutenant W.T. Blunt, recalled that Phillips 'at no time displayed any expectation that air cover could be expected'.[30]

Goodenough's second point, that Phillips did not ask for fighters because he had already done so, is difficult to understand; Phillips had asked for air cover off Singora, not Kuantan, and if he really believed the RAF could have provided air cover at Kuantan on the morning of the 10th, there is no reason to think the same air cover could not have been provided if he had called for it at 1020 on the 10th – unless, of course, he saw the lack of air cover that morning as an indication that it would not be available if he called for it. Perhaps, but it is at least as likely he would think there was no fighter cover off Kuantan because the report of a landing there had turned out to be false and that Palliser was expecting Force Z to be off Singora; why else would Admiral Palliser have sent the signal received at 0952 reporting the strength of Japanese forces off Singora?[31]

Nevertheless, there seems to have been a belief among some on the *Prince of Wales*'s compass platform that air cover was not possible. Lieutenant Blunt again:

I do not recall any discussion re air cover. I think that it had been accepted from the outset that the RAF could not provide any effective cover. There would therefore have been no occasion or point in such a request.[32]

Blunt was not alone in this. According to Lieutenant-Commander Harland, who was on the bridge of the *Prince of Wales* at least during the first torpedo attack,

From what I have heard [of Middlebrook and Mahoney's book *Battleship*], it contains some suggestion that air support would have been forthcoming if Admiral Phillips had asked for it in time. This is of course nonsense.[33]

Finally, Tom Phillips's assistant secretary, who was not with him at the end, wrote that 'we had been told (as we left Singapore) that aircraft could not after all be made available', and with respect to the decision not to call for fighters, 'I can only surmise that T.P. thought it pointless to call for something which was not available (so he thought).'[34] It is thus quite possible that, in spite of the fact Phillips had requested fighter protection *off Singora*, he and others on the bridge of the *Prince of Wales* understood that fighter protection simply could not be provided anywhere at all on 10 December, even though Force Z was much closer to Singapore than Singora or Kota Bharu. If that is what happened, a tragic miscommunication took place, since fighter protection from Singapore *was* available. If a miscommunication took place, it is difficult to understand why it did, in view of the way the 'No fighter protection' signal was worded. If it indeed occurred, it would provide a better explanation for not breaking radio silence than a good reason.

Sixthly, it has been suggested, or could be suggested, that Admiral Phillips's decision was affected by a variety of factors other than cool reason. Phillips was no doubt operating under great physical and mental strain and with little sleep, including a long trip to Manila and back, the hectic period before sailing, and the long night before the battle. There has even been a suggestion that Phillips was taking pills to keep him going,[35] but that has not been substantiated, and may have been mistaken for an 'addiction' to, of all things, chocolates.[36] Tom Phillips may not have been a well man even under the best of circumstances,[37] though a story about his having a bad toothache seems questionable. The signal about the impossibility of fighter protection on the 10th must have been discouraging, even though in context it applied to fighter protection off Singora. Tom Phillips could not have been heartened by the signal from Admiral Palliser that Brooke-Popham was hinting that he would concentrate all air efforts on Singapore. The seemingly irrelevant message from the First Sea Lord about torpedo attacks in harbour must have been mystifying. Admiral Phillips had probably expected to have a go at the Japanese off Kuantan, and he must have been disappointed when he found no Japanese there. If he had really expected air cover off Kuantan, the lack of it must have been more disappointing. Since Admiral Phillips had asked the RAF for air cover before he sailed, it seems unlikely that he was 'determined not to ask a sister service for help', but he could have become sick and tired of asking that sister service for help. Taking all these factors together, once can imagine that a tired, unwell, frustrated, and discouraged Tom Phillips felt that he and Force Z had been abandoned and were on their own, and saw no point in calling for help. Such a reaction would have been understandably human, but to conclude that Admiral Phillips did not break radio silence for this reason would do a serious disservice to the coolly analytical and professional admiral, as well as to Captain Leach and the staff who were there to advise him, especially since there are still other, more rational reasons to consider.

Seventhly, probably the best reason advanced to date has to do with Admiral Phillips's evaluation of the risk of air attack at that point in the operation. He had been led to expect that in flying skill the Japanese were almost equal to the Italians but less skilful than the Germans.[38] That was not intended as much of a compliment, even though Italian fliers had already managed to torpedo the battleship *Nelson* and the cruisers *Kent, Liverpool* and *Glasgow*,[39] all but the latter while at sea. Nor did Admiral Phillips believe his force would be exposed to the types of aircraft most dangerous to ships; he told General MacArthur and Admiral Hart, 'The thing that worries us is the dive bombers, rather [than] the high level bombers, and the torpedo planes.'[40] Phillips may well have known that the Japanese had no dive-bombers at all in the area, believed that high-level bombing was an inevitable but acceptable risk, perhaps because it had been largely ineffective against ships at sea to that point in the war, and believed that the ships were beyond the effective range, though *not* the theoretical maximum range, of Japanese torpedo-bombers.[41] He certainly did not expect Japanese torpedo-planes off Kuantan, as shown by his remark to Lieutenant-Commander Harland at the time of the first attack, and as Captain Bell later recalled.[42] In sum, according to Commander Goodenough, Admiral Phillips thought Force Z was 'outside really effective air striking range'.[43] Accordingly, as some historians have put it, the most likely explanation for the decision not to break radio silence is that Tom Phillips 'was confident his ships could defend themselves . . .',[44] or that he 'was clinging to the hope that all the Force was likely to encounter was a short series of high-level bombing runs, which the capital ships could ride off, if not completely without damage'.[45] In other words, he did not ask for air cover because he did not think he had to. Unfortunately for him, the attack force did include torpedo-bombers, and it subjected Force Z to an air attack that was delivered with greater skill, in greater numbers, and from a greater distance than any air attack at sea to that date in history.

There is, however, another reason, heretofore not considered, to explain why Tom Phillips did not break radio silence when sighted by Ensign Hoashi's single plane on 10 December, and it can be found in the Royal Navy's tactical doctrine of the day. That doctrine was set out in the 'Fighting Instructions', the first of which dates to the year 1545, and the most recent version of which dated from March 1939.[46] During the Second World War, some Royal Navy officers ignored them, but some took them more seriously.[47] They were not far from Phillips's mind, for on 9 December he sent for a copy, which was taken to him by Paymaster Sub-Lieutenant R.E.F. Peal, RNVR.[48]

One of the Fighting Instructions addresses the use of radio (W/T) and keeping radio silence:

THE USE OF W/T
10. W/T messages may be intercepted or D/F'd by the enemy, so putting him on his guard and giving him valuable information as to the position of our forces. When in doubt in regard to making a signal by W/T, Captains should balance the advantages to be gained by rapid communication against the possible loss of surprise. The detailed instructions on this matter are contained in the Signal Manual, Chapter XVII.

Turning to Chapter XVII of the then-current Signal Manual,[49] there are several articles that address radio silence, especially Articles 553 (W/T silence) and 605 (Complete W/T silence).[50]

Perhaps most importantly, Article 570 addressed whether to break radio silence when a single aircraft was sighted:

570. Reports of single enemy aircraft

These reports are made under the same instructions as those for reporting surface ships, except that W/T silence should not be broken to report a single enemy aircraft unless the Commanding Officer considers that its presence is a first indication that there are enemy surface forces in the area, of which the Admiral is not already aware.

Taken together, the Fighting Instructions and the Signal Manual emphasize the importance of keeping radio silence, which, while at sea, was the rule rather than the exception. Radio silence could be broken under certain circumstances, such as for reporting formations of aircraft, but not for single aircraft. There is no explanation in Article 570 for the caution against breaking radio silence for a single aircraft, but it may have been based on the assumption that a single aeroplane could not do enough damage to warrant the breaking of radio silence. On the other hand, there would seem to be no point in maintaining radio silence if even a single aircraft knew where you were, even if its sighting report were not perfectly accurate, and a single aircraft could call in many more that could do real damage – which is, of course, exactly what happened to Force Z on 10 December 1941.

While we have no evidence that it was because of Article 570 that Phillips did not break radio silence, the possibility that it was is not that far-fetched. The same policy of not breaking radio silence for a single aircraft actually played a part in another tragic episode almost five months later. On 5 April 1942, the British cruisers *Dorsetshire* and *Cornwall* were in the Indian Ocean on their way to rendezvous with the rest of Admiral James Somerville's Eastern Fleet when they were sighted by a search plane from Admiral Nagumo's carrier strike force. The senior officer of the force, Captain Augustus Agar, VC, at first maintained radio silence, but finally decided to break radio silence, even though his navigator 'pointed out there was a strict rule against this when reporting a single aircraft only. . . .'[51] Unfortunately, the message was passed to Admiral Somerville in a garbled state, and by the time anyone realized it was from the *Dorsetshire* it was too late;[52] the two cruisers had been sunk by Nagumo's aircraft in one of the most impressive dive-bombing attacks of the war. When Japanese aircraft were sighted from the *Cornwall*, Lieutenant B.M. Holden, a survivor of the *Repulse*, was heard to say, 'Surely not another bombing.'[53] Indeed it was, but Lieutenant Holden survived again.

Nevertheless, even after considering the Fighting Instructions and the Signal Manual, Admiral Phillips's decision not to break radio silence to call for air cover when sighted by Ensign Hoashi was an unfortunate decision. As the C-in-C of the Eastern Fleet, Tom Phillips was not a slave to the Fighting Instructions or the Signal Manual, and he could have disregarded them as circumstances demanded. He knew that he had been sighted, and he knew that there was *some* danger from air attack, certainly from high-level bombing, and torpedo-bombing could not be ruled out; by maintaining radio silence, he was living dangerously. While no one can deny that keeping radio silence was a very important consideration in operations at sea, it was not the only important consideration; having adequate air cover was certainly another. If Phillips really believed that air cover was impossible, he was being more pessimistic than the situation warranted. Moreover, as *Prince of Wales* survivor Geoffrey Brooke has said, 'There is no advantage in wireless silence once the enemy know where you are, and even if no fighters were available the correct procedure was simply to report the state of affairs and leave it to the shore authority to do something if he could.'[54] The mere possibility that Hoashi's sighting report might have been inaccurate was not enough to justify keeping radio silence. That Phillips did not disregard the Signal Manual may have been due to his tendency to be more theoretical than practical, and perhaps also to his evaluation of the risks of air attack based on what he thought he knew of the air threat; he may have thought that the level of risk was not high enough to justify disregarding the Signal Manual. Viewed in this light, Phillips's decision was an understandable one, but not the best one. Still, the decision was not one that should have earned him a court martial, much less the judgement that 'two great ships and many good men were lost because one stubborn sea-dog refused to acknowledge he had been wrong'.[55]

It has been suggested, perhaps as a way of excusing Phillips's decision not to break radio silence to call for fighters, that it would have made no difference because of the shortcomings of the Brewster Buffaloes and No. 453 Squadron.[56] There are, however, some good reasons to question this. In the first place, although it cannot be known for sure, it has been demonstrated that if Admiral Phillips had called for fighters immediately after being sighted at 1015, the Buffaloes should have been able to reach Force Z just prior to the torpedo attack that crippled the *Prince of Wales*.[57] And while the Buffalo has often been maligned, primarily because it was unable to take on the Japanese Zero, and its landing gear was too weak for carrier landings, there is no reason to believe it would have been totally ineffective against unescorted

Japanese bombers on 10 December. Indeed, on 20 February 1942, fifteen of seventeen unescorted Bettys were shot down or forced to ditch by US Navy F4F Wildcat fighters, which were little better than the Buffalo, and SBD Dauntless dive-bombers, which saved the aircraft carrier *Lexington* with the loss of but two Wildcats.[58] Thirdly, while No. 453 Squadron was not a crack squadron or a very happy unit,[59] some of its pilots were veterans of the Battle of Britain. Also on the scene were Buffaloes from No. 243 Squadron, one of which was flown by Geoff Fisken, the only ace in the Pacific to fly Buffaloes. He believed that the Japanese bombers, 'laden with their deadly cargo, would have been easy targets for a Buffalo'.[60] Finally, to make the difference on 10 December, the Buffaloes did not have to shoot down every Japanese bomber; all they had to do was to disrupt the attacks, particularly the first torpedo attack on the *Prince of Wales*. It would not have been an easy task, especially without any practice in working with Force Z on fighter direction operations, but it should have been possible for even the Buffaloes of Nos 453 and 243 Squadrons. Unfortunately, they never got the chance.

Even one of Admiral Phillips's staunchest defenders,[61] Commander Goodenough, recognized that the Admiral had not made the best decision and that he should have called for air cover. In a letter to naval historian Captain Roskill, he said, 'In the event, it is of course proved that he should have broken silence and sent a signal, anyhow after the first attack, when W/T silence was no longer necessary.'[62] In a letter to the widowed Lady Phillips, he said, 'Looking back now with the knowledge of the muddle on shore [probably a jab at Admiral Palliser, whom he blamed], I think the Admiral would have been wise to ask for them [fighters],' and added 'yet again',[63] presumably referring to Phillips's request for fighter protection before he sailed.

Tom Phillips was certainly not the only admiral in the Second World War to face a difficult decision on whether to break radio silence. Some admirals broke radio silence and got away with it. In May 1941, Admiral Lütjens broke radio silence to make a long signal from the *Bismarck*, but the cross-bearings on the signal were misplotted in Admiral Tovey's flagship and Lütjens did not immediately suffer the consequences of the mistake. In December 1943, Admiral Sir Bruce Fraser broke radio silence twice at the beginning of the Battle of the North Cape, but, even though the Germans plotted his signals,[64] he got away with it, and went on to sink the German battlecruiser *Scharnhorst*. On the other hand, Tom Phillips was not the only admiral in the Second World War to pay a price for not breaking radio silence. At the Battle of Midway, Admiral Yamamoto's flagship, the battleship *Yamato*, several hundred miles behind Admiral Nagumo's carrier striking force, intercepted American radio transmissions indicating that an American aircraft carrier was already at sea near Hawaii. Yamamoto chose to maintain radio silence,[65] and Nagumo had to find out about the American aircraft carriers the hard way, and lost four carriers himself. The Battle of Midway cost Japan the war; the loss of the *Prince of Wales* and *Repulse* was a devastating blow, but even if it helped cost Britain Singapore and eventually her Empire, it did not cost her the war.

Notes

1   Stephen, *The Fighting Admirals*, at 114–37.
2   Fleet Gunnery Officer Commander Henry Brown, related in a letter to Arthur Marder of 31 January 1979. Marder Papers.
3   Middlebrook and Mahoney, *Battleship*, at 305.
4   As suggested by Lieutenant G.P. Allen, a survivor of the *Prince of Wales*. Unpublished Memoirs of Lieutenant G.P. Allen, at 25. Papers of Lieutenant G.P. Allen. Imperial War Museum, Department of Documents.
5   According to Sub-Lieutenant Geoffrey Brooke, a warrant telegraphist told him he went to the Admiral's bridge during the action and was told by his 'seniors' that efforts to persuade the Admiral to call for air cover had failed, and that, when he approached the Admiral for permission, Phillips shook his head. Brooke, *Alarm Starboard!*, at 112. Interestingly, during the battle Phillips was on the compass platform, or bridge, not the admiral's bridge, one level below.
6   Letter from L.H. Bell to A.J. Marder of 31 July 1978, in reply to letter from Marder to Bell of 17 July 1978. Marder Papers.
7   Letter of 8 May 1951. Roskill Papers. Goodenough was the unnamed staff officer referred to in Roskill's account of the battle in *The War at Sea*, vol. 1, at 565. Letter from S.W. Roskill to Professor Marder of 20 January 1979. Marder Papers.
8   Letter of 6 June 1947. T.S.V. Phillips Papers.
9   Goodenough referred to the letter to the Admiralty in his testimony before the Bucknill Committee. Adm 116/4554, at 156.
10 Cecil Brown wrote that, between entries for 1106 1/2 and 1107, 'We're told that Admiral Phillips has just sent a signal to Singapore asking for aircraft protection.' Brown, *Suez to Singapore*, at 314. Brown was misinformed!
11 Letter from Paymaster Captain Dougal Doig to Arthur Marder of 6 December 1978. Marder Papers.
12 It would have been possible for Admiral Phillips to send a message back to Singapore with Lieutenant Bateman's Walrus without breaking radio silence. Indeed, Lieutenant Bateman was asked by Captain Leach to take a sealed envelope

to Singapore, but its contents, and ultimate fate, are not known. Letters from Mrs Philippe Bateman and Mr Piers Bateman to the author of 19 November 1997 and 23 July 1998, respectively.

13 Letter from Captain L.H. Bell to Arthur Marder of 14 July 1978. Marder Papers.

14 Letter from Captain L.H. Bell to Arthur Marder of 14 July 1978. Marder Papers.

15 TNA Adm 199/1149, at 230–2.

16 Grenfell, *Main Fleet to Singapore*, at 127.

17 Middlebrook and Mahoney, *Battleship*, at 211.

18 Stephen, *The Fighting Admirals*, at 135.

19 See Appendix, Nos 57–60.

20 Letter from Commander T.V.G. Phillips to Captain Roskill of 10 February 1962. Roskill Papers.

21 Letter from Roskill to Marder of 27 June 1979. Marder Papers.

22 Letter from Michael Goodenough to Lady Phillips of 6 June 1947. T.S.V. Phillips Papers.

23 Report of Conference, 6 December 1941, at 5–6, 7. Hart Papers, Box 3, Naval Historical Center, Operational Archives Branch, Washington Navy Yard.

24 See Appendix, No. 44.

25 Letter from Goodenough to Stephen Roskill of 8 May 1951. Roskill Papers.

26 Letter from Goodenough to Lady Phillips of 6 June 1947. T.S.V. Phillips Papers. The letter is dated 6 June with no year indicated, but since it was written on the stationery of HMS *Pelican*, and Goodenough commanded HMS *Pelican* from August 1946 to November 1947, the letter to Lady Phillips must have been written in 1947.

27 This argument is implied in Louis Allen, *Singapore 1941–42*, Newark, University of Delaware Press, 1977, at 144, relying on Captain Roskill's quoting of Goodenough (without naming him) in volume 1 of *The War at Sea*.

28 Letter from Goodenough to Lady Phillips of 6 June 1947. T.S.V. Phillips Papers.

29 Letter from Goodenough to Captain Roskill of 8 May 1951. Roskill Papers.

30 Letter from W.T. Blunt to the author of 27 January 1999.

31 See Appendix, No. 57.

32 Undated letter from W.T. Blunt to the author in reply to letter of 8 December 1998.

33 Letter from R.F. Harland to A.J. Marder of 5 February 1979. Marder Papers.

34 Letter from K.H. Farnhill to A.J. Marder of 9 August 1978. Marder Papers.

35 Hough, *The Hunting of Force Z*, at 178.

36 Marder, *Old Friends, New Enemies*, at 369; letter from Commander T.V.G. Phillips to Arthur Marder of 1 August 1979. Marder Papers.

37 Admiral John Godfrey, who had known Phillips since they were term-mates at HMS *Britannia*, said later, 'As V.C.N.S. [Vice-Chief of the Naval Staff], his great qualities were rather marred by ill health. . .'. J.H. Godfrey, 'The Navy and Naval Intelligence 1939–1942: Afterthoughts', 1947. TNA Adm 223/619. An officer who served with him said he had a chronic 'catarrh' for which he sniffed some kind of 'alleviant'. Letter from Admiral John Litchfield to Arthur Marder of 14 May 1975. Marder Papers.

38 Letter from L.H. Bell to Marder of 14 July 1978. Marder Papers.

39   Smith and Dominy, *Cruisers in Action 1939–1945*, at 188.

40   Report of Conference, 6 December 1941. Admiral Hart Papers, Naval Historical Center, Operational Archives Branch, Washington Navy Yard.

41   Letters from L.H. Bell to Marder of 14 and 31 July 1978. Marder Papers.

42   Letter from L.H. Bell to Arthur Marder of 14 July 1978. Marder Papers.

43   Letter from Goodenough to Lady Phillips of 6 June 1947. T.S.V. Phillips Papers.

44   Middlebrook and Mahoney, *Battleship*, at 305.

45   Marder, *Old Friends, New Enemies*, at 439, quoting 'Misfortune off Malaya', an attachment to a letter from Paymaster Captain Dougal Doig to Marder of 8 September 1978. Marder Papers.

46   S.W. Roskill, *The War at Sea, Vol. 3: The Offensive*, pt 2, London, HMSO, 1961, at 406. The 1939 version is found at TNA Adm 239/261.

47   Arthur Marder, 'The Influence of History on Sea Power', in *From the Dardanelles to Oran: Studies of the Royal Navy in War and Peace 1915–1940*, London, Oxford University Press, 1974, at 53–4.

48   Attachment to letter from R.E.F. Peal to the author of 26 November 1997.

49   The Signal Manual of the day can be found at TNA Adm 186/786.

50   These two articles read as follows:

553. W/T silence

(a) *General.* – Since it is necessary to use W/T for the majority of enemy reports, the following instructions are laid down in regard to breaking W/T silence for making such reports.

Nothing in these instructions precludes the use of W/T during W/T silence should the commanding officer consider that the importance of the occasion justifies the risk of disclosing the presence and position of his ship, and possibly of the fleet.

(b) *Standing instructions.* – W/T silence may be broken for the purpose of enemy reporting, on the following occasions:

By Ships in Company with the Admiral (e.g., in a Fleet Cruising Disposition).

(i) To report enemy surface craft, or formations of enemy aircraft. Submarines may be reported *at night* if in the opinion of the commanding officer, W/T involves less risk than V/S [visual signalling].

(ii) To make negative reports on occasions laid down in Art. 562(b).

(iii) To answer reports in (i) and (ii).

By Detached Ships and Aircraft

(iv) To report all enemy ships (including submarines) and formations of aircraft.

(v) To make negative reports on occasions laid down in Art. 562(b).

(vi) To answer reports in (iv) and (v).

(c) *Special orders.* – The standing instructions may be amended as required for particular circumstances, e.g., the Commander-in-Chief may order that W/T is to be used by ships for reporting the sighting of, or asdic [sonar] contact with, submarines threatening the fleet.

(d) *W/T organisation for enemy reports.* – A brief outline of the general principles is given at the end of this chapter.

For full details of W/T organisation, *see* General Signalling Instructions.

605. Complete W/T silence

(a) Owing to the danger of D/F, 'complete' W/T silence is automatically imposed when the fleet proceeds to sea, until, or unless, the Admiral considers that the enemy will gain nothing from D/F, or that the need for using W/T outweighs the risk from D/F.

In the latter circumstances, the Admiral 'relaxes' W/T silence by ordering 'Negative W/T silence.'

(b) While complete W/T silence is in force, individual ships or aircraft may 'break' W/T silence for enemy reporting (see Art. 553). It is further permissible for any ship, at the discretion of the commanding officer, to use W/T if it is essential to make a signal by W/T, e.g., manoeuvring in a fog, when as high a frequency as possible is to be employed.

51 Augustus Agar, VC, *Footprints in the Sea*, London, Evans Brothers Ltd, 1959, at 306.

52 Donald MacIntyre, *Fighting Admiral*, London, Evans Brothers Ltd, 1961, at 192.

53 Ken Dimbleby, *Turns of Fate: The Drama of HMS Cornwall 1939–1942*, London, William Kimber, 1984, at 164.

54 Correspondence, *Naval Review* 80 (April 1992), at 171.

55 Middlebrook and Mahoney, *Battleship*, at 305.

56 Marder, *Old Friends, New Enemies*, at 480.

57 Middlebrook and Mahoney, *Battleship*, at 306. The book's calculation is a bit off, as it does not allow the same amount of time for No. 453 Squadron to take off (the actual time was 22 minutes, but the hypothetical time was only 12 minutes), but even so the squadron would have arrived at 1140, just as the first torpedo attack on the *Prince of Wales* was about to begin.

58 John Lundstrom, *The First Team: Pacific Naval Air Combat from Pearl Harbor to Midway*, Annapolis, Naval Institute Press, 1984, at 95–107.

59 It is said that No. 453's squadron leader, RAF Flight Lieutenant W.J. Harper, had gone to Australia to find more suitable pilots. Gillison, *Royal Australian Air Force 1939–1942*, at 197. But according to the Australian members of the squadron, he disliked and was biased against Australians and the RAAF. John Bennett, *Defeat to Victory: No. 453 Squadron RAAF*, Royal Australian Air Force Museum, 1994, at 61–2.

60 Cull, *Buffaloes over Singapore*, at 54.

61 As mentioned, when Mr Churchill was writing his history of the Second World War, his naval assistant, Captain G.R.G. Allen, consulted Commander Goodenough and modified the account of Force Z to make it more favourable to Admiral Phillips. Letter from Captain Allen to Mr Churchill of 23 November 1948. Ismay Papers.

62 Letter from Goodenough to Roskill of 8 May 1951. Roskill Papers.

63 Letter of 6 June 1947. T.S.V. Phillips Papers.
64 Beesly, *Very Special Intelligence*, at 220, 224.
65 H.P. Willmott, *The Barrier and the Javelin*, Annapolis, Naval Institute Press, 1983, at 342; Walter Lord, *Incredible Victory*, New York, Harper & Row, 1967, at 43–4.

Part IV

The Aftermath

CHAPTER FIFTEEN

The Days and Years after the Battle

Of course, at the time no one in Tokyo, Singapore, London or anywhere else knew that the loss of the *Prince of Wales* and *Repulse* would not cost Britain the war.

The Japanese learned that both the *Prince of Wales* and the *Repulse* had been sunk from aircraft that had stayed just long enough to see the end of the *Prince of Wales*. The British in Singapore learned the awful news from the *Electra*'s signals, and from Singapore Admiral Palliser then informed the Admiralty. After he had heard the news from the First Sea Lord, Mr Churchill went at once to inform the House of Commons. Reactions to the news of such a momentous event were often remarkable.

In Japan, there was naturally great jubilation at the victory. The news broke the tension at Japanese Combined Fleet Headquarters, where the feeling had been, 'If we failed in this battle and the Malay landing operation came to a screeching halt, even *hara-kiri* would not be a sufficient apology.' When Admiral Yamamoto heard the news, his usually nearly expressionless face broke into a big smile, even though the news meant he had lost a bet on the outcome of the battle and owed a subordinate ten dozen bottles of beer.[1] Later, however, Yamamoto confided to a fellow chess player:

In spite of this new victory today, our success cannot possibly continue for more than a year. . . . I feel great sympathy for the British commander who apparently went down with the *Prince of Wales*. The same thing may happen to me someday in the not-too-distant future.[2]

Admiral Yamamoto's reaction was as prophetic as it was gracious; in 1943, he died when his aircraft was ambushed and shot down by American P-38 fighters while he was on an inspection tour of the Solomon Islands.

In Singapore, Duff Cooper, who had just been appointed Resident Cabinet Minister at Singapore for Far Eastern Affairs, later wrote that the loss of the ships 'was the single worst piece of news I have ever received'.[3] It fell to Duff Cooper to make the official announcement in Singapore that evening. At the Cricket Club in Singapore, the announcement brought a shocked silence of perhaps thirty seconds, until an older member dropped his glass.[4]

In Britain, the reaction can well be imagined. As one newspaper columnist recalled, 'That day's news was among the worst and saddest in the life-time of any of us.'[5] Winston Churchill's reaction to the news has often been quoted, but it is nevertheless worth repeating. He wrote,

> I was opening my boxes on the 10th when the telephone at my bedside rang. It was the First Sea Lord. He gave a sort of cough and gulp, and at first I could not hear quite clearly. 'Prime Minister, I have to report to you that the *Prince of Wales* and *Repulse* have both been sunk by the Japanese – we think by aircraft. Tom Phillips is drowned.' 'Are you sure it's true?' 'No doubt at all.' So I put the telephone down. I was thankful to be alone. In all the war I never received a more direct shock. The reader of these pages will realise how many efforts, hopes, and plans foundered with these two ships. As I turned over and twisted in bed the full horror of the news sank in upon me. There were no British or American capital ships in the Indian Ocean or the Pacific except the American survivors of Pearl Harbour, who were hastening back to California. Over all this vast expanse of waters Japan was supreme, and we were everywhere weak and naked.[6]

One of his secretaries remembers being present when he heard the news; trying to make herself as small as possible, she recalled him saying, 'Poor Tom Phillips.'[7]

The King revealed his reaction to the loss of the ships in a letter to Mr Churchill:

> The news of the loss of the 'Prince of Wales' and 'Repulse' came as a great shock to the Queen & me when we were on our tour in S. Wales today. For all of us it was a national disaster. . . . I thought I was

getting immune to bad news, but this has affected me deeply as I am sure it has you. There is something particularly 'alive' about a big ship, which gives one a sense of personal loss apart from considerations of loss of power.[8]

Mr Churchill replied,

I realized how deeply Your Majesty would feel the loss of your two splendid ships. Quite apart from the sorrow it is a heavy blow, and our combinations formed in the Far East with so much difficulty from limited resources have been disrupted. . . . Taking it altogether, I am enormously relieved at the extraordinary changes of the last few days.[9]

Naturally, such a calamity provoked some questioning. The loss of the two ships prompted an uproar in the British press,[10] and when Mr Churchill spoke to the House of Commons again, there were some hard questions asked, including a few by Admiral of the Fleet Sir Roger Keyes,[11] who was by then a Member of Parliament. However, there was never a full-fledged inquiry into the loss of the ships. There was an internal Admiralty inquiry headed by Captains William Davis and Angus Nicholl, but their report, dated 20 January 1942, maintained that they had insufficient information to make a full and detailed report.[12] The First Sea Lord and the First Lord then signed off on a report to the Prime Minister on the loss of the *Prince of Wales* and *Repulse* on 25 January 1942.[13] The report to the Prime Minister was based in part on the Davis-Nicholl report, but, perhaps not surprisingly, it did not adopt the conclusion that the stationing of such an unbalanced force at Singapore was 'strategically unsound'.[14]

There were two additional inquiries that were restricted to the technical aspects of the loss of the *Prince of Wales*, a formal one by the Second Bucknill Committee, which had earlier investigated the 'Channel Dash' of the German warships *Gneisenau*, *Scharnhorst* and *Prinz Eugen* up the English Channel in February 1942, and another one by the Admiralty Construction Department.[15] Neither went into any of the political or strategic aspects of the battle, but they did make a number of recommendations for modifications to the surviving ships of the 'King George V' class.[16] These modifications were eventually made, but were never really put to the test; the only battle damage suffered by a sister ship of the *Prince of Wales* was at the Battle of North Cape in December

1943, when the *Duke of York* had a leg of her foremast clipped by an 11in shell from the German battlecruiser *Scharnhorst*.

While people around the world digested the news, the grim business of war continued. On 11 December, just a day after the Battle off Malaya, an event of much greater military significance to the outcome of the campaign in Malaya took place when the 11th Indian Division was soundly defeated by the Japanese in northern Malaya at the Battle of Jitra. Another event even more important to the outcome of the war also occurred on 11 December, an event that made victory for the Allies all but inevitable when, after Germany, Japan and Italy had signed a wartime alliance as an amendment to the Tripartite Pact, Germany and Italy declared war on the United States.[17] Such a momentous event should not, however, have been unexpected; for months, the Japanese ambassador to Germany had been relaying to Tokyo German assurances that she would declare war on the United States if Japan did, and his messages had been intercepted and decoded by the Americans and presumably the British as well.[18]

The loss of the *Prince of Wales* and *Repulse* was a hard blow to Allied morale in Singapore and Malaya, but otherwise their loss had little effect on the outcome of the campaign for Malaya and Singapore. They could not have stayed at Singapore, and in any event would have been of little use in what became a land and air campaign, as the Japanese Army worked its way down the Malay peninsula. The Admiralty appointed Admiral Sir Geoffrey Layton to replace Tom Phillips as C-in-C Eastern Fleet. Layton promptly asked to be relieved, ostensibly because he had lost the confidence of the Admiralty,[19] but after his plea had gone unnoticed, he left for Colombo 'to collect a new fleet'. Major warships from the Royal Navy and the Imperial Japanese Navy played no part in the campaign until the desperate and heroic attempts to escape Singapore just before its fall,[20] and otherwise the only other real naval battle of the campaign was fought off Endau on 26 January 1942, when the Japanese tried to land urgently needed ammunition by sea. The Japanese force was attacked by Allied aircraft, which suffered severe losses, and by the destroyers HMAS *Vampire*, once of Force Z, and HMS *Thanet*, which was lost in the action.[21] After British forces had evacuated Malaya, the Japanese invaded Singapore, which surrendered on 15 February 1942. Allied naval fortunes in the area fell to their nadir with the Battle of the Java Sea, fought from 27 February to 1 March 1942, when a force of British, Dutch, American, and Australian cruisers and destroyers was almost completely annihilated.

One remaining ship of Force Z, the *Electra*, as well as the *Exeter*, *Jupiter* and *Encounter*, fought gallantly, but were sunk in that same Battle of the Java Sea. The *Vampire* and the *Tenedos* were not involved in the Battle of the Java Sea, but were sunk by Japanese carrier aircraft in Admiral Nagumo's raid on Ceylon in April 1942. The *Tenedos* was caught in harbour and the *Vampire* was sunk off the coast in company with the aircraft carrier *Hermes*, which had finally completed the refit she began when the *Prince of Wales* left Cape Town in November 1941.

And what of HMS *Express*? How she survived has been explained by Captain O.W. Phillips, who was Admiral Tom Phillips's Fleet Engineer Officer:

The 'Express', which had previously had her bows blown off [by a mine in 1940] and rebuilt, stayed alongside 'Prince of Wales' until the last minute, and was lifted bodily out of the water by the ship's bilge keel as she rolled over, straining the forward boiler-room bulkhead, on the forward side of which was a deep oil tank. Cracks started to seep oil through this bulkhead. . . .

I had a difference of opinion with the Chief Constructor at the base over the repairs to the damaged bulkhead in 'Express'. The worst crack was just a[t] mid-sprayer level, and any trouble due to the bulkhead giving in a seaway, it had been already weakened by 'Express's' previous accident, might end in a disastrous boiler-room fire. So, despite the extra work necessary to remove fittings to do a good job, I was insistent that the C.C. [Chief Constructor] should fit a doubling plate to the bulkhead inside the fuel tank. This he utterly refused to do despite my warning. As he was the 'expert', I could not take it any further. Actually a bad fire in 'Express', due to the repair giving, did occur quite shortly afterwards.[22]

The *Express* suffered a boiler fire on 6 February 1942, and as a result she had to leave the Far East for repairs in South Africa,[23] thus escaping almost sure destruction in the Battle of the Java Sea three weeks later.

The survivors of the *Prince of Wales* and *Repulse*, shortly after their return to Singapore, were treated to a heartening speech by Captain Tennant, and then to a thoroughly depressing one by Admiral Layton, who informed them they would no longer be known as the ship's companies of the *Prince of Wales* and *Repulse*, and that they would be sent hither and thither in Singapore and the Malay peninsula 'to help us out of this infernal muddle'.[24] A few survivors, such as Captain

Tennant, were ordered to return to Britain, but most were denied survivor's leave, and either joined other ships or stayed to help in the defence of Malaya and Singapore.

The fates of those who stayed were many and varied. Some of the men were posted to HMS *Exeter*, and became prisoners of war after she had been sunk in the Battle of the Java Sea. Royal Marines from the *Repulse* and *Prince of Wales* fought very well in Malaya and Singapore, after combining with a British Army unit, the Argyll & Sutherland Highlanders, and, in a play on the name of a famous football team, becoming known as the 'Plymouth Argylls'. Some of the survivors of Force Z were captured by the Japanese, and some of those, such as Lieutenant Richard Pool, were sent to work on the Burma–Siam Railway.[25] Other survivors were able to escape from Singapore to the Dutch East Indies and beyond. Lieutenant Geoffrey Brooke was able to escape from Singapore, and then he and a few others sailed across the Indian Ocean from Sumatra to Ceylon in a small fishing boat.[26] Some survivors fought on in other theatres of the war. Bill Uren, seen in the famous last photograph of the *Prince of Wales*, won a Distinguished Service Medal in the escort destroyer HMS *Bramham* for his bravery during the valiant struggle to get the tanker *Ohio* into Malta in August 1942.

There were many extraordinary stories. Paymaster Lieutenant Joe Blackburn survived the sinking of the *Prince of Wales* and was able to make his way to Australia, but in May 1942 he was aboard the steamer *Nankin* in the Indian Ocean when it was captured by the German raider *Thor*. Blackburn and his fellow passengers were then delivered by the Germans to Japan, where they remained prisoners of war for the duration.[27]

Apart from a heroic British-Australian commando-style raid that destroyed shipping at Singapore in 1943,[28] and the submarines that operated out of Trincomalee and Australia, the Royal Navy did not reappear in Far Eastern waters until 1944. When it did, it exacted a measure of revenge when the destroyers *Saumarez*, *Virulam*, *Vigilant*, and *Virago* sank the Japanese heavy cruiser *Haguro* on 16 May 1945, and the submarine *Trenchant* sank the heavy cruiser *Ashigara* on 7 June 1945.[29] The Royal Navy provided aircraft carriers, escorted by sister ships of the *Prince of Wales*, as part of Task Force 57 for the assault on Okinawa and raids on Japan, when the armoured decks of the British carriers impressed American observers with their ability to shrug off kamikaze attacks.[30] After the Japanese surrender, Singapore passed once again into British hands in September 1945.

After the battle the Japanese escort ship *Shumushu* located the *Prince of Wales* and *Repulse*,[31] but the Japanese never succeeded in salvaging either one. In April 1954, HMS *Defender* located the final resting place of the *Prince of Wales*.[32] In 1965 and 1966, Royal Navy divers of the Far East Clearance Diving Team, led by Lieutenant-Commander David Lermitte, were sent down to examine first the *Repulse* and then the *Prince of Wales*. The divers found the *Repulse* lying on her port side at a mean depth of 180 feet and at a heading of 196 degrees, and the *Prince of Wales* lying almost completely capsized, and at a heading of 020 degrees, her shallowest part 150 feet below the surface.[33] Most importantly, the divers discovered the devastating torpedo hit on the port quarter of the *Prince of Wales*.

Though resting beneath the waves for decades, the *Prince of Wales* and *Repulse* have not been forgotten. From time to time, Royal Navy and Commonwealth divers visit the ships and ensure that the Royal Navy flag, the White Ensign, still flies from the ships, even though beneath the waves, secured to the propeller shafts of each vessel. In 2002, the ship's bell of the *Prince of Wales* was recovered and brought back to Britain.[34] More recently, the ships have been designated as 'protected areas', along with such famous ships as the *Hood* and the *Hampshire*.[35]

The names *Repulse* and *Prince of Wales* have lived on in the Royal Navy. In 1968, the nuclear submarine HMS *Repulse* was commissioned. In 2003, at long last, Buckingham Palace announced that the new aircraft carriers to be built for the Royal Navy would be named *Queen Elizabeth* and *Prince of Wales*, a name first used in the Royal Navy in 1763.[36] When completed, it can sail with the USS *Winston Churchill*. . . .

Notes

1 Official Japanese History, at 484.
2 Marder, *Old Friends, New Enemies*, at 511.
3 Duff Cooper, *Old Men Forget*, London, Rupert Hart-Davis, 1953, at 301.
4 Noel Barber, *A Sinister Twilight: The Fall of Singapore 1942*, Boston, Houghton Mifflin Co., 1968, at 47.
5 J.L. Garvin in the *Observer* of 14 December 1941, as quoted in Marder, *Old Friends, New Enemies*, at 494.
6 Churchill, *The Grand Alliance*, at 620.
7 Martin Gilbert, *Churchill: A Life*, New York, Henry Holt & Co., 1991, at 712.
8 Wheeler-Bennett, *King George VI: His Life and Reign*, at 533. With the gracious permission of Her Majesty the Queen.
9 Letter of 12 December 1941. Royal Archives. With the gracious permission of Her Majesty the Queen.

10 Burt, *British Battleships 1919–1939*, at 400.

11 Great Britain, Parliamentary Debates, Commons, 5th ser. vol. 376 (1941–2), col. 1698.

12 At least part of the report is found in TNA Adm 199/1149, and the rest is located in Captain Roskill's papers on the subject. Roskill Papers 4/79.

13 TNA Prem 3/163/2.

14 Roskill Papers 4/79.

15 The two reports can be found together in a single booklet. TNA Adm 239/349.

16 TNA Adm 239/349.

17 Carl Boyd, *Hitler's Japanese Confidant: General Oshima Hiroshi and Magic Intelligence, 1941–1945*, University of Kansas Press, 1993, at 37.

18 *Ibid.* at 31, 35, 36.

19 Letter from Geoffrey Layton to Dudley Pound of 18 December 1941. Layton Papers, British Library.

20 For an account, see Geoffrey Brooke, *Singapore's Dunkirk*, London, Leo Cooper, 1989, reprinted 2003.

21 G. Hermon Gill, *Royal Australian Navy 1939–1942*, Canberra, Australian War Memorial, 1957, at 559–60.

22 Unpublished Memoirs of Rear Admiral O.W. Phillips, at 338, 339. Papers of Rear Admiral O.W. Phillips. Imperial War Museum, Department of Documents.

23 John English, *Amazon to Ivanhoe: British Standard Destroyers of the 1930s*, Kendal, England, World Ship Society, 1993, at 74.

24 Hayes, *Face the Music*, at 149.

25 Pool, *Course for Disaster*.

26 Brooke, *Alarm Starboard!*, at 172–95.

27 Joe G. Blackburn, 'From Capital P.O.W. to a very small p.o.w.', undated memorandum for the author.

28 Ronald McKee, *The Heroes*, Sydney, Angus & Robertson, 1960.

29 A.J. Watts, *Japanese Warships of World War II*, London, Ian Allen, 1966, at 370.

30 Norman Friedman, *British Carrier Aviation: The Evolution of the Ships and their Aircraft*, Annapolis, Naval Institute Press, 1988, at 147.

31 Official Japanese History, at 483.

32 TNA Adm 1/25572.

33 Lieutenant-Commander D.P.R. Lermitte, RN, 'With All Flags Flying – 200 Feet Down', in Kendall McDonald, ed., *The Second Underwater Book*, London, Pelham Books, 1970, at 56, 58, based on articles by Lieutenant-Commander Lermitte that first appeared in the *Royal Navy Diving Magazine*.

34 'Prince of Wales bell saved by divers', *Navy News* (UK) (September 2002), at 3.

35 The designation was mainly due to efforts of Ken Byrne, secretary of the Prince of Wales & Repulse Survivors' Association, and Alan Matthews, son of *Repulse* survivor Ted Matthews.

36 Steve Bush, 'Naval Scene', *Warship World* 8 (January 2004), at 4.

CHAPTER SIXTEEN

In Retrospect: Men and Machines

The Battle off Malaya was a supreme test for the men from Britain and Japan who opposed each other and for their machines, especially their ships and aircraft. No study of the battle would be complete without an appraisal of how they did.

On the Japanese side, their surface forces never got a chance to prove their mettle, or their metal. While their submarines and submariners performed very valuable reconnaissance, their signal procedures were not what they should have been, and it was fortunate for the British that *I-58* was not quick enough to put any torpedoes into any of the British ships at very close range. The search planes from the Japanese cruisers did their job well enough on the evening of 9 December, and the next day Ensign Hoashi had a true hero's day. The aircrews and bombers of the 22nd Air Flotilla performed one of the most extraordinary feats of arms in history, in endurance (in flying over 400 miles) and skill, even aside from wasting bombs on the *Tenedos* and later wasting more bombs on innocent fish in the South China Sea. The tendency for the G4M Betty to explode into flames and earn its reputation as the 'No. 1 Lighter' had no effect on the outcome. All in all, however, the Japanese richly deserved their victory.

As for the British, looking first at the destroyers, then the *Repulse*, and, last but not least, the *Prince of Wales*, the story of their men and machines is a bit more complicated, as one might expect in what was for them a very long, hard day.

The four destroyers performed at least as well as could have been expected. The lack of dual-purpose main guns that could be used against both ships and aircraft, and more and better close-range anti-aircraft weapons, was keenly felt. The destroyers' ship handling, on the other hand, was uniformly excellent: the *Tenedos* skilfully evaded heavy air attack on her solitary way back to Singapore, and the *Electra*, *Vampire* and *Express* carried out brilliant rescue work after the *Prince of Wales* and *Repulse* were sunk. The seamanship shown by Lieutenant-Commander Cartwright of the *Express* in going alongside the *Prince of Wales* and staying there to the last possible moment was exceptional.

As to the performance of the *Repulse* and her men on 10 December, no one would dispute that the vessel was beautifully handled by Captain Tennant, who managed to avoid nineteen torpedoes in the first torpedo attacks, including some that had missed the *Prince of Wales*. The *Repulse* did not suffer her first torpedo hit until a group of torpedo-planes switched their target from the *Prince of Wales* to the *Repulse* after the *Repulse* had already committed herself to avoiding another set of torpedoes. The *Repulse* finally succumbed to an extraordinarily skilfully delivered attack that came from three directions: there was absolutely nothing Captain Tennant could have done to avoid them all.

Unfortunately, the *Repulse*'s anti-aircraft guns were incapable of doing what needed to be done on 10 December, which was to shoot down Japanese aircraft before they could launch their bombs or torpedoes. Their gunners did their best under the most difficult of conditions, but they were sorely handicapped by the limitations of their weapons and directors.

As regards the staying power of the *Repulse*, she stood up well to the bomb hit from the first attack, and did better than many might have expected, thanks to the thicker deck armour fitted between the wars. In the case of the first torpedo hit, the anti-torpedo bulges added between the wars contained the damage well, and she continued to sail and fight. Although she sank within five minutes of being hit by four more torpedoes, no more could have been expected of her; no other ship of her era could have been expected to stay afloat much longer than that. Up to that point in the Second World War, a number of British capital ships had withstood single torpedo hits,[1] but none had survived three or more, specifically the *Royal Oak* in October 1939 and the *Barham* in November 1941.[2]

Nor could more have been expected of the *Repulse*'s damage control. Her crew dealt very well with the bomb hit, and evidently dealt well enough with the first torpedo hit. When the *Repulse* was hit by four more torpedoes, there was absolutely nothing damage control could have done to save the ship. Their job was over, and it was time to abandon ship.

In her first and last major battle of the Second World War, the *Repulse*, her captain and ship's company had fought well and had done themselves proud.

With respect to the performance of the *Prince of Wales* and her men on 10 December, they hardly got a chance to shine except in adversity, as she was unable to avoid two torpedoes in the very first attack on her; this was the critical event in her loss, since not only was she severely damaged, she was also unable to steer to avoid further attacks. The *Prince of Wales* had fended off Italian torpedo-bombers when she escorted a convoy to Malta in September 1941, and had then seen the battleship *Nelson* torpedoed in the bow, but on 10 December the Japanese torpedo-bombers were much more numerous, and their crews and aircraft were among the very best in the world.

What caused the *Prince of Wales* to be hit in the first attack? It was not that she turned too late to avoid the torpedoes; indeed, Captain Leach may have begun his turn to avoid torpedoes even before all were launched, since his turn caused one Nell to abort its attack. Instead, two other factors were most likely responsible, namely (a) the skilful manner in which the attack was delivered and perhaps (b) the poor turning performance of the ships of her class, the 'King George V' class.

Although not the 'pincer' attack that finished off the *Repulse*, the first torpedo attack on the *Prince of Wales* was very skilfully delivered by nine bombers that came in off her port bow and launched their torpedoes in a fan-shaped pattern on courses that converged on the *Prince of Wales*.[3] According to Captain Leach's secretary, Paymaster Lieutenant W.T. Blunt, it was impossible to comb all the tracks because they were coming from all angles.[4] The fact that the ship was hit twice on the port side and another torpedo almost hit her on the starboard side aft[5] shows that the torpedoes were not running parallel to each other and therefore would have been extremely difficult to avoid.

As for the *Prince of Wales*'s turning radius, a ship's turning radius is a function of her hull form aft (the 'deadwood'), the number of propellers and rudders she has and the positioning of the rudders *vis-à-vis* the propellers.[6] Perhaps because they had only one rudder, the *Prince of Wales* and her sister ships had a poor turning radius as compared to some other American and British capital ships. One Admiralty study determined that, at a speed of 14½ knots and with 35° of rudder, the battleship USS *Washington* had a turning radius of 575 yards and the *King George V* had a turning radius of 930 yards.[7] According to other Admiralty records, the battleship *Nelson* had a turning radius of 625 yards at 35° rudder and 14 knots, but the battlecruiser *Renown*, the sister ship of the *Repulse*, had a turning radius of 1,000 yards at 35° rudder and a speed of 15 knots.[8]

To sum up, while the Japanese torpedo-bombers had already given Captain Leach an extremely difficult problem, the *Prince of Wales*'s poor turning radius may have made his job impossible. Under such circumstances, there was probably nothing Captain Leach could have done to avoid the torpedoes that crippled the *Prince of Wales* in the first torpedo attack. The *Repulse* was able to avoid a number of torpedoes in spite of her equally poor turning radius, but, without detracting from the remarkably skilful handling of Captain Tennant, the first torpedo attacks on the *Repulse* were launched from one direction and, as far as we know, with the torpedoes running parallel to each other, rather than on converging courses toward their target.

As with the *Repulse*, the anti-aircraft guns of the *Prince of Wales* were incapable of doing what needed to be done on 10 December, which was to shoot down Japanese aircraft before they could launch their bombs or torpedoes. To make matters worse, the pom-poms suffered a number of jams because of problems with their ammunition.[9] Her gunners did their best under the most difficult of conditions, particularly after the first torpedo hits, and deserve great credit for damaging five of the Japanese bombers in the last high-level attack of the day, but they were still handicapped by their weapons and directors, by the lack of opportunity for target practice on the way out to the Far East, and then by the catastrophic damage she suffered in the first attack.

In the matter of the staying power of the *Prince of Wales*, much was expected of her, and at the time some thought she had succumbed too easily, especially compared to the astonishingly robust *Bismarck*. That was hardly a fair comparison: the *Prince of Wales* had been designed to meet the limit of 35,000 tons standard displacement set by the Washington Naval Treaty (and to fit existing British docks), but the *Bismarck*, at 41,673 tons standard displacement,[10] far exceeded treaty limits. Much of the *Bismarck*'s extra displacement went into her beam, 118 feet v. 103 feet for the *Prince of Wales*, which was a critical factor in a ship's ability to absorb torpedo hits.

Even more importantly, at the time no one understood that the worst damage to the *Prince of Wales* was caused by a freakish yet devastating torpedo hit on her stern, which opened the ship to the sea through a shaft alley. The *Prince of Wales* was hardly alone among capital ships in the Second World War in suffering crippling damage from torpedo hits in the stern.

The most famous example of such hits occurred in May 1941, when the *Bismarck* was crippled by damage to her rudders caused by a torpedo hit in the stern. Another example occurred on 6 April 1941, when the German battlecruiser *Gneisenau* was hit in the stern by an aerial torpedo that caused extensive flooding through a collapsed shaft alley. Unlike the *Prince of Wales*, she was in port at the time and was never in serious danger.[11] On 12 August 1945, the old American battleship *Pennsylvania* was at anchor when she was hit by a Japanese aerial torpedo that damaged three shafts, one of which was thrown out of alignment; if it had been turning, it would have caused damage similar to that suffered by the *Prince of Wales*.[12] On 8 June 1940, the *Gneisenau*'s sister ship *Scharnhorst* was hit near the stern by a torpedo from the destroyer *Acasta* off Norway. The extensive damage included a bent shaft, but the *Scharnhorst* was able to reach port.[13] Finally, on 28 March 1941, the Italian battleship *Vittorio Veneto* was hit by an aerial torpedo on the port quarter during the Battle of Matapan. The damage included a fractured port outer shaft and leaks that forced the inner port shaft to shut down. At first all her engines were stopped and her steering was out of action, but with time she was able to restart her starboard engines, rig emergency steering, and limp home.[14]

The simple fact was that no battleship, or any other ship for that matter, could be completely protected from crippling damage to her stern, whether through damage to the shafts, propellers or rudders, or to a part of the ship where the hull narrows and the ship's side protection is less effective or is absent. The difference is that the other battleships to suffer severe torpedo damage to the stern, with the notable exception of the *Bismarck*, were either in port or were given time without further torpedo attack to tend their wounds and return safely to port.

When a torpedo hit the *Prince of Wales* on the port side near her after 5.25in turrets, her side protection system failed, but this damage was much less important in the loss of the ship than the hit on her stern. The extent of the damage from this hit could have been exacerbated by damage suffered by the *Prince of Wales* in almost exactly the same place in August 1940, before she was completed, when a bomb exploded about 6 feet from her hull when she was in a basin fitting out.[15] Once again, the experience of the *Prince of Wales* was not unique among capital ships of the Second World War: the side protection system of the battleship USS *North Carolina* failed when she was hit by a Japanese submarine torpedo on 15 September 1942,[16] and the side protection system of even the Japanese super-battleship *Yamato* failed when she was hit by an American submarine torpedo on 25 December 1943.[17]

Because the nature of the torpedo damage to the *Prince of Wales* was not understood until after the diving operation in 1966, it is not surprising that extraordinary qualities were attributed to the torpedoes used by the Japanese. The Japanese torpedoes were not super-torpedoes with warheads of 867lb, as attributed to them by the Admiralty,[18] or of 1,210lb, as attributed to them by some postwar sources; instead, they were 17.7in torpedoes with warheads of 330lb used by the Genzan and Mihoro Groups, and 452lb used by the Kanoya Group.[19] While they weren't super-torpedoes, they were still excellent torpedoes and worked very, very well.

Regarding damage control, the *Prince of Wales* had a relatively new damage control officer, Lieutenant Peter Slade, who was faced with what were extraordinarily difficult problems after the first torpedoes had hit. The oppressive heat and the loss of electrical power that hampered communication and lighting could not have made the damage control job any easier, but they probably made no difference to the final result. With time, such as that enjoyed by the *Vittorio Veneto*, damage control efforts *might* have borne some fruit.

Although in general the ship's damage control efforts were determined and heroic, there were several lapses by other men. For example, after the first torpedoes had struck, men escaping from some compartments may not have closed watertight doors behind them, resulting in some unnecessary progressive flooding.[20] There was also the unauthorized and unnecessary flooding of several magazines, presumably to avoid an explosion, which adversely affected the ship's remaining buoyancy and reduced her freeboard by perhaps 15in at the stern.[21] It is impossible to know whether either error made any difference to whether the *Prince of Wales* survived or not, and the errors of others should not overshadow the heroic damage control efforts of Lieutenant Slade or of Commander Lawson, who both went down with the ship.

Because the loss of the *Prince of Wales* was such a shock and its causes were not well understood at the time, it was perhaps natural that other causes were blamed, such as the lack of a long, interrupted period to work up. That, however, would imply or suggest that she was not as efficient as she should have been, and that would not be fair. No doubt the *Prince of Wales* had been denied the long, uninterrupted time that new warships are normally given to 'work up' to full fighting efficiency. She was completed in March 1941 and had to face the *Bismarck* and *Prinz Eugen* in May 1941. In contrast, the *Bismarck* was commissioned in August 1940, but did not see combat until her sortie into the Atlantic in May 1941. The lack of an uninterrupted work-up was a concern to both Admiral Phillips[22] and Captain Leach,[23] but their concern seems to have been with the ship's anti-aircraft efficiency, not with the overall efficiency of the entire ship's company. One senior survivor believed that she was 'fully worked up and long before December 1941 was a finely tuned fighting unit with battle experience', but also recognized the faults in her anti-aircraft armament and the lack of anti-aircraft practice on the way to the Far East.[24] The *Prince of Wales* had actually had three weeks of concentrated exercises before Operation Halberd in September 1941, and was then 'on top form'; however, because classes for advancement and seamanship were given priority over gunnery drills on the way to the Far East, she should have had a gunnery work-up before her final operation; but there was no time.[25]

It is difficult to see how the lack of an uninterrupted work-up actually caused the loss of the *Prince of Wales*; the key event in her loss, the devastating torpedo hits in the first attack, certainly had nothing to do with the lack of an uninterrupted work-up, as the most efficient ship's company in the world would probably have been overwhelmed. Even if the *Prince of Wales*'s gunnery had been on top form on 10 December (and it probably wasn't), it would probably not have made a difference, given the problems with her anti-aircraft guns and directors and the Japanese tactics, dropping torpedoes from long range and, in the first attack, from many different directions. Certainly the lack of an adequate, uninterrupted period to work up was not the ideal way to treat a new ship, but it is to her credit that the *Prince of Wales* still managed to become a relatively efficient fighting unit in spite of it.

The *Prince of Wales* was one of the most powerful and famous ships of her time, but in later years it has been suggested or implied that she was an 'unlucky ship', or a 'Jonah', and that she was an unhappy ship.[26] Both suggestions have caused great offence to survivors of the *Prince of Wales*,[27] and upon closer examination neither is fair.

If it is asked whether the *Prince of Wales* was considered a Jonah, it is true that there were at least a few superstitious seamen[28] who regarded her as an unlucky ship, either unlucky herself or unlucky to the battlecruisers she sailed with.[29] It is rather doubtful, however, that many did, or that they thought so very seriously, since the men of the *Prince of Wales* were quite unaware of such feelings at the time. At least some of those who considered her a Jonah were from the *Repulse*,[30] whose crew was not exactly inclined to think kindly of the more publicized *Prince of Wales*.

There was no reason to consider *Prince of Wales* an unlucky ship, any more than any other warship sunk in the Second World War. After some initial minor mishaps[31] that were probably not well known, she was actually quite lucky, given the defects in her main armament, to have seriously damaged the *Bismarck* and to have escaped destruction by the *Bismarck* and the cruiser *Prinz Eugen*. She was especially lucky that a 15in shell from the *Bismarck* that hit her below the waterline near some vital compartments did not explode.[32] She did succumb to an 'unlucky' hit on her port quarter in the first torpedo attack, but this hit was no more unlucky than the torpedo that doomed the *Bismarck*, which has never been known as an unlucky ship.

Nor was there good reason to label the *Prince of Wales* as unlucky to the battlecruisers she sailed with. It was merely a coincidence that two battlecruisers were lost while in company with her, and she was certainly not to blame for the loss of the *Hood* or the *Repulse*. The *Hood* and *Repulse* were lost because of their own weaknesses, lack of sufficient armour in the *Hood* and lack of modern protection against torpedoes and adequate anti-aircraft armament in the *Repulse*, and because of the dangers to which they were exposed in spite of their known weaknesses.

Instead of being considered an unlucky ship, the prevailing image of *Prince of Wales* at the time was a much more positive one, that of a powerful and battle-tested battleship, or it was like that of a sailor on the *Repulse*, who, as the ships were leaving Singapore, said, 'Just look at her, boy! Churchill's yacht. The glamour ship. Look at her!'[33] Certainly, the Japanese did not see her as an unlucky ship; to them, she was the 'unsinkable battleship'.[34]

Nor was there any reason for the *Prince of Wales* to be an unhappy ship. She had one of the finest captains in the Royal Navy, who had a reputation for always running a happy ship in spite of being a firm disciplinarian,[35] as well as one of the finest executive officers, Commander Lawson. Survivors of the *Prince of Wales* have vehemently insisted that she was a happy ship that her men were proud of.[36] Perhaps some of the ship's company might have preferred to stay in home waters rather than go out to the Far East,[37] but that alone would not have made her an unhappy ship. Lieutenant Wildish recalled,

> We had the finest of Captains, much loved by his ship's company . . . a splendid Commander who was a real leader of men; and a united and supremely happy Wardroom. . . . Prince of Wales was a very happy ship. Within the limitations imposed on a 'Treaty Compliance' battleship we had done our stuff, first in the Bismarck action, and then in Operation Halberd. Our very young junior crewmen were getting their sea and battle legs, were proud of themselves, and morale was rising.[38]

There seems to be plenty of reason to believe she was a happy ship, in spite of having a large proportion of 'hostilities only' men, i.e. in the Royal Navy only for the duration of the war, who would normally be less enamoured of shipboard life in wartime than career sailors.

Although the *Prince of Wales* seems to have been a happy enough ship, she does not seem to have been 'a happy flagship', if that can be said of a ship. Indeed, the main suggestion that the *Prince of Wales* was an unhappy ship came from one of the eight cipher officers on Admiral Phillips's staff, Sub-Lieutenant H.J. Lock, who thought the staff were shunned by the other officers in the wardroom,[39] and at least a few others felt there was feeling against them.[40] As Admiral Phillips's assistant secretary recalled, 'For all the evidence that PoW was a happy ship, I did not find it so and there seemed to me to be a considerable rift between the ship's officers and the staff who had of course been imposed upon them.'[41] One of the officers of the *Prince of Wales* later wrote that the ship's company did not welcome the arrival of yet another flag officer (i.e. admiral), as she had not been a 'private ship' (i.e. not a flagship) since her initial work-up.[42] Regardless of who may have been to blame, something of a rift between the ship's officers and the Admiral's staff officers does seem to have existed.

Whatever rift there might have been, it was not limited to junior officers; Admiral Phillips and Captain Leach do not seem to have hit it off very well either. According to the engineer officer of the *Prince of Wales*, Commander L.J. Goudy, the two men were 'obviously not hand in glove together'. Perhaps this is not surprising, given the difference in their personalities, but even Goudy, who knew both well, said he did not understand the difference between the two men.[43] Goudy recalled an incident in which he went to the compass platform to make a report about the ship's boilers to Captain Leach, but the Captain waved him over to Admiral Phillips, saying, 'Tell him, he's the boss.'[44]

Perhaps too much can be made of talk of a rift. The staff had only been on board a short time, and any ill feelings may have been limited to just a few. Furthermore, Paymaster Lieutenant W.T. Blunt, Captain Leach's secretary, has said that the relationship between Phillips and Leach was 'entirely one of mutual respect and confidence', with 'no sort of friction between the men',[45] and Captain L.H. Bell, Phillips's Captain of the Fleet, was a longtime personal friend of Captain Leach.[46] Nevertheless, for whatever reason, something of a rift does seem to have existed. Not only is it unfortunate that the rift came to exist at all, it is even more unfortunate that it led to the unfair implication that the *Prince of Wales* was an unhappy ship.

In the light of all this, it would be unfair to remember the *Prince of Wales* as an unlucky or unhappy ship. Instead, she should be remembered as the ship that damaged the *Bismarck* and forced her to head for France, the ship that carried Winston Churchill to a historic meeting with President Roosevelt, and as a ship that was lost in a courageous attempt to stem an unstoppable Japanese tide. She was also the first British, or indeed Allied, warship to face all three members of the Axis, the Germans, the Italians and then the Japanese.[47] The *Prince of Wales* was a powerful and extraordinary ship, manned by some exceptional men, which in a short life of less than a year enjoyed one of the most amazing careers of any warship ever built.

The men of the Imperial Japanese Navy and the Royal Navy fought hard and well in the Battle off Malaya. Their machines had performed well, or as well as could have been expected.

Notes

1 They were the *Barham* in 1939, the *Resolution* in September 1940, the *Malaya* in March 1941, and the *Nelson* in September 1941. Raven and Roberts, *British Battleships of World War II*, at 343, 346, 359, 367.

2 *Ibid.* at 343, 359.

3 Memoirs of Captain C.D.L. Aylwin, RM, at 14. Papers of Captain C.D.L. Aylwin, RM. Imperial War Museum, Department of Documents.

4 Letter from Blunt to the author of 27 January 1999, and conversation of 5 May 1999.

5 Testimony of Lieutenant-Commander R.F. Harland before the Second Bucknill Committee. TNA Adm 116/4554, at 158.

6 Thomas C. Gillmer, *Fundamentals of Construction and Stability of Naval Ships*, Annapolis, Naval Institute Press, 1959, at 127–9.

7   Report, 'Detailed Comparison between United States and British Warships', 1943, TNA Adm 1/15578.

8   TNA Adm 239/43.

9   The jams were caused by shells separating from their casings. Some of the pom-poms on the *Repulse* suffered stoppages, though not always from the same problem. Jacobs, 'The Loss of Repulse and Prince of Wales', at 28.

10 Garzke and Dulin, *Battleships: Axis and Neutral Battleships in World War II*, at 208.

11 *Ibid.* at 143–4.

12 Friedman, *U.S. Battleships: An Illustrated Design History*, at 417.

13 M.J. Whitley, *German Capital Ships of World War Two*, London, Arms and Armour Press, 1989, at 124.

14 Garzke and Dulin, *Axis and Neutral Battleships in World War II*, at 387–9.

15 Garzke and Dulin, *Allied Battleships in World War II*, at 177, 245.

16 Garzke and Dulin, *United States Battleships in World War II*, at 38–9.

17 Garzke and Dulin, *Axis and Neutral Battleships in World War II*, at 54–5.

18 Technical Report on Damage to and Loss of H.M.S. 'Prince of Wales'. TNA Adm 239/349, at 10.

19 Campbell, *Naval Weapons of World War Two*, at 209.

20 Report of the Second Bucknill Committee, at 23. TNA Adm 239/349.

21 Letter from Commander (E) L.J. Goudy to Marder of 12 September 1978. Marder Papers.

22 Letter from Michael Goodenough to Stephen Roskill of 8 May 1951. Roskill Papers.

23 Letter from L.H. Bell to Arthur Marder of 24 March 1975. Marder Papers. Captain Leach told Captain Doig in Singapore, 'You know, Douglas, they've never really given me a chance with this ship.' Doig, 'Misfortune off Malaya', at 11.

24 Letter from Vice-Admiral D.B.H. Wildish to the author of 24 June 2003.

25 Letter from Colin McMullen to Arthur Marder of 3 March 1976. Marder Papers.

26 The suggestions arose in the book *Battleship* by Martin Middlebrook and Patrick Mahoney.

27 e.g. Admiral D.B.H. Wildish, Captain C.W. McMullen, Commander A.G. Skipwith and Lieutenant-Commander Geoffrey Brooke.

28 Just how superstitious seamen can be is well illustrated by a story from HMS *Mauritius*, which was tied up near the *Prince of Wales* in Singapore before she sailed. The *Prince of Wales*'s black cat left the ship before she sailed and was adopted by the *Mauritius* after the *Prince of Wales* was sunk. Later, when the men of the *Mauritius* could not find her, they thought she had left the ship, and took it as a portent of their doom as well. Luckily, the cat was found, and normal shipboard routine could resume. Leach, *Endure No Makeshifts*, at 12–13.

29 At least so thought a yeoman on HMS *Electra*. Cain and Sellwood, *H.M.S. Electra*, at 158.

30 Middlebrook and Mahoney, *Battleship*, at 114.

31 *Ibid.* at 46.

32 She was even lucky not to have been named *King Edward VIII*, a name proposed by the Admiralty but refused by King Edward VIII himself, who, shortly before his abdication, insisted that the ship be named after his brother, the Prince of Wales

(and future King George VI). George L. Moore, 'Warship Names', *Warships*, No. 126 (Autumn 1996), at 25, 26–7.

33 Gallagher, *Action in the East*, at 39.

34 Official Japanese History, at 437.

35 Admiral Sir Ronald Brockman, attachment to letter to A.J. Marder of 31 December 1975. Marder Papers.

36 e.g. Letter from Captain D.G. Roome to Arthur Marder of 30 May 1975. Marder Papers. One of her survivors, Paymaster-Lieutenant W.T. Blunt, described her as a 'happy enough' ship. Author's notes of conversation of 5 May 1999.

37 Lieutenant D.B.H. Wildish, quoted in Middlebrook and Mahoney, *Battleship*, at 62.

38 Letter from Admiral D.B.H. Wildish to the author of 10 August 1999.

39 Middlebrook and Mahoney, *Battleship*, at 60. Lock was a survivor of the destroyer HMS *Kelly*, Lord Louis Mountbatten's most famous ship. Letter from Joe G. Blackburn to the author of 10 August 1999.

40 Letter from R.E.F. Peal to the author of 26 November 1997.

41 Letter from Rear Admiral Kenneth Farnhill to Arthur Marder of 17 September 1979. Marder Papers.

42 Letter from later-Commander Rodney Wrightson to Arthur Marder of 28 November 1978. Marder Papers. The *Prince of Wales* had worn Admiral Curteis's flag during Operation Halberd in September. V.E. Tarrant, *King George V Class Battleships*, at 88.

43 Letter from L.J. Goudy to Arthur Marder of 7 May 1975. Marder Papers.

44 Letter from L.J. Goudy to Arthur Marder of 28 May 1975. Marder Papers.

45 Undated letter from Commander W.T. Blunt to the author, in reply to letter of 8 December 1998.

46 Letter from L.H. Bell to Arthur Marder of 24 March 1975. Marder Papers.

47 Letter from L.J. Goudy to Arthur Marder of 28 May 1975. Marder Papers.

CHAPTER SEVENTEEN

In Retrospect:
Causes and Responsibility

As with any important battle, the outcome was influenced or caused by a number of factors, including fortune, the performance of men and machines, and the decisions of commanders. It is worth recalling the prescient words of Captain William Davis:

> We in Plans and Operations Foreign [in the Admiralty] were solidly against sending out *Prince of Wales* to the Far East, as it were almost by herself, as also was the First Sea Lord who argued strongly against the unwisdom of despatching a wholly [*sic*] unbalanced force into an area where we did not know the strengths or capacities of the potential enemy. We suggested that such action would make *Prince of Wales* a hostage to fortune.[1]

The *Prince of Wales*, and the *Repulse* as well, were indeed to be made hostages to fortune, by command decisions that matched up the strengths and capacities of the men and machines of the British Empire against the unknown strengths and capacities of the Japanese Empire.

To begin with the role of fortune, there were certainly times that fortune, or, as some would call it, luck, chance, or Providence, seemed to be against Force Z. For instance, the Pacific war came swiftly, too swiftly, after the *Prince of Wales* and *Repulse* arrived at Singapore, before adequate plans could be made for their use or a balanced force assembled. Their arrival at Singapore in time for war was more of a curse than the blessing it first seemed to be. Once the ships sailed, if

I-58 had not sighted Force Z just before midnight on 9 December, it might have enjoyed an undisturbed voyage back to Singapore. If any one of the RAF aircraft sent to Kuantan early on 10 December had sighted and reported Force Z, some air cover could have been provided. If the weather on 10 December had been as nasty as it usually was at that time of year, Force Z might never have been found by Ensign Hoashi or by the rest of the 22nd Air Flotilla. Fortune was most unkind when the *Prince of Wales* suffered a freak, crippling hit that must have been a few feet from missing her altogether. If the Bettys of the Kanoya Group had not sighted the *Repulse*'s Walrus, and then Force Z, the ships might well have survived, especially if the *Prince of Wales* had been able to regain her steering and head for Singapore.

It was also unfortunate that the pre-Pearl Harbor discussions between Great Britain and the United States resulted in nothing to help Force Z, even though they laid the groundwork for an alliance that eventually defeated Italy, Germany and Japan. The sighting of Japanese convoys off Indo-China induced Admiral Hart to release four US destroyers to Admiral Phillips, but even that came too late. Even worse was the decision to transfer US warships such as the carrier *Yorktown* and her cruisers and destroyers to the Atlantic. The old British battleships freed up by the transfer were of no use to Force Z, and the transfer made it impossible to revive the idea of an American 'Asiatic reinforcement', which could have combined with Force Z to defend the Malay Barrier in the event of war. Such a combination would have made for a much more balanced force and given the Allies a fighting chance of slowing down the Japanese.

Seeing the role of fortune in a different way, some have said that the *Prince of Wales* and *Repulse* were doomed, and that if they had escaped destruction on 10 December they would have been hunted down and sunk another day.[2] That is hardly certain; indeed, if the *Prince of Wales* and *Repulse* had survived to return to Singapore, they might well have been withdrawn to a safer location (such as Colombo) for safety's sake or for repairs. Even if they had remained in the immediate area, in the Dutch East Indies or at Darwin in north-western Australia, the Japanese might never have found them again in sufficient strength to sink them: they had a difficult enough time locating them on 10 December. The Japanese had little margin for error: at the beginning of December 1941, the 22nd Air Flotilla had only one torpedo per bomber.

On the other hand, fortune was not always all that unkind to Force Z; it did provide perfect weather for rescue operations on 10 December.

In a perverse way, fortune also saw to it that Force Z was sighted by Japanese search planes the evening of the 9th. If they had not, Force Z would have continued on to Kota Bharu, and, although it would have sold itself dearly, it would have found itself up against not only the aircraft of the 22nd Air Flotilla, but against every Japanese battleship, cruiser, destroyer, and submarine in the South China Sea. Surely continuing would have carried the direst of consequences for every ship and man in Force Z.

That is not to say that the outcome of the battle was caused by fortune alone. Far from it. The men and machines that fought the battle, with all their strengths and weaknesses, played an important part in the outcome of the battle. As Captain Davis foresaw, in this first clash between new enemies, the British could not know the strengths or capacities of the Japanese, and had to learn about them the hard way. On the Japanese side, their aircraft and their torpedoes performed very well, and with hardly an exception their bombers crews exhibited astonishing skill and endurance, greater than anyone could have predicted, since up to that time the Japanese themselves had had no occasion to attack, much less sink, major warships at sea. The Japanese submarines scouted well, though their reports sometimes went astray.

On the British side, all in all the captains and crews of the British ships fought very well under the most difficult of circumstances. The destroyers could do little more than perform brilliant rescue work. Both the *Prince of Wales* and *Repulse* lacked anti-aircraft guns and directors sufficient to deal with Japanese aircraft dropping torpedoes at long range. No one could have expected the *Repulse* to do better than she did, given her First World War-era hull design. A planned refit would have given her a better chance. The performance of the *Prince of Wales* was disappointing to some, since she did not withstand as many torpedoes as expected, but it was not known until years later that she had suffered a devastating hit aft that would have crippled almost any battleship. Disaster could still have been averted if the *Prince of Wales* had avoided the first torpedoes launched at her, but she did not, because of a very skilful attack and perhaps because of her poor turning radius. The loss of the *Prince of Wales* was due much more to the skill of the Japanese and the devastating damage they inflicted than to the design of the *Prince of Wales* or the actions of her captain or her men. The men of the *Repulse* and *Prince of Wales* emerged from the action with much to be proud of.

Aside from the roles played by fortune and the performance of men and machines, key command decisions on both sides played a crucial role in outcome of the battle. On the Japanese side, the decisions and dispositions of Admirals Ozawa, Kondo, and Matsunaga served them well enough, although Kondo and Ozawa showed a tendency to disperse forces that would cost Japan dearly in later battles in the Pacific. The truly outstanding decision on the Japanese side was Admiral Yamamoto's coolly calculated decision to transfer part of the Kanoya Group to Indo-China to counter the well-publicized arrival of the *Prince of Wales* at Singapore.

On the British side, there were a number of key decisions that led to the tragedy. First, the decision to send the *Prince of Wales* initially to Cape Town, instead of to the Far East, was a muddled compromise, suggested by Pound but in response to Churchill's insistence on sending the ship to Singapore. If the question of sending the *Prince of Wales* to the Far East had been squarely faced, a reasoned decision could have been made on what would be done with her and the *Repulse* if deterrence failed. Secondly, the decision to send the *Prince of Wales* and *Repulse* on to Singapore to deter Japan, most likely made by Churchill with Pound's acquiescence after Churchill's Guildhall speech, was an example of wishful thinking. Militarily, it was dangerous to send the ships out without planning for the possibility that deterrence would fail, and the start of war would find them in a forward area from which withdrawal was not easy and without a more balanced force. Worse, the desire to deter the Japanese led to the publicity given to the arrival of the *Prince of Wales* at Singapore, which triggered the transfer of the Kanoya Group to Indo-China. When it became clear that deterrence had failed, the question of what to do with the ships had to be faced, with very little time and with a great distance between Churchill and the Admiralty and Tom Phillips, and possibilities were rife for misunderstanding or for making the wrong decision. Thirdly, prodded and put in an impossible situation by Churchill and the Admiralty, Admiral Phillips made a brave, calculated, but nevertheless risky decision to sail to attack the Japanese off the invasion beaches. In spite of Churchill's later subtle suggestion to the contrary in his memoirs, he and the First Sea Lord knew of, and were probably in accord with, if not enthusiastic about, the decision to go on the attack. Fourth, while Tom Phillips was probably justified in not calling for air cover before he was sighted by Ensign Hoashi on the 10th, once he was sighted the better decision would have been to call for air cover, in spite of the rule against breaking radio silence to report a single aircraft; it might well have made a difference.

Of course, the roles played by the different types of factors can be hard to separate. The sighting of Force Z by *I-58* was ill fortune, but it was also good Japanese planning that put *I-58* where she could spot Force Z. The devastating torpedo hit on the stern of the *Prince of Wales* was perhaps in part due to ill fortune, but it was also in part due to great Japanese skill and perhaps in part due to the ship's poor turning radius. If the Japanese aircrews had been less skilful or if their torpedoes had been defective, the worst British decisions would have been of no consequence. In putting Admiral Phillips in a position to decide whether to break radio silence to call for air cover, fortune may have unkindly placed Tom Phillips, a remarkable and brilliant officer, in the wrong place at the wrong time. Even if he had changed his earlier views on the ability of ships to stand up to air power, he may have been the British admiral least likely to call for fighters on 10 December. Since he had pressed for Hurricanes to be sent to the Far East instead of Buffaloes, he may have also been the British admiral most likely to distrust the abilities of the Brewster Buffalo. Finally, with his penchant for the theoretical over the practical, he may have been more likely to go by the book and keep radio silence when a single aircraft was sighted.

After considering together the roles of fortune, of the men and machines that fought the battle, and of the command decisions that played a part in the outcome of the battle, it is now possible to discern what the most important factors in the outcome of the battle were. First, there was the series of British decisions to send the ships to Singapore to deter the Japanese, with the publicity that led to the transfer of the decisive Kanoya Group to Indo-China and to Admiral Phillips having to undertake a risky operation without a balanced force. Secondly, there was the unseasonably beautiful weather on 10 December that revealed Force Z to Ensign Hoashi and then the rest of the 22nd Air Flotilla. Thirdly, there was Admiral Phillips's understandable but unfortunate decision not to break radio silence, even though there were fighters ashore that could have been sent to help him. Fourthly, there was the astonishing ability of the Japanese to mount massed and skilled torpedo bombing attacks at long range, a capability the British could not have known about beforehand. Fifthly, there was the devastating torpedo hit on the stern of the *Prince of Wales*. The grounding of the *Indomitable* was not a factor in the outcome of the battle since she could not have arrived in time anyway.

A review of the most important factors, especially the most important British decisions, leads inevitably to the question of who on the British side was to bear the responsibility (a kinder word than 'blame') for the tragedy. The 'usual suspects' have been Admiral Phillips, Admiral Palliser, First Sea Lord Dudley Pound and Winston Churchill.

If responsibility is to be assessed, it should fall, not upon Admiral Phillips or Admiral Palliser, but upon Winston Churchill and the First Sea Lord. Admiral Palliser[3] did the best he could with the information he had, which gave him no warning that Phillips had abandoned the operation and headed for Kuantan. Tom Phillips did the best he could in the impossible position into which he was put; his only really questionable decision was the one to maintain radio silence.

Another possible suspect is First Lord A.V. Alexander, but, perhaps because he was not known for standing up to Churchill, little was expected of him, and he has not been blamed for the loss of the ships. To his credit, he did oppose the dispatch of the *Prince of Wales* in the October 1941 meetings, but after that he seems to have been left 'out of the loop' by Churchill and Pound, except to be present at the meeting on the night of 9 December.

The lion's share of the blame should instead attach to Pound and Churchill. Neither did anything to extricate Tom Phillips from the situation he found himself in at Singapore as war was breaking out. Pound dispatched the Churchillian prodding signal to Phillips, and, perhaps thinking the ships would face only the *Kongo*, and mindful of the great victory won at the Falklands exactly twenty-seven years before, both Churchill and Pound seem to have been all in favour of the risky operation that resulted.

Pound no doubt thought the compromise decision to send the *Prince of Wales* to Cape Town was the best he could do under the circumstances; but this was the one occasion he should have stood up to Churchill and forced the issue. If he had prevailed, the *Prince of Wales* would not have gone to Singapore; if he had failed, he could have at least obtained a commitment that the ships would be withdrawn if deterrence failed and if they could not be made part of a balanced force, either on 20 October or at a subsequent Defence Committee meeting. Instead, he allowed Admiral Phillips and the *Prince of Wales* and *Repulse* to go on to Singapore, where they were drawn into an impossible situation.

The decision to send the *Prince of Wales* and *Repulse* to Singapore and the subsequent disaster to the convoy PQ-17 to the Soviet Union in

1942 has caused some, like historian Stephen Roskill, to question Pound's fitness for the position of First Sea Lord. This question ignited a long-running war of words between two of the great naval historians of the twentieth century, Captain Stephen Roskill and Professor Arthur Marder. Fuelled in part by personal animosity and professional rivalry, the feud centred on whether Churchill dominated Pound and his other service advisers, whether Pound's health affected his performance as First Sea Lord, and whether Churchill unduly interfered in naval matters when he was First Lord at the Admiralty and as Prime Minister. This duel went through many rounds, beginning in 1972 and ending in 1981 with Marder's death and the posthumous publication of his *Old Friends, New Enemies*,[4] and brought out much information on Churchill and his relationship with Pound.

Without declaring a winner of the match, it is fair to say that, while to some extent Churchill 'dominated' almost everyone, including his service advisers, Pound was not a 'yes man', and handled the difficult Mr Churchill well on most matters, avoiding a direct 'no' whenever possible and eventually dissuading the PM from his most impractical or dangerous schemes. The dispatch of the *Prince of Wales* was an unfortunate exception, but Pound was first backed into a corner in the 20 October meeting after resolutely opposing Churchill, and then after the meeting Churchill wore him down until he agreed that the ships should be sent to Singapore. As for Pound's health, although there were conflicting accounts, it is fair to say that Pound was physically and mentally up to the job of First Sea Lord, in spite of an arthritic hip and the consequent lack of sleep, until he fell seriously ill with a fatal brain tumour in 1943. Finally, it is safe to say that Churchill interfered unduly in naval matters both as First Lord of the Admiralty from 1939 to 1940 and then as Prime Minister, the campaign in Norway in 1940 and the dispatch of the *Prince of Wales* being prime examples.

In the end, it is Winston Churchill who should shoulder the largest share of the blame. He was the driving force behind the faulty political decision to send the ships to Singapore to deter Japan, and, as a political decision, it was arguably one that he and the Cabinet were entitled to make. However, once it became clear that the political purpose of deterrence had failed, he should have been the driving force behind the decision to get them away from Singapore when they were in harm's way. Instead, Mr Churchill left them in a position where they were truly 'hostages to fortune'. And he was not unfamiliar with the concept; in

1935, he gave a speech warning Mussolini not to attack Abyssinia (Ethiopia), and said:

> I am surprised that so great a man, so wise a ruler, as Signor Mussolini should be willing, even eager, to put his gallant nation in such an uncomfortable military and financial position. To cast an army of nearly a quarter of a million men, embodying the flower of Italian manhood, upon a barren shore 2,000 miles from home against the good will of the whole world and without command of the sea, and then, in that position, to embark on what might well be a series of campaigns against a people and in regions which no conqueror in 4,000 years ever thought it worth while to subdue – to do that is to give hostages to fortune unparalleled in all history.[5]

Mussolini would have done well to have heeded Churchill's warning, but Churchill would have done well to remember his own words.

That Mr Churchill was able to wear Pound down in order to get his agreement to send the ships on to Singapore is hardly to his credit. Moreover, he should have learned from his mistake in wearing down First Sea Lord Jackie Fisher to get him to agree to the Dardanelles operation in the First World War, an operation that ended in failure and the resignations of Fisher and then Churchill. In *The World Crisis*, Churchill did not conceal 'the great and continuous pressure' he had put on Fisher, but justified it by saying that 'war is a business of terrible pressures, and persons who take part in it must fail if they are not strong enough to withstand them'; only in a draft did Churchill admit that this had been 'his greatest mistake', but the passage was deleted before publication.[6] It was likewise a mistake to pressure Pound into agreeing to send the ships on to Singapore.

In making decisions about the *Prince of Wales* and *Repulse*, Churchill and Pound were operating under extremely difficult conditions, trying to deter and then fight a new enemy, Japan, when they already had their hands full with Germany and Italy, and were no doubt doing their best. The errors of judgement they committed were not 'culpable, but such as men, being human, make under the stress of war'.[7] The road to Hell – or, in this case, hot and steamy Singapore – was no doubt paved with good intentions.

Still, men can and should be judged more critically by what they say and write about their deeds after the fact. Neither Churchill nor Pound ever publicly accepted any blame for the loss of the *Prince of Wales* and

Repulse, but at least Pound appreciated the difficult position Tom Phillips had been put in and took every opportunity he could to staunchly defend him.

In contrast, while Mr Churchill at first defended Tom Phillips, in his *The Second World War* he committed a number of sins, to wit: he described the meeting of 9 December in such a way as to leave the false and unfair impression that the operation Phillips had embarked upon was the last thing he would have done and that he had known nothing of it, and misleadingly characterized the attendance at the meeting as 'mostly naval'; he glossed over his role in the decision to send the *Prince of Wales* and *Repulse* to the Far East; he exaggerated the role planned for the *Indomitable*; and finally, he omitted parts of speeches that tied him to Force Z's march to the Battle off Malaya. Surely this is not coincidental. As one historian has written about Churchill's use of documents in *The World Crisis*, 'The reader is never sure that the version given by Churchill is complete, or if material damaging to the case Churchill is building up has been omitted, or if any deletions made have been indicated in the text.'[8]

In Churchill's defence, in the preface to the first volume of *The Second World War*, he did not claim it was history, but a contribution to history, and once even said 'This is not history, this is my case.'[9] Many would not expect any detachment from a politician's account of a war in which he played so central a part, but in many ways *The Second World War* takes, or appears to take, a detached view rather than a personal view, and it is easy for a reader to see it as history rather than a politician's memoir.[10] Even if it is treated as the latter, its sins with respect to the story of the loss of the *Prince of Wales* and *Repulse* simply go too far. That their loss was a painful memory for him is no excuse. All this was unworthy of a man whom many look up to, and justifiedly so, as one of the greatest wartime leaders of the twentieth century.

Notes

1 'Loss of "Prince of Wales" and "Repulse" 10th December 1941: Notes from Diaries of Captain William Davis, Deputy Director of Plans, Admiralty', attachment to letter from Admiral William Davis to Arthur Marder of 3 April 1975. Marder Papers.

2 Marder, *Old Friends, New Enemies*, at 506; Stephen, *Fighting Admirals*, at 114.

3 Coincidentally, Admiral Palliser's son Sir Michael became the head of the British Diplomatic Service, Commander Goodenough's son Sir Anthony became the UK High Commissioner to Canada, and Admiral Phillips's grandson Tom, T.R.V. Phillips, is at present the Director South Asia and UK Representative for Afghanistan with the Foreign and Commonwealth Office.

4 Marder, 'Winston is Back', *English Historical Review* Supplement 5 (1972); Roskill, 'Marder, Churchill and the Admiralty 1939–42', *RUSI Journal* 117 (December 1972): 49–53; Marder, *From the Dardanelles to Oran*, at 173–8; Roskill, *Naval Policy between the Wars, Vol. 2: The Period of Reluctant Rearmament*, at 465 n. 3; Roskill, *Churchill and the Admirals*, at 283–99; Marder, *Old Friends, New Enemies*, at 233–9.

5 James, ed., *Winston S. Churchill: His Complete Speeches 1897–1963; Vol. 6: 1935–1942*, at 5673.

6 Robin Prior, *Churchill's World Crisis as History*, London, Croom Helm, 1983, at 76–7.

7 Bennett, *The Loss of the Prince of Wales & Repulse*, at 56.

8 Prior, *Churchill's World Crisis as History*, at 281.

9 Warren F. Kimball, 'Churchill and Roosevelt', in Robert Blake and Wm Roger Lewis, eds, *Churchill: A Major New Assessment of his Life in Peace and War*, New York, W.W. Norton & Co., 1993, at 294, quoting Sir William Deakin, who helped with the research for Churchill's war memoirs.

10 See Prior, *Churchill's World Crisis as History*, at 281.

Conclusion

The Battle off Malaya was a momentous struggle between two empires – the British Empire represented by a small force that was both powerful and vulnerable, and the Japanese Empire by a powerful force fighting at the time and place of its choosing. Although it did not cost the British Empire either Malaya or Singapore, it was still a very important battle because it cost Britain two very valuable capital ships that she could have used elsewhere at a critical point in the war, and because it demonstrated beyond any doubt the ability of aircraft to sink even capital ships at sea without air cover.

Whatever the causes of the outcome of the battle, no matter who was to blame, there can be no sugarcoating the result of the battle: even though Force Z had managed to disrupt the Japanese timetable for the unloading of supplies for the invasion, the battle was certainly not a draw. To Britain and her allies, the loss of the *Prince of Wales* and *Repulse* must have seemed like losing one's queen in the opening moves of a chess game. Still, the men of Force Z had nothing to be ashamed of. They fought bravely and well, and, like the men of the Mediterranean Fleet off Crete in May 1941, they made great sacrifices to uphold a long Royal Navy tradition of going to the aid of the Army no matter what the cost. Nor did their sacrifices go unappreciated by the British Army: Lieutenant-General A.E. Percival wrote in his postwar dispatch, 'I wish to pay tribute to the gallant manner in which the C-in-C Eastern Fleet endeavoured to assist the land and air forces by attacking the enemy's sea communications.'[1] General Percival, like Admiral Phillips, had served primarily as a staff officer before he became General Officer Commanding Malaya, and, while he did not make the ultimate sacrifice Phillips made, he had to endure years as a prisoner of war under the Japanese after the fall of Singapore.

Both the British and Japanese had to evaluate the lessons of the battle. The British should have learned the obvious lesson that maintaining radio silence could be overrated. Both sides should have learned that warships should not be exposed to enemy air power without adequate air cover of their own. Neither would always observe the lesson, the Japanese on many occasions from the Guadalcanal campaign on, and the British in May 1942, when three valuable destroyers were lost to German bombers in the Mediterranean, and in October 1943, when a number of warships were sunk and damaged by German bombers in the Aegean.

One of the most important lessons for both the British and the Japanese was the need to re-evaluate the place of the battleship *vis-à-vis* aircraft. To some, the loss of the *Prince of Wales* and *Repulse* meant the end of the era of the battleship. According to one historian, 'The battleship had been toppled from the lordly position it had retained for three centuries.'[2] Perhaps, but the point may have been a bit overstated. Certainly, more than any other single event in the Second World War, the Battle off Malaya brought home, once and for all, the vulnerability of battleships to aircraft at sea, but battleships had already shown their vulnerability to air attack in the war; to date, even apart from the Japanese air attack on Pearl Harbor several days before, British aircraft had torpedoed three Italian battleships in harbour at Taranto, had crippled the *Bismarck* in the Atlantic and had nearly crippled the Italian battleship *Vittorio Veneto* off Matapan. Ironically, the only battleships sunk by aircraft at sea during the rest of the war were Japanese, the *Musashi* in 1944 and the *Yamato* in 1945, and to add to the irony, neither of them had any appreciable air cover at the time.

Battleships were not, however, consigned to idly riding at anchor for the rest of the war. Aside from serving as anti-aircraft escorts for aircraft carriers, they were still able to find some traditional employment. In November 1942, the American battleship *Washington* sank the Japanese battleship *Kirishima* off Guadalcanal, in December 1943 the British battleship *Duke of York* crippled the battlecruiser *Scharnhorst* at the Battle of North Cape, and in October 1944, at the Battle of Leyte Gulf, American battleships helped sink the Japanese battleship *Yamashiro*, and Japanese battleships mauled some American escort carriers and nearly broke through to attack transports off Leyte. The lesson of the loss of the *Prince of Wales* and *Repulse* should not have been that battleships no longer had a role to play in the war at sea, but that battleships could be sunk by aircraft at sea, and that no warship, battleship or otherwise, should be risked in waters ruled by hostile aircraft without adequate air cover.

It is a tribute to the men of the *Prince of Wales* and *Repulse* that the Royal Navy applied the main lesson of the tragedy more than forty years later when the British sent a task force to retake the Falkland Islands from Argentina in 1982. Harrier jets from two aircraft carriers, the *Invincible* and the *Hermes*, provided critical air cover against brave and determined Argentinian air attacks. The First Sea Lord of the Royal Navy at the time was Admiral of the Fleet Sir Henry Leach, whose father, Captain John Leach, would no doubt have been proud.

Leaving aside lofty questions of the role of fortune, the performance of ships and men, the decisions made, and the lessons to be learned, there is perhaps a deeper essence of the battle that should not be overlooked. Terrible as it was, at least the Battle off Malaya was a hard-fought contest that was unmarred by the savagery that marked so many other battles in the Pacific War. Credit must go to the Japanese for not interfering with the rescue of survivors.

Perhaps this sense of the battle has been best captured by the sons of two of the key participants. On the British side, Captain Leach's son, Admiral of the Fleet Sir Henry Leach, wrote, 'The Japanese conducted an honourable action from which they emerged with professional credit. They displayed resolute courage and skill, and magnanimity in victory.'[3] On the Japanese side, after the battle was over Admiral Matsunaga told his son Ichiro, who had been aboard the battleship *Haruna* in the South China Sea during the battle, 'In this naval battle both the combatant vessels and aircraft on both sides fought fair and square with all their might – great significance lay in this.'[4] Amen.

Notes

1 A.E. Percival, 'Operations of Malaya Command, from 8th December 1941 to 15th February 1942', Supplement to the *London Gazette* of 26 February 1948. TNA ZJ 1/1029, at 1272.

2 Marder, *Old Friends, New Enemies*, at 514.

3 Leach, *Endure No Makeshifts*, at 9.

4 Statement of Ichiro Matsunaga for Professor Marder, 23 July 1976. Marder Papers.

Appendix

IMPORTANT SIGNALS AND MESSAGES

What follows is a listing of the most important messages and signals concerning the *Prince of Wales* and *Repulse*, organized as best they can be in chronological order by times of origin (T.O.O.), though exact times are not always available. The designation '1548Z/21/10/41' means that the signal or message originated at 1548Z, or 3.48 p.m. Greenwich Mean Time, on 21 October 1941. The time of receipt (T.O.R.) is given when available, but that is rare. Many abbreviations are given at the beginning of the book. The source for each signal or message is given, and the most important ones are BS14 (Battle Summary No. 14, TNA Adm 234/330), PWTM (Principal War Telegrams & Memoranda: Far East 1940–43, TNA Cab 105/20), and AWD (Admiralty War Diary for October and December 1941, TNA Adm 199/2232 & 2234).

21 October 1941
No. 1: 1548Z/21/10/41

From the Admiralty, A.C.N.S. (F)   To All Stations at Home and Abroad (?)

Prince of Wales wearing the flag of Admiral Sir Tom Phillips, Commander-in-Chief, Eastern Fleet, and escorted by *Electra* and *Express* will leave U.K. shortly for Singapore via the Cape.

(AWD & BS14)

6 November 1941
No. 2: 1200Z/6/11/41

From S.O. Force 'G'   To the Admiralty

Following are my proposals for movements of Force 'G' after arrival at the Cape.

2. I am assuming that it remains the intention to give publicity to arrival of Force 'G' at the Cape and accordingly propose to remain in that area from 17 to 21 November. Should early arrival at Singapore be more important than publicity this time could be reduced to 48 hours at some inconvenience to engine room and store departments.

3. Following is the form of publicity it is proposed to grant at the Cape. Facilities to be given to Press photographers and controlled interviews to be given by selected officers and men on *Bismarck* action and Atlantic Meeting. No mention to be made of destination of ship. Result to be released when decided by Admiralty.

4. Program after leaving Cape depends on need for early arrival Singapore.

5. If earliest possible arrival at Singapore is desired, H.M.S *Prince of Wales* could arrive there 12 days after leaving the Cape, destroyers being left behind when clear of the Cape area.

6. If earliest arrival at Singapore is not essential, it would be of advantage to meet C.-in-C., East Indies at Ceylon, remaining 3 days. H.M.S. *Prince of Wales* could then arrive at Singapore 16 days after leaving the Cape, destroyers rejoining at Ceylon.

7. If destroyers remain in company throughout, H.M.S. *Prince of Wales* could arrive Singapore 19 days after leaving Cape.

8. In any case propose H.M.S. *Repulse* arrive Singapore (corrupt group)* H.M.S. *Prince of Wales*.

9. Request Their Lordships instructions as to (a) policy concerning stay at Cape and publicity at that place, (b) need for early arrival after leaving Cape.

T.O.O. 1200Z/6/11/41.

*Admiral Phillips 1637Z/8/11 (*see* postea, signal [4]) leaves no doubt that 'with' or 'in company with' was intended.

(BS14)

No. 3: 1848Z/6/11/41

From the Admiralty

To S.O. Force 'G'.
Repeated C.-in-C., South Atlantic.
C.-in-C., China.
C.-in-C., East Indies.

IMMEDIATE

What are your views as to movements of *Prince of Wales*, *Revenge* and *Repulse* in the immediate future?

To save time you might consider going on ahead of your destroyers after passing 45 degrees E.

T.O.O. 1948A/6/11/41
(for 1st Sea Lord.)

Note:- This signal crossed the preceding one, 1200Z/6 from S.O. Force 'G'.

(BS14)

8 November 1941
No. 4: 1637Z/8/11/41

From S.O. Force 'G'   To the Admiralty

Your 1950* and your 1948/6, and my 1200Z/6 to Admiralty only and C.-in-C., East Indies 0752/7.

[Paragraphs 1,2,3,4 referred to arrangements for meeting with Field Marshal Smuts and movements at the Cape.]

5. Reasons for suggesting in my 1200Z/6 that H.M.S. *Repulse* only should accompany H.M.S. *Prince of Wales* to Singapore in the first instance were as follows.
   (A) A force of 2 fast battleships at Singapore should cause Japan concern but should be regarded by her more as a raiding force than as an attempt to form a line of battle against her.
   (B) The addition of one 'R' class might give the impression that we were trying to form a line of battle, but could only spare 3 ships, thus encouraging Japan.
6. For the above reasons I felt that unless events precipitate matters it might be best for *Revenge* to remain in Indian Ocean until she was joined by *Royal Sovereign* and *Ramillies*, when the 3 ships might come to Singapore towards (? end of) January.
7. If there were a suitable convoy from Australia during the period *Revenge* is available, it might be of advantage for her to proceed to Western Australia and escort it. I do not however consider it desirable that she should at the present time proceed to Australia to fit R.D.F. etc. as was, I believe, contemplated at one time.
8. Admiralty pass to C.-in-C., South Atlantic and C.-in-C., East Indies.

T.O.O 1637Z/8/11/41.

*Informing Admiral Phillips that Field-Marshal Smuts would be very pleased to see him.

(BS14)

9 November 1941

No. 5: 1845Z/9/11/41

From the Admiralty, 1st Sea Lord   To N.O.I.C., Simonstown

Urgency of F.O. Force 'G''s arrival at Singapore necessitates stay of *Prince of Wales* being as short as possible over 48 hours. Request air passage for Admiral Phillips to Pretoria to be ready as soon after his arrival as he may require it.

2. Facilities for Press photographers and controlled interviews will be afforded on board. Date of release will be communicated to you by F.O., Force 'G'.

T.O.O. 1945A/9/11/41.
(BS14)

11 November 1941

No. 6: 1416Z/11/11/41

From the Admiralty   To S.O. Force 'G'
                                    Repeated C.-in-C., East Indies.
                                    C.-in-C., China.
                                    C.-in-C., Mediterranean

A.T. 1954/9 to S.O. Force 'G' only.

As it has been necessary for political reasons to announce the strengthening of our forces in the Eastern area, it is considered undesirable for capital ships to arrive at Singapore without a destroyer screen.

2. The following movements are therefore to be carried out:-

A. *Prince of Wales* is to leave Capetown with destroyers and proceed to Ceylon. Destroyers may be slipped when clear of Cape area if S.O. Force 'G' wishes to prolong his time in Ceylon to meet C.-in-C., East Indies.
B. *Repulse* is to proceed to Ceylon as proposed by C.-in-C., East Indies to arrive by 1st December. She is to form part of Force 'G' from her time of arrival.

C. *Prince of Wales* and *Repulse* screened by the 4 destroyers referred to in A.T. 0155/29th October are to proceed in company to Singapore as soon as practicable after arrival of the destroyers in Ceylon.

D. *Revenge* is to arrive at Ceylon at an early date after the departure of Force 'G', convenient to her convoy duties.

T.O.O 1516A/11
1st Sea Lord.
Approved 1st Lord (BS14)

24 November 1941

No. 7: 1039Z/24/11/41

From the Admiralty.   To A.I.G.21, A.I.G.13*

A. C.-in-C., Eastern Fleet, is expected to arrive Singapore about 6/12. He will assume duties laid down in paragraph B of A.T. 1719/28/10** at 0800 Local Time on day following his arrival, except that the command and administration of naval forces and establishments at present carried out by C.-in-C., China, will not come under his command until the flag of C.-in-C., China, is struck in accordance with A.T. 1151/23/10 (C.-in-C., China only).

B. Reference paragraph F. of A.T. 1719/28/10 the following units are to be considered as forming part of the Eastern Fleet:- *Prince of Wales*. *Repulse*, *Revenge*, *Electra*, *Express*, *Encounter*, *Jupiter*, and such other units of the China Station as desired by C.-in-C., Eastern Fleet.

T.O.O 1139A/24/11/41

*All Commanders-in-Chief, and certain other Flag Officers and Commonwealth Naval Authorities directly concerned.
**This signal laid down the duties and responsibilities of the C.-in-C., Eastern Fleet, so far as they could be foreseen.[1]

(BS14)

28 November 1941

No. 8: 1804Z/28/11/41

From the Admiralty   To S.O. Force 'G'

A. In view of the unsatisfactory situation vis a vis Japan it is considered desirable (unless you see reasons for not doing so) that you should fly to Singapore so as to get on with your planning and be ready to assume command in the Eastern theatre, should war develop.

B. It is also hoped that by doing this you may be able to get contact with the Admiral commanding U.S. Pacific Fleet* or his representative as early as practicable.

T.O.O. 1804/28/11/41

*Amended to read Asiatic Fleet, 1051A/29/11/41.

(BS14)

1 December 1941

No. 9: 0951Z/1/12/41

From S.O. Force 'G'   To the Admiralty

IMMEDIATE

Personal for First Sea Lord. Admiralty message 1139/24 November paragraph (a). Intend to assume duty referred to at 0800, Wednesday, 3rd December. Present intention is that flag of C.-in-C., China, shall remain flying until completion of Naval Conference.

2. In view of Admiralty Message 1804A 28th November it appears that the situation after preliminary British Conference might then preclude my visit to Manila.
3. After discussion with United States Naval Liaison Officer I considered it of great importance that I should make contact with Admiral Hart.
4. Intend, therefore, unless you see reason to contrary, to proceed to Manila ex-officio on Thursday 4th returning on Sunday 7th accepting the (? fact) that I shall not at the time be fully informed on the questions concerning Dominions. Admiral Palliser will remain Singapore.
5. Preliminary British Conference to begin Monday 8th December.
6. Questions whether a further visit to Manila is necessary after the preliminary British Conference for conference referred to in one (b) of Admiralty Message 0104, 26th November, can be decided later.

T.O.O 0951Z/1/12/41.

(BS14)

No. 10: 1743Z/1/12/41

From the Admiralty   To S.O. Force 'G'.

IMMEDIATE

Personal from First Sea Lord.

Your 0951Z/1.

(A) Paragraphs 1, 5 & 6 are noted.
(B) Paragraphs 2, 3 & 4 – Concur.
(C) You and I are in agreement that C.-in-C., Eastern Fleet, should normally be afloat. It is possible, however, that during the present period of uncertainty whilst conferences are in progress you might consider it desirable to send *Prince of Wales* and/or *Repulse* away from Singapore in order that the uncertainty of their whereabouts would disconcert the Japanese.

Under these circumstances you might find it necessary to hoist your flag on shore temporarily.

T.O.O. 1843A/1/12/41.
Asst. Secretary to 1st Sea Lord.
(BS14)

3 December 1941

No. 11: 0057Z/3/12/41

From the Admiralty   To S.O. Force 'G'.

IMMEDIATE

Personal from First Sea Lord.

A.   C.-in-C., Asiatic Fleet, has no doubt informed you that three Japanese submarines were sighted off Saigon proceeding South.
B.   It seems likely their task will be to watch Singapore.
C.   Request you will consider the following alternatives:–
  1. To ask Admiral Hart if he could send the 8 U.S. destroyers to Singapore on a visit so that they would be immediately available if the balloon went up.
  2. To get the *Prince of Wales* and/or *Repulse* away from Singapore to the Eastward.

T.O.O. 0157A/3/12/41.
(BS14)

No. 12: 0923Z/3/12/41

From C.-in-C., Eastern Fleet   To the Admiralty

IMPORTANT

Personal for First Sea Lord. Your 1843/1(?1)

It has been necessary to put in hand retubing of distiller of H.M.S. *Prince of Wales* today 3rd December. Work should be completed in 7 days and distiller at maximum (?72) hours notice during work. Ship capable of proceeding for 48 hours on reserve feed tanks.

Intend to send H.M.S. *Repulse*, H.M.A.S. *Vampire* and H.M.S. *Tenedos* on short visit Port Darwin leaving Singapore Friday 5th December.

T.O.O., 0923Z/3/12/41.

(BS14)

No. 13: 1213Z/3/12/41

From C.-in-C., Eastern Fleet   To the Admiralty

IMMEDIATE

Personal 1st Sea Lord.

My 0923Z 3rd was despatched before receipt of your 0157A 3rd.

2.   I will discuss your paragraph C(i) with Admiral Hart.

T.O.O. 1213Z/3/12/41.

(BS14)

4 December 1941
No. 14: 0925Z/4/12/41

From Commander-in-Chief, Eastern Fleet   To the Admiralty

(0925Z/4.)
Personal for First Sea Lord:

My 0923Z 3rd. I think visit of H.M.S. *Repulse* to Darwin at the moment may be useful in connection with Australian Government attitude regarding release of any cruiser to serve with Fleet. From what I have heard here I anticipate difficulty in this respect, especially since loss of H.M.A.S. *Sydney*, on whom I was counting.

(PWTM)

5 December 1941

No. 15: 5/12/41

From the War Office   To the Commander-in-Chief, Far East.

(55982 (M.O. 10.) 5/12.)
Following from Chiefs of Staff C.O.S. F.E. No. 50:–
Reference our 54850* of 29th November.
His Majesty's Government have now received an assurance of American armed support in the following contingencies:

(a) If we undertake 'Matador' either to forestall a Japanese landing in the Kra Isthmus or as a reply to a Japanese violation of any other part of Thailand (Siam).
(b) If the Japanese attack the Dutch East Indies and we go at once to their support.
(c) If the Japanese attack us.

2. Accordingly you should order 'Matador' without reference home in either of the two following contingencies –

(a) You have good information that a Japanese expedition is advancing with the apparent intention of landing on the Kra Isthmus.
(b) The Japanese violate any other part of Thailand (Siam).

3. In the event of a Japanese attack on the Netherlands East Indies you have authority without reference home immediately to put into operation the plans which you have agreed with them.

4. Commander-in-Chief, Far East, pass to Commander-in-Chief, China, who is to pass to Commander-in-Chief, Eastern Fleet, as from Chiefs of Staff.

*Not reproduced.

(PWTM)

7 December 1941

No. 16: 0421Z/7/12/41

From C. in C. E.F., 0421Z/7   To Admiralty

Personal for 1st S.L.

Adm. Phillips arrived back at Singapore at 0230Z/7th.

(AWD)

No. 17: 0611Z/7/12/41

C.O.I.S. Singapore   To C. in C. Asiatic Fleet, Admiralty, etc.

Further to C. in C. China's 0745/6. Escort of first named force consists of 1 battleship, 5 cruisers, 7 destroyers. From description and W/T traffic, battleship is almost certainly *Kongo*. 2 of cruisers are 'Zintu' class, probably *Zintu* and *Naka*, flagship of second and fourth destroyer squadrons.

Description of remaining cruisers corresponds to 'Kako' class but from W/T traffic second fleet cruisers considered more likely, probably *Atago*, *Tyokai* and *Maya*. Convoy now reported as 22 10,000-ton M/Vs.

Second named force. No description of escort available. Convoy now reported as 21 M/Vs. Third named force reported as 1 cruiser and 3 10,000 ton M/Vs. During last 24 hours majority of signals originated by C. in C. Combined Fleet, whereabouts unknown.

Result of aircraft R/C since first sighting negative.

0611Z/7
(AWD)

No. 18: 1055Z & 1825GH/7/12/41

From The Commander-in-Chief, Far East   To the War Office

(409/6. 7/12.)
1. Enemy information as in C/S Singapore's 0611Z/7 to Admiralty.
2. First location Japanese convoys at over 300 miles from Malayan coast was very good piece of work by No. 1 Squadron R.A.A.F. (Hudson). Impracticable to hand over shadowing to relief aircraft, since patrolling aircraft at limit of their range.
3. Attempt being made to use Beaufort for high photography. Weather in Gulf of Siam now, on the whole, bad for air reconnaissance. One torpedo-bomber squadron is now at Kota Bharu.
4. Malaya is at first degree of readiness and 'Matador' force standing by. Some road blocks are reported in construction by the Thais on the road between Kedah frontier and Singgora and on Kroh road near Betong.

(PWTM & TNA WO 172/15)

No. 19: 1229Z/7/12/41

From the Admiralty   To C.-in-C., Eastern Fleet

MOST IMMEDIATE

Pass to C.-in-C. Far East.

A. No decision has yet been taken by H.M. Government but on the
    assumption that it may be decided that if a Japanese expedition is located
    in the South China Sea in such a position that its course indicates that it is
    proceeding towards Thailand, Malaya, Borneo or Netherlands East Indies,
    report what action it would be possible to take with naval or air forces.
B. Was any co-operation with U.S. Forces in such an eventuality arranged as
    a result of C.-in-C. Eastern Fleet's visit to Manila?

T.O.O. 1329A/7/12/41.

(BS14)

No. 20: 1405Z/7/12/41

From the C-in C, Eastern Fleet   To the Admiralty, repeated C-in-C,
                                          United States Asiatic Fleet

(1405Z/7.)
Your 0950* 7th December, not to other addressees. Presuming you have
received Commander-in-Chief, China 1431,* 6th December, and Captain on
Staff 0622,* 7th December.

2. Aircraft reconnaissance to-day, Sunday, over Gulf of Siam between 101?
    and 104? East as far as 011? North handicapped by poor visibility.
3. One Catalina operating off south-west coast Cambodia has made no report
    and is now overdue.
4. Report from Hudsons:-
    (a) One merchant ship 010? North 101? 30? East, course 270? at 1345.
    (b) One armed Merchant ship 005? 40? North, 106? 30? East, course
        045? at 1430.
    (c) One cruiser, one transport 008? North, 102? 30? East, course 340? at
        1835, aircraft was fired at.
    (d) 4 destroyers 008? 10? North, 101? 15? East, course 180? at 1848.
5. No further contact with convoy previously sighted.
6. Above times zone minus seven and half.
7. Further signal follows regarding 'B' of your 0950Z* 7th December.

* Not reproduced.

(PWTM)

No. 21: 1423Z/7/12/41

From the C-in-C, E. F., C-in-C, F.E.   To the Admiralty for C.O.S.
Committee, with reference to
Telegram No. [15].

(1423Z/7.)

Reference Chief of Staff, Far East, No. 50, paragraph 2 (a). Our reading of instruction is that Naval and Air action against such expedition is not at present authorised. Request confirmation.

(PWTM)

No. 22: 1601Z/7/12/41

From the C. in C. Eastern Fleet   To the Admiralty

MOST IMMEDIATE

Your 1329A 7th.

(a) Naval Forces. If the relative strength of the enemy forces permit endeavour would be made to attack expedition by day or night.

If we are in inferior strength raid will be attempted and Air Force will attack with bombs and torpedoes in conjunction with our naval forces within limit of aircraft radius of action.

(b) Co-operation of (corrupt group) and Dutch forces already fully arranged by C. in C. China and issued in agreed publication entitled 'Plans for employment of naval and Air Forces of associated powers in Eastern Theatre in the event of war with Japan.' Short title 'PLENAPS'.

This publication is in course of transmission to Admiralty by air and left Singapore 30 November.

I fully concur with these plans, though they will of course require modification in detail as strength of Eastern Fleet grow.

Reconnaissance and disposition of naval and Air Forces provided for in these plans is already in force.

T.O.O. 1601Z/7
T.O.R. 1913[A or Z?]/7

(TNA Cab 121/114)

No. 23: 1605Z/7/12/41

From the C-in-C, Far East   To the Admiralty

(1605Z/7.)
Reference Commander-in-Chief, Eastern Fleet's 1431/7,* and Chief of Staff, Far East 50.

(A) Have decided not to operate 'Matador' for following reasons:-
  1. Conditions for reconnaissance were very bad and there can be no real certainty that ships seen were an expedition.
  2. If expedition is, in fact, aimed at Singgora Region it can reach there before we arrive. 'Matador' is designed only to forestall a connection expedition.
  3. · If conclusions drawn from reconnaissance prove incorrect we should incur all disadvantages of first breaking Thai neutrality.
  4. Switch movements are consistent with a deliberate attempt to induce us to violate Thai neutrality.

(B) If Japanese do land in Southern Kra Isthmus is it to be assumed we are at war with Japan? Commander-in-Chief, Eastern Fleet, concurs.

*Not reproduced.

                                                                    (PWTM)

No. 24: 1710Z/7/12/41

From Opnav   To the Admiralty

(1710Z/7.)
Personal from Chief Naval Officer[2] for First Sea Lord:-
  Have you received copy of agreement between Admiral Hart and Phillips?
                                                                    (PWTM)

No. 25: 1731Z/7/12/41

From The Eastern Fleet   To the Admiralty, repeated
                                               Commander-in-Chief, Far East, &c.

(1731Z/7.)
Chief of Staff, Far East, 50, reached me at Manila, when I was in conference with Admiral Hart, P.M. 6th December, and I showed it to him. He had not then received corresponding instructions from Chief Naval Officer.

He asked what 'Matador' was, and I showed him on map.
In neither case was anything given to him in writing.

(PWTM)

No. 26: 1733Z/7/12/41

From C.-in-C., Eastern Fleet   To the Admiralty

Personal for 1st Sea Lord.

63.1 Discussion with Admiral Hart very friendly and we can expect full co-operation.
   2 Draft of points of agreement, transmitted via C.N.O. was originally drawn up to provide discussion, but at conclusion Admiral Hart was very anxious to telegraph this to Washington and London.* I reluctantly agreed, making it clear that I had not yet met Dominion and Dutch and would have preferred to do so before sending any signal home.
   3 Admiral Hart was reluctant to part with his destroyers even when at war and this is referred to in point of agreement. He was not willing to send them to Singapore at once but I have again asked him today to send four in view of situation.
   4 Dutch Admiral arrives tomorrow Monday and I hope to make sufficient progress with Dominion representative to be able to ask him and U.S. representative to meeting in the afternoon.

T.O.O. 1733Z/7 [0103/GH/8/12].
T.O.R. 1230Z/11/12/41.

*This signal is omitted, as the points agreed on were rendered nugatory by the Japanese action.[3]

(BS14)

No. 27: 1746Z/7/12/41

From the Commander-in-Chief, China   To the Admiralty

(1746Z/7.)
Report from Kota Bharu an attempt is being made to land from 3 or 5 ships, one landing craft already approaching mouth of river. Kota Bharu 006? North, 102? 10? East.

(PWTM)

No. 28: 1848Z/7/12/41

From The Admiralty   To the Commander-in-Chief, Eastern Fleet.

(1948A/7.)
Following from Chiefs of Staff to Commander-in-Chief, Eastern Fleet, pass to Commander-in-Chief, Far East:-

1. Following is present state of negotiations in Washington and is for your personal information only:-
2. As reported in the press, the President addressed to the Japanese a direct question as to the reason for their concentration of troops in Southern Indo-China. The reply to this question was evasive and unsatisfactory. The President accordingly has sent a message to the Emperor of Japan recounting the long history of peace between the two countries, drawing attention to the unjustifiable concentration of troops in all parts of Indo-China and urging him to withdraw in the interests of peace.
3. If the President receives no answer by Monday evening (Washington time) he will publish the message. If by Tuesday afternoon no reply is received, or if the answer is unsatisfactory, President will send a warning to the Japanese Government that if the Japanese make an attack on Thailand, Malaya, Burma or the Netherlands East Indies, it will be regarded as a hostile act. This warning would be followed on Wednesday morning by similar warnings from ourselves and the Dutch. This time-table is subject to speeding up if the Japanese move faster.
4. In the meanwhile, the President sent a confidential message to the Thai Prime Minister to the effect that the United States would regard it as a hostile act if the Japanese invaded Thailand, Malaya, Burma or the East Indies. A similar message is now being conveyed to the Thai Prime Minister on our behalf.
5. The way is thus clear for us to act against the Japanese in the event of –
   (a) An attack on British or United States territory,
   (b) An attack on Dutch territory
   (c) An attack on, or entry by invitation into any part of Thailand, with the knowledge that we shall be certain of United States armed support.
6. Instructions for carrying out 'Matador' contained in War Office telegram 55982* (M.O. 10) of 5/12 hold good. Further instructions will shortly be sent as to whether or not a Japanese expedition can be attacked at sea before any hostile act against the United States, the Dutch or ourselves or any Japanese entry into Thai territory has taken place.

*Telegram No. [15]

(PWTM)

No. 29: 1925Z/7/12/41

From Opnav, 1925/7   To D.N.I. Admiralty

Hostilities with Japan commenced with air raid on Pearl Harbour at 1830Z. Inform British, Dutch, and Spenavo.
Note: No action by War Registry to inform Dutch Authorities.

(AWD)

No. 30: 2043Z/712/41

From The Admiralty   To A Message Home and Abroad.

(2143A/7.)
Commence hostilities against Japan at once.
Note.-Above message has been passed to Spenavo.

(PWTM)

No. 31: 2054Z/7/12/41

From the Commander-in-Chief, China   To the Admiralty.

(2054Z/7.)
Air attack by 18 aircraft carried out in Singapore Island at 2030Z/7.

(PWTM)

No. 32: 2200Z/7/12/41

From The Admiralty   To Opnav in reply to telegram No. [24]
(2200Z/7.)
Personal for C.N.O. from 1st Sea Lord:-
    Your 1710Z/7.
    No; but I am expecting it at any moment. In any case, as long as you are happy about it, I have complete confidence in anything Admiral Phillips has agreed to, and I am sure we can rely on our representatives on the spot to acquit themselves forcefully.

(PWTM)

No. 33: 2247Z/7/12/41

From C. in C. E.F., 2247Z/7   To C. in C. E.I.

Revenge is to proceed to Colombo at best speed.

(AWD)

No. 34: 2249Z/7/12/41

From C. in C. E.F., 2249Z/7   To C. in C. E.I. [East Indies]

Exeter is to leave her convoy and proceed Singapore at best speed reporting E.T.A.

(AWD)

8 December 1941
No. 35: 0014Z/8/12/41

From 1st S.L. 0114A/8   To C. in C. E.F.

Cancel Adm. 2336/7, as report has now been received through Opnav.

(AWD)

No. 36: 0204Z/8/12/41

From C. in C. E.F.   To the Admiralty

0204Z/8
(1) (corrupt group: (?) Provided that) as I hope I can make 4 destroyers available intended to proceed with *Prince of Wales* and *Repulse* dusk tonight 8/12 to attack enemy force off Kota Bharu daylight Wednesday 10th. (2) Endevours will be made to estimate strength of enemy naval forces by air R/C, but large proportion of aircraft are naturally required for attack.

(AWD & BS14)

No. 37: 0251Z/8/12/41

From C. in C. E.F., 0251Z/8   To the Admiralty

My 0204Z/8.
1. All water in South China Sea is readily minable and need for more T.S.D.S. destroyers is urgent. *Jupiter* has been a notorious crock for some months and is liable to stop suddenly at any moment. I am putting her in hand for re-riveting oil tank, time required about 3 weeks. *Encounter* has had to be docked for renewal of stern bush(es) but will be completed 11/12.
2. I have ordered 2 S class destroyers from Hong Kong to Manila if possible for them to sail.
3. I have ordered *Exeter* to Singapore and N.B. Wellington have been asked to send *Achilles* to Singapore.
4. *Mauritius* refit is being hastened as much as possible.

5. Request *Hobart* be ordered East, question of her destination is being discussed with N.B. Melbourne.
6. Need for further modern cruisers is great.
7. Request reply to my 1015/3 re *Royal Sovereign*.

(AWD)

No. 38: 0254Z/8/12/41

From C. in C. E.F. 0254Z/8   To Admiralty

My 2030/7, 2054 intended. No damage H.M. ships or Naval establishments.

(AWD)

No. 39: 0322Z/8/12/41

From Spenavo   To the Admiralty

(0322/8.)

Following is paraphrase of message from Opnav to Spenavo, London:-

'Admiral Bloch talked on the telephone with Admiral Stark at 1820. G.C. T. 7th December. The following is a synopsis of the conversation:

At 1830 G.C. T. Japanese attacked with bombs and torpedoes from submarines and aircraft. On two of the planes were swastikas. In the two attacks made the severe damage inflicted by the Japanese:-

(1) In Pearl Harbour the *Oklahoma* turned over. The *Tennessee* has a bad list and is on fire and attempting to dock her. *Pennsylvania* was in No. 1 dry dock, which was hit by bombs, but the *Pennsylvania* is apparently undamaged. Two destroyers in dry dock were hit, one of which has blown up. In the floating dock one destroyer is on fire. The dock is being flooded in an effort to save her. The sea wall between the *Helena* and the *Oglala* was hit by torpedoes. The *Oglala* is on fire and badly listed. She probably cannot be saved.
(2) The power-house at Pearl Harbour was bombed but was not made inoperative. The Oahu Power Company evidently hit because no civilian power in Honolulu.
(3) Kaneohoe Wheeler, Ford Island and Hickham airfields attacked. Hangars set on fire, those at Hickham very bad. Patrol planes on the apron at Ford Island set on fire. At Kaneohoe patrol planes also burning.
(4) Number of personnel casualties apparently heavy.
(5) Honolulu evidently not attacked.
(6) Earliest notice of danger came from a plane which spotted some Jap submarines off the Pearl Harbour entrance; these submarines were

attacked by destroyers with results unknown to Admiral Bloch. One Jap submarine was sunk by aircraft.

(7) Kimmel is at sea with two task forces, each with a carrier. What action he has taken Bloch did not know.

(8) The Japs were attacked by United States fighter planes and Bloch knows of at least two Jap planes brought down.'

(PWTM)

No. 40: 0452Z/8/12/41

From C-in-C E.F. C-in-C F.E.   To C.Z.M. (R)[4] A.O.C.F.E., G.O.C. Malaya

Intend sailing at 1100Z/8/12/41 with *Prince of Wales*, *Repulse* and four destroyers with the object of attacking enemy transports reported between Singora and Pattanni.

2. This force will be known as Force Z.
3. Speed of advance will be 17 knots and course will be shaped through:-
     Point A 02 degs. 37'N. 106 degs. 28'E.
     Point B 03 degs. 25'N. 106 degs. 40'E.
     Point C 06 degs. 15'N. 103 degs. 17'E.
4. Anticipate arrival off objective dawn 10th December.
5. Request all Dutch forces concerned may be informed accordingly.
Acknowledge.

T.O.O. 0452Z/8/12/41
(TNA Adm 199/1149, at 42 & Air 23/4745)

No. 41: 0505Z/8/12/41

From C. in C. E.F., 0505Z/8   To C. in C. Pacific Fleet

After recent discussions with C. in C. U.S. Asiatic Fleet and Australian and New Zealand Naval authorities a redistribution of Aust. and N.Z. cruisers has been proposed in an endeavour to collect cruisers for operation with British Battle Fleet and as a striking force along Malay Barrier.

2. This will leave insufficient escort for following:-
     (a) Trans-Pacific shipping between N.Z. and Panama.
     (b) Air trainees in Matson liners from Auckland to San Francisco.
     (c) Shipping between Torres Strait and U.S.A.
3. As majority of this shipping passes through the Pacific area as defined in A.B.C. 1, of which portions have now been classified as danger areas, it

would be very much appreciated if any assistance could be given for escorting this shipping. I should be grateful if you would communicate your intentions in this manner direct to A.C.N.B.

(AWD)

No. 42: 0530Z/8/12/41

From The Commander-in-Chief, Far East   To the War Office,
repeated Commander-in-
Chief, Asiatic Fleet, &c.

(422/6. 8/12.)
Following for Chiefs of Staff from Commanders-in-Chief Far East, and Eastern Fleet:-
Far Eastern situation report. 0930 hours local time, 8/12.

1. *Malaya.*–Landing occurred from about five Japanese ships between Kelatan River and Sabak shortly after 0130 hours, 8/12. Later force of ten merchant ships was seen some ten miles to the south. Considerable fighting took place north of Kota Bharu aerodrome, details of which will follow. By 0800 hours all surface craft retiring course 330. Mopping up operations in progress on shore. Air attacks at night claim hits on two ships, which were left on fire. Attacks by Wildebeest Torpedo Aircraft and Blenheims have also been made, results not yet known. Two Hudsons and one Catalina so far reported missing from operations. Gong Kedak and Machang aerodromes in Kelantan bombed this morning. No damage reported. Machang unoccupied. Light scale air raid on Singapore Island at 0415 hours, 8 12, concentrated mainly on Seletar and Tengah Aerodromes. No appreciable damage reported.
2. *Hong Kong.* . . .
3. No news from Thailand. Reconnaissance to the northward including Singgora left 0730 local time, has reported landings at Patani and was attacked by six fighters at Singgora. Further reconnaissance at Singgora area being made by Buffaloes.

(PWTM & TNA WO 172/15)

No. 43: 0540Z&1310GH/8/12/41

From the Commander-in-Chief, Far East   To the War Office

(423/6. 8/12.)
For Chiefs of Staff Committee from C-in-C, Far East, and C-in-C, Eastern Fleet:-

1. It appears to us that outcome of battle in Northern Malaya will largely turn on number of available aircraft.
2. Should Japan gain air superiority situation would be very difficult.
3. With our present reserves it is unlikely to be practicable to maintain present effort for more than two or three weeks. We consequently wish to emphasise the need for the maximum practicable air reinforcements as early as possible. Particular types required are long-range bomber and night fighter. We require two squadrons of each of these, with adequate reserves and spares.

(PWTM)

No. 44: 1521Z/8/12/41

From Chief of Staff, Eastern Fleet   To C.-in-C., Eastern Fleet

My 2253/8th Part 1 begins. R.A.F. reconnaissance to depth of 100 miles to the north-westward of you will be provided by 1 Catalina from 0800 onwards tomorrow 9th.

(ii) It is hoped that a dawn reconnaissance of coast near Singora can be carried out on Wednesday 10th.

(iii) Fighter protection on Wednesday 10th will not, repeat not, be possible. My 2253/8th Part 1 end. Part 2 follows.

T.O.O. 2251 GH/8.

T.O.R. 0106/9/12.

(BS14)

No. 45: 1523Z/8/12/41

From Chief of Staff, Eastern Fleet   To C.-in-C., Eastern Fleet

My 2253/8th Part 2.

(iv) Japanese have large bomber forces based Southern Indo-China and possibly also in Thailand. C.-in-C., Far East, has requested General MacArthur to carry out attack with his long-range bombers on Indo-China aerodromes as soon as possible.

(v) Kota Bharu aerodrome has been evacuated and we seem to be losing grip on other northern aerodromes due to enemy action.

(vi) Military position near Kota Bharu does not seem good, but details are not available.

T.O.O. 2253 GH/8.

T.O.R. 0125/9/12.

(BS14)

No. 46: 2351Z/8/12/41

From 1st S.L., 0051A/9   To C. in C. E.F.

Your 0251Z/8.

A. Your para. 7 (your 1015/3 also refers) *Royal Sovereign* arrives Durban with W.S.12 Z on 17/12. At the moment we do not know what scale of attack the Japanese are likely to bring on to our convoy routes. From C. in C., E. I. 0454Z/6 it appears that the only alternative escort that he can provide is *Emerald* as far as Mombasa and then Colombo; this appears inadequate if there is any chance of a Japanese 8-inch cruiser being in the area. It would appear therefore that *Royal Sovereign* should remain with W.S. 12 Z at least as far as Seychelles.

B. *Royal Sovereign* is more or less worked up but before joining you, she should do one further series of practice shoots, which presumably can be done at Trincomalee.

C. *Ramillies* is bringing out W.S.14 which is a large convoy of 32 ships. Weather conditions at Scapa prevented her completing her work up and she needs further shoots of all types.

D. *Resolution* is working up now and will escort W.S. 15 leaving 7/1. She will have had 6 weeks working up.

E. Your para 1. We have now had to send Force 'H' destroyers to Eastern Mediterranean to assist with our supply routes and to cut the enemy's. At least until the Cyrenaican situation is cleared up it will not be possible to send you any more British destroyers. As Americans are not now taking over Force H., so enabling us to send you 8 Destroyers, I am asking C.N.O. if the 6 American destroyers now escorting W.S. 12 X. could join you as part of the additional reinforcements and in addition to the 8 they have already allocated to you.

F. Your para. 5. This will be done.

G. Your para. 6. It is regretted that no further cruisers can be sent to join Eastern Fleet.

(AWD)

9 December 1941

No. 47: 0530Z/9/12/41

From the Commander-in-Chief, Far East To the War Office. Addressed all concerned.

(Unnumbered. 9/12.)
Following from Commanders-in-Chief, Far East and Eastern Fleet. for Chiefs of Staff: -

Situation report local time 0900 hours.

1. *Malaya* – Now three areas of land operations. Kelantan. South Thailand, immediately north of Kedah frontier. South Thailand, north-east of Kroh. Further landings took place at Badang.

   Kelantan. – All aircraft left Kota Bharu aerodrome, which was threatened by enemy ground troops, at 1620 hours 8th December and flew to Kuantan. At 0800 hours 9th December Kota Bharu aerodrome had been demolished and 8th Brigade holding line just north of Kota Bharu. Kemassin Beach evacuated. Considerable infiltration and working round flanks by well-armed enemy. Position confused. No activity front from Melawi to Semerak. Enemy believed to have ships behind Perhentian Islands, from which they are landing troops and stores by lighters. No. A.F.Vs. yet known to have landed. One battalion and one field battery ordered to Kelantan.

   South Thailand.-11th Division Reconnaissance crossed frontier P.M. 8th December and made contact with enemy at Ban Sadao. Enemy had ten A.F.V.'s; after inflicting casualties our forces withdrew, destroying two major bridges between Ban Sadao and frontier. Klong Neagh railway bridge demolished by our armoured train 0500 hours. Krohcol crossed frontier P.M. 8th December. Advance to ledge position, initially opposed by Thai police, now been resumed.

2. *Air.*-Enemy have concentrated on our aerodromes, and during 8th December bombed Kota Bharu, Gong Kedak, Maching, Alor Star, Sungei Patani, Butterworth and Penang. Heaviest attacks were at Sungai Patani, where number of our fighters destroyed on ground and most buildings destroyed. Alor Star and Sungei Patani aerodromes unable to operate and have been evacuated. 18 Dutch bombers arrived Sembawang to-day.

   Search at sea by two Vildebeests from Kuantan commenced 0200 hours. Negative report.

   Three air raid warnings at Singapore during night 8th/9th and early 9th, but no raids developed.

   To sum up. The success of the attacks on our northern aerodromes is handicapping our air action and this will have an effect upon the fighting on land.

3. *Thailand.*-In addtion to landings at Singgora and Pattani. Burma report, 0113 9th December, local wireless intercept stating landings at Huahin Prachuabkirikhan, which may be a threat to Mergui. Another intercept stated Thais ordered to cease fire at 0730 hours 8th December.

4. *Hong Kong.* . . .

5. *Naval.* – Our forces are operating in the South China Sea.

(PWTM & TNA WO 172/15 at 209)

No. 48: 0545Z/9/12/41

From C.-in-C., Eastern Fleet   To Force 'Z'

Besides a minor landing at Kota Bharu which was not followed, landings have been made between Patani and Singora and a major landing 90 miles north of Singora.

2. Little is know of enemy major forces in the vicinity. It is believed that *Kongo* is the only capital ship likely to be met. Three *Atago* type, one *Kako* type, and two *Zintu* type cruisers have been reported. A number of destroyers possibly of Fleet type are likely to be met.

3. My object is to surprise and sink transports and enemy warships before air attack can develop. Objective chosen will depend on air reconnaissance. Intend to arrive objective after sunrise tomorrow 10th. If an opportunity to bring *Kongo* to action occurs this is to take precedence over all other action.

4. Subject to C.O.'s freedom of manoeuvre in an emergency, Force 'Z' will remain in close order and will be manoeuvred as a unit until action is joined. When the signal 'Act independently' is made or at the discretion of C.O., *Repulse* will assume freedom of manoeuvre remaining in tactical support but engaging from a wide enough angle to facilitate fall of shot.

5. Intend to operate at 25 knots unless a chase develops and subsequently to retire at maximum speed endurance will allow.

6. Capital ships should attempt to close below 20,000 yards until fire is effective, but should avoid offering an end on target. Ships must be prepared to change from delay to non-delay fuzes according to target.

7. *Prince of Wales* and *Repulse* are each to have one aircraft fuelled and ready to fly off if required. If flown off aircraft must return to land base. Kota Bharu aerodrome is understood to be out of action.

8. *Tenedos* will be detached before dark to return independently to Singapore.

9. Remaining destroyers may be detached during the night of 9th/10th should enemy information require a high speed of advance. In such case these destroyers are to retire towards Anamba Island at 10 knots until a rendezvous is ordered by W/T.

1315 GH/9/12/41.
(BS14)

No. 49: 1125Z/9/12/41

From Chief of Staff, Eastern Fleet   To C.-in-C., Eastern Fleet.

MOST IMMEDIATE

One battleship, 'M' class cruiser, 11 destroyers and a number of transports reported close to coast between Kota Bharu and Perhentian Island by air reconnaissance this afternoon.

> T.O.O. 1125 Z/9/12/41 (1855 GH/9/12).
> T.O.R. 1147Z/9/12/41 (1917 GH/9/12)
> (BS14)

No. 50: 1155Z/9/12/41

From Chief of Staff, Eastern Fleet   To C.-in-C., Eastern Fleet.

Correct my 1125/9.   Force was sighted at 0900 Z/9 (1925 GH/9).

> T.O.O. 1155Z/9/12/41 (1925 GH/9).
> (BS14)

No. 51: 1415Z/9/41

From Chief of Staff, Eastern Fleet   To C.-in-C., Eastern Fleet

IMMEDIATE

To C.-in-C., E.F. Only significant enemy reports is [sic] contained in my 1126 Z 9th. Enemy apparently continuing landing in Kota Bharu area which should be fruitful as well as Singora.

(1) On the other hand enemy bombers on South Indo-China aerodromes are in force and undisturbed. They could attack you five hours after sighting and much depends on whether you have been seen to-day.
      Two carriers may be in Saigon area.
(2) Military situation at Kota Bharu appears difficult. Aerodrome is in enemy hands.
(3) All our northern aerodromes are becoming untenable due to enemy air action. C.-in-C., F.E. hints he is considering concentrating all air efforts on defence of Singapore area.
(4) Extremely difficult to give you clearer picture because air reconnaissance communications are so slow due to damage to aerodromes.

> T.O.O. 1415 Z/9 (2145 GH/9).
> T.O.R. 1532 Z/9 (2302 GH/9).
> (BS14)

No. 52: 1501Z/9/12/41

From the Chief of Staff, Singapore   To the Admiralty for D.N.I.

(1501Z/9)
From W/T Traffic.

Saigon Area.-Third Aircraft Carrier Squadron, Commander-in-Chief Southern Expeditionary Fleet, Commander-in-Chief Combined Air Force, one Seaplane Tender Squadron.

Sama Area.-Commander-in-Chief Combined Fleet, Commander-in-Chief Third Fleet, some unidentified Auxiliaries and Naval Units.

Hong Kong Area.-Flagship Commander-in-Chief South China Fleet.

Truk Area.-Flagship of Commander-in-Chief Fourth Fleet. Aircraft concentrations in Formosa. Air W/T traffic generally heavy. Large volume of W/T traffic originating in Jaluit addressed to Commander-in-Chief Combined Fleet.

From Aircraft Sighting: P.M. 9th December one Battleship, three Cruisers, eleven Destroyers and a number of transports reported close to coast between Kota Bharu and Perhentian Islands. No details received.

(PWTM)

No. 53: 1515Z/9/12/41

To C.-in-C., Eastern Fleet   From Chief of Staff, Eastern Fleet

IMMEDIATE.

Enemy reported landing Kuantan, latitude 03° 50' North.

T.O.O. 1515 Z/9/12/41 (2235 GH/9)
T.O.R. 1605 Z/9/12/41 (2355 GH/9)
(BS14)

No. 54: 1729Z/9/12/41

From the Admiralty   To C.-in-C., E.F.

IMPORTANT

Personal from First Sea Lord.

As torpedo aircraft attack on ships at anchor in Johore strait cannot be ruled out, I am sure you have in mind, M/LD. 02033/41, Dated 22 April 1941, Paragraph 18-(14), which you took so much interest in.

T.O.O. 1829A/9
T.O.R. 2210Z/9/12/41
(TNA Adm 199/1149, at 85)

10 December 1941

No. 55: 0517Z/10/12/41

From The Commander-in-Chief, Far East To the War Office, repeated All
Concerned.

(463/6. 10/12.)
Following from Commanders-in-Chief, Far East and Eastern Fleet for Chiefs of
Staff:-
    My 441/6 9/12.* Sitrep's local time 0400 hours 10th December.

1. *Malaya.*-During 9th December Air Reconnaissance reported one battleship,
    two cruisers, seven destroyers and number of transports off Kota Bharu, one
    transport off Kuantan and fifteen transports and one aircraft carrier off
    Singgora. Eleven Blenheims bombed Singgora Aerodrome, where forty
    bombers were seen on ground and approximately forty fighters were
    airborne. Result of raid not observed. Five Blenheims lost. Heavy enemy
    attacks on Alor Star, Sungei Oatani, Butterworth and Kuantan Aerodromes.
    At Sungei Patani five enemy planes brought down, four by A.A. guns;
    Kuantan Aerodrome evacuated by our aircraft. Dutch fighter squadron has
    arrived Singapore. Kedah 11th Division no change. Seven enemy light tanks
    destroyed. Krohcol at Betong 1800 hrs. 9th December. Kelantan 8th
    Brigade now on line Peringat-Mulong. Reinforcements have arrived.
    Kuantan at 2200 hrs. 9th December enemy landed in small numbers just
    north of Beserah. These were driven off and 0845 10th December all quiet.
    One battalion ordered to Jerantut to reinforce Kuantan if required. Sarawak-
    Miri oil denial scheme completed and destruction of aerodrome proceeding.
    To sum up, enemy primary object appears to be to establish aerodromes in
    Northern Malay and at same time he is testing our defences on wide front.
2. *Hong Kong.* . . .

*Not reproduced.

(PWTM)

No. 56: 0030Z&0800GH/10/12/41

From C.-in-C. [E.F.]   To Chief of Staff, Eastern Fleet

IMMEDIATE

Earliest time Force 'Z' is likely to reach point B1 of my 1340 GH/8 is 0630/11
and point A2 at 0900/11. You should send as many effective destroyers,

including U.S., as available, to pass through point A and meet me at daylight 11th if possible. Point B will probably be approached on course 130? Acknowledge.

T.O.O. 1455 GH/9/12/41.

Note: This signal was given to the *Tenedos* at 1625/9 for transmission at 0800/10, by which time she would be off the Anambas. The *Tenedos* was detached from Force 'Z' at 1835/9.

(BS14)

No. 57: 0141Z/10/12/41

From Chief of Staff, Eastern Fleet   To C-in-C, Eastern Fleet

IMMEDIATE

Enemy forces 15 transports and an aircraft carrier reported off SINGORA at 1600GH/9th December.

T.O.O. 0141Z/10
T.O.R. 0222Z/10
(TNA Adm 199/1149, at 86)

Nos. 58–61: 0225Z to 0300Z/10/12/41
(Signals from HMS *Tenedos*)

From HMS *Tenedos*   To Singapore

58. T.O.O. 0955GH   Am being attacked by Enemy A/C in position 2 08N 105 78E.

59. T.O.O. 1005GH   24 Enemy Aircraft bearing 350 degrees 15 miles course 020. My position 080 41 miles from 2 105 E

60. T.O.O. 1020GH   15 Enemy _ 220 degrees 10,000 feet My position 088 38 miles from 2 N 105E.

61. T.O.O. 1030GH   OEAB. Enemy Aircraft dropping bombs.
(TNA ADM 199/1149)

Nos. 62–70: 0428Z to 0548Z/10/12/41
(Signals from Force Z)

62. T.O.O. 1158GH   From *Repulse* to Any British Man-of-
                                          War

Enemy aircraft bombing. My position 134 NYTW 22 x 09.

                                          T.O.R. 1204GH

63. T.O.O. 1220GH   From (?) *Prince of Wales* to (?)

EMERGENCY. Have been struck by a torpedo on port side. NYTW 0222 RO6 4
torpedoes. *Repulse* hit by 1 torpedo. Send destroyers.

                                          T.O.R. 1240GH

64. T.O.O. 1252GH   From Senior Officer, Force 'Z' to Any
                                          British Man-of-War

EMERGENCY. Send all available tugs. My position 003° 40' N. 104° 30' E.

                                          T.O.R. 1304GH

65. T.O.O. 1300GH   From *Electra* to (?) Any British Man-of-
                                          War

MOST IMMEDIATE. H.M.S. *Prince of Wales* hit by 4 torpedoes in position
003°45' N. 104° 10' E. *Repulse* sunk. Send destroyers.

                                          T.O.R. 1310GH

66. T.O.O. 1300GH   From Senior Officer, Force 'Z' to Any
                                          British Man-of-War

IMMEDIATE. H.M.S. *Prince of Wales* disabled and out of control.

                                          T.O.R. 1310GH

67. T.O.O. 1301GH.   From *Prince of Wales* to Any British
                                          Man-of-War

EMERGENCY. Send all available tugs. My position now is EQTW 40 (?).

                                          T.O.R. 1311GH

68. T.O.O.1307GH?   From C-in-C, Eastern Fleet to Chief of
                                          Staff, Singapore

MOST IMMEDIATE. Am disembarking men not required for fighting ship. Send – (?) – (?) – fast as possible.

T.O.R. 1317GH

69. T.O.O. 1307GH?   From *Electra* to Any British Man-of War

MOST IMMEDIATE. My 0530 send tugs. (?)

T.O.R. 1317GH

70. T.O.O. 1318 GH   From *Electra* to Any British Man-of War

IMMEDIATE. H.M.S. *Prince of Wales* sunk.

T.O.R. 1321GH
(BS14)

No. 71: 0615Z/10/12/41

From the Chief of Staff, Eastern Fleet   To the Admiralty

(0615Z/10)
H.M.S. *Prince of Wales* and H.M.S. *Repulse* sunk by torpedoes at about 1317GH/10 in position 003? 40? North, 104? 30? East.

(PWTM)

No. 72: 0807Z/10/12/41

From the Chief of Staff, Eastern Fleet   To the Admiralty

(0807Z/10)
My 0615Z, 10th. Details not available, but will be forwarded as soon as possible. It will be impossible to keep news secret locally for more than a few hours. Commander-in-Chief, Far East, concurs.

(PWTM)

No. 73: 0956Z/1012/41

From the Admiralty

To the Chief of Staff, Eastern Fleet, repeated Commander-in-Chief, East Indies

(1056A/10)
Following from First Sea Lord for Admiral Layton. Pending information as to casualties in *Prince of Wales* you should remain at Singapore. Pass to Commander-in-Chief, Far East.

(PWTM)

No. 74: 1710Z/10/12/41

From C. in C. E.F., 1701Z/10

To the Admiralty

My 1555. Capt. L.H. Bell, Capt. of Fleet, has been interviewed on landing. His account of todays proceeding indicates that the C. in C's intentions were, up to about 1700/9 to attack transport off Songhkla, relying on surprise failing the provision of fighter protection which in fact could not be provided. Up to that time he had not as far as he knew been located by air R/C owing to low clouds. At that time clouds cleared and three Japanese A/Cs were sighted. As a result of this he decided to return at full speed to Singapore. About midnight he received information that a seaborne attack was developing on Kuantan and decided to investigate and attack. On arrival (of) at Kuantan 0800 nothing was in sight but he had passed (corrupt group) down a tug with possible landing craft in tow and so turned back to deal with them. It was approx. at this time that first attack by H.L.B took place. Attack was well carried out at about 11,000 feet and hits scored abreast main mast of *Repulse*. This was followed by air attack by 9 (?torpedo/bombing aircraft) on *Prince of Wales*. Attack was pushed well home and skilfully carried out. One if not 2 hits were scored and extensive flooding caused, 2 engine rooms being put out of action and speed reduced to 12 knots. A second attack by 9 torpedo bombing aircraft on *Prince of Wales* scored a further 2 hits. A third T/B aircraft attack, again by 9 aircraft, but this time on *Repulse* scored 2 or 3 hits and she turned over and sank in a few minutes. A H.L.B attack was then carried out on *Prince of Wales* from 10,000 feet and one hit with probably 1000lb bomb was obtained. Finally another T.B attack was carried out which scored at least one more hit and ship heeled slowly to port and capsized in about 20 minutes. Captain Bell emphasized skill with which all attacks were carried out and determination with which they were pressed home. About 7 aircraft were shot down. By direction of V.A. Sir G. Layton fact finding enquiry will be started tomorrow to obtain fullest possible information.

(AWD)

No. 75: 2025Z/10/12/41

From 1st Sea Lord   To C-in-C A.W.I. [American West Indies]

A.M.1809A/7. On completion of visit to Trinidad C.-in-C. A.W.I. is requested to sail *Indomitable* for Durban [South Africa] direct.

2. C. in C. S.A. [South Africa] is requested to arrange onward route within his command.

(AWD)

No. 76: 2150Z/10/12/41

From lst S.L. 2250A/10   To C.O.S., Eastern Fleet

Personal for Vice Adm. Layton.

Until it is known whether Adm. Sir Tom Phillips is one of the survivors you are to carry out the duties of: C. in C. Eastern Fleet, and have discretion whether to fly your flag on shore or afloat.

(AWD)

Notes

1 A copy of this signal is found in TNA Adm 116/4877, at 86–88.

2 Author's note: Should read 'Chief of Naval Operations'.

3 So noted by the Naval Historical Branch. The message can be found in *Pearl Harbor Hearings*, vol. 4, at 1933–5.

4 Commander-in-Chief Netherlands Naval Forces in the East Indies. Compare entries in Admiral Layton's war diaries, TNA Adm 199/1185, with Adm 199/1473, e.g. 4 December 1941.

Select Bibliography

BOOKS

Ash, Bernard, *Someone Had Blundered*, Garden City, NY, Doubleday & Co., 1961

Barnett, Correlli, *Engage the Enemy More Closely*, New York and London, W.W. Norton & Co., 1991

Beesly, Patrick, *Very Special Intelligence: The Story of the Admiralty's Operational Intelligence Centre 1939–1945*, Garden City, NY, Doubleday & Co., 1978

Bennett, Geoffrey, *Loss of Prince of Wales and Repulse*, Annapolis, Naval Institute Press, 1973

Bix, Herbert P., *Hirohito and the Making of Modern Japan*, New York, HarperCollins Publishers Inc., 2000

Brodhurst, Robin, *Churchill's Anchor: Admiral of the Fleet Sir Dudley Pound, OM, GCB, GCVO*, Barnsley, South Yorkshire, Leo Cooper, 2000

Brooke, Geoffrey, *Alarm Starboard!: A Remarkable True Story of the War at Sea*, Cambridge, Patrick Stephens, 1982

Brown, Cecil, *From Suez to Singapore*, New York, Random House, 1942

Burt, R.A., *British Battleships 1919–1939*, London, Arms and Armour Press, 1993

Cain, T.J. and Sellwood, A.V., *H.M.S. Electra*, London, Frederick Muller Ltd, 1959

Campbell, John, *Naval Weapons of World War Two*, London, Conway Maritime Press, 1985

Chapman, John W.M., ed. and trans. *The Price of Admiralty: The War Diary of the German Naval Attaché in Japan, 1939–1943, Vols 2 and 3 (23 August 1940 to 9 September 1941)*, Ripe, East Sussex, Saltire Press, 1984

Churchill, Winston S., *The Second World War, Vol. 3: The Grand Alliance*, Boston, Houghton Mifflin Co., 1950

Costello, John, *Days of Infamy*, New York, Pocket Books, 1994

Elphick, Peter, *Far Eastern File: The Intelligence War in the Far East 1930–1945*, London, Hodder & Stoughton, 1997

Falk, Stanley, *Seventy Days to Singapore*, New York, G.P. Putnam's Sons, 1975

Forester, C.S., *Sink the Bismarck!*, New York, Bantam Books, 1959

Franklin, Alan, and Franklin, Gordon, *One Year of Life*, Edinburgh and London, William Blackwood & Sons Ltd, 1944

Gallager, O'Dowd, *Action in the East*, New York, Doubleday, Doran & Co., 1942

Gannon, Michael, *Pearl Harbor Betrayed*, New York, Henry Holt & Co., 2001

Garzke, William H. Jr and Dulin, Robert O. Jr, *Battleships: Allied Battleships of World War II*, Annapolis, Naval Institute Press, 1980

Gilbert, Martin, *Winston S. Churchill, Vol. 6: Finest Hour 1939–1941; Vol. 7: Road to Victory 1941–1945; Vol. 8: 'Never Despair' 1945–1965*, Boston, Houghton Mifflin Co., 1983, 1986, 1988

Gilchrist, Sir Andrew, *Malaya 1941: The Fall of a Fighting Empire*, London, Robert Hale, 1992

Gill, G. Hermon, *Royal Australian Navy 1939–1942*, Canberra, Australian War Memorial, 1957

Gillison, Douglas, *Royal Australian Air Force 1939–1942*, Canberra, Australian War Memorial, 1962

Gray, Edwyn, *Operation Pacific*, Annapolis, Naval Institute Press, 1989

Green, William, *Warplanes of the Second World War: Fighters*, vol. 4, New York, Doubleday & Co., 1961

Grenfell, Russell, *Main Fleet to Singapore*, London, Faber & Faber Ltd, 1951

Haggie, Paul, *Britannia at Bay: The Defence of the British Empire against Japan 1931–1941*, Oxford, Clarendon Press, 1981.

Hayes, Vice-Admiral John, *Face the Music: A Sailor's Story*, Edinburgh, Pentland Press Ltd, 1991

Hobbs, David, *Aircraft Carriers of the Royal and Commonwealth Navies*, London, Greenhill Books, 1996

Hough, Richard, *The Hunting of Force Z: Britain's Greatest Modern Naval Disaster*, London, Collins, 1963

Howse, Derek, *Radar at Sea: The Royal Navy in World War 2*, Annapolis, Naval Institute Press, 1993

Irving, David, *Churchill's War, Vol. 2: Triumph in Adversity*, London, Focal Point Productions Ltd, 2001

Kirby, S. Woodburn, *The War Against Japan, Vol. 1: The Loss of Singapore*, London, HMSO, 1957

Kirby, S. Woodburn, *Singapore: The Chain of Disaster*, New York, Macmillan Co., 1971

Leach, Admiral of the Fleet Sir Henry, *Endure No Makeshifts: Some Naval Recollections*, London, Leo Cooper, 1993

Lenton, H.T., *British and Empire Warships of the Second World War*, London, Greenhill Books, 1998

Leutze, James, *A Different Kind of Victory: A Biography of Admiral Thomas C. Hart*, Annapolis, Naval Institute Press, 1981

McIntyre, W. David, *The Rise and Fall of the Singapore Naval Base*, Hamden, CT, Archon Books, 1979

Marder, Arthur J., *From the Dardanelles to Oran: Studies of the Royal Navy in War and Peace 1915–1940*, London, Oxford University Press, 1974

Marder, Arthur J., *Old Friends, New Enemies: The Royal Navy and the Imperial Japanese Navy, Vol. 1: Strategic Illusions 1936–1941*, Oxford, Oxford University Press, 1981

Matthews, Alan, *Sailors' Tales: Life on Board H.M.S. Repulse during World War II*, Wrexham, Wales, 1997

Middlebrook, Martin and Mahoney, Patrick, *Battleship: The Loss of the Prince of Wales and the Repulse*, London, Allen Lane, 1977

Miller, Edward S., *War Plan Orange*, Annapolis, Naval Institute Press, 1991

Montgomery, Brian, *Shenton of Singapore: Governor and Prisoner of War*, Singapore, Times Books International, 1984

Morison, Samuel Eliot, *History of United States Naval Operations in World War II, Vol. 3: The Rising Sun in the Pacific 1931–April 1942*, Edison, New Jersey, Castle Books, 1948

Okumiya, Masatake, Horikoshi, Jiro and Caidin, Martin, *Zero!*, New York, E.P. Dutton & Co., Inc., 1956

Ong Chit Chung, *Operation Matador: Britain's War Plans against the Japanese 1918–1941*, Singapore, Times Academic Press, 1997

Pool, Richard, *Course for Disaster: From Scapa Flow to the River Kwai*, London, Leo Cooper Ltd, 1987

Prados, John, *Combined Fleet Decoded*, New York, Random House, 1995

Raven, Alan and Roberts, John, *King George V Class Battleships*, London, Bivouac Books, 1972

Raven, Alan and Roberts, John, *British Battleships of World War II*, Annapolis, Naval Institute Press, 1976

Roskill, Stephen, *The War at Sea, Vol. 1: The Defensive; Vol. 2: The Period of Balance*, London, HMSO, 1954, 1956

Roskill, Stephen W., *Naval Policy between the Wars, Vol. 2: The Period of Reluctant Rearmament 1930–1939*, Annapolis, Naval Institute Press, 1976

Roskill, Stephen W., *Churchill and the Admirals*, New York, William Morrow & Company, Inc., 1978

Shores, Christopher, Cull, Brian, and Izawa, Yazuho, *Bloody Shambles, Vol. I: The Drift to War to the Fall of Singapore*, London, Grub Street, 1992

Smith, Peter, and Dominy, John, *Cruisers in Action 1939–1945*, London, William Kimber, 1981

Stephen, Martin, *The Fighting Admirals*, Annapolis, Naval Institute Press, 1991

Stephen, Martin, and Grove, Eric, ed., *Sea Battles in Close-Up: World War II*, Annapolis, Naval Institute Press, 1988

Tagaya, Osamu, *Mitsubishi Type 1 Rikko 'Betty' Units of World War 2* (Osprey Combat Aircraft 22), Botley, Oxford, Osprey Publishing Limited, 2001

Tarrant, V.E., *King George V Class Battleships*, London, Arms and Armour Press, 1991

ARTICLES

Armstrong, Ken, 'The Sinking of HMS Repulse: Memories of 60 Years Ago', *Warship World 7* (November 2001): 18–19

Bell, Christopher, 'The "Singapore Strategy" and the Deterrence of Japan: Winston Churchill, the Admiralty and the Dispatch of Force Z', *The English Historical Review* CXVI (June 2001): 604–34

Brooke, G.A.G. 'The Loss of the Prince of Wales and Repulse', *Warship World* 5 (Autumn 1997): 24–5

K.R.B. [Kenneth R. Buckley], 'A Personal Account of the Sinking of H.M.S. Repulse', *Naval Review* 30, No. 3 (August 1942): 197–200

Cowman, Ian, 'Main Fleet to Singapore? Churchill, the Admiralty, and Force Z', *Journal of Strategic Studies* 17 (June 1994): 79–93

Jacobs, A.E., 'The Loss of the Repulse and Prince of Wales, December 10, 1941: A Participant's Account', *Warship International* 23 No. 1 (1986): 12–28

Plenty, H.C., 'The End of Force Z', *Sabretache* 27 (July/September 1986): 29–32

Roskill, S.W., 'Marder, Churchill and the Admiralty 1939–42', *RUSI Journal* 117 (December 1972): 49–53

OFFICIAL HISTORIES, REPORTS, AND DISPATCHES

Brooke-Popham, Sir Robert, 'Operations in the Far East, from 17th October 1940 to 27th December 1941', Supplement to the *London Gazette* of 22 January 1948, TNA ZJ 1/1028

Headquarters, US Army Far East & US Eighth Army (Rear), *Japanese Monograph No. 107: Malaya Invasion Naval Operations* (rev. edn), Washington, DC, Office of the Chief of Military History, Department of the Army, 1958

Joint Committee on the Investigation of the Pearl Harbor Attack, *Hearings before the Joint Committee on the Investigation of the Pearl Harbor Attack*, Washington, DC, GPO, 1946

Layton, Geoffrey, 'Loss of H.M. Ships Prince of Wales and Repulse, December 17, 1941', Supplement to the *London Gazette* of 20 February 1948, TNA Adm 1/2006

Ministry of Defence, Admiralty Historical Section (Naval Historical Branch), 'The Loss of H.M. Ships *Prince of Wales* and *Repulse*, 10th December, 1941', Battle Summary No. 14, BR 1736(8)/1955, TNA Adm 234/330

Ministry of Defence, Naval Historical Branch, *War with Japan*, vols 1 and 2, London, HMSO, 1995

Ohtsuka Bunichi, trans. Military History Office, National Defense College, *Daitoa (Taiheiyo) Senso Kokan Senshi sosho (Greater East Asia War), Vol. 24: Hito Mare kaigun shinko sakusen (Naval Advance Operations into the Philippines and Malay Area)*, Tokyo, Asakumo Shimunsha, 1969

Percival, A.E., 'Operations of Malaya Command, from 8th December 1941 to 15th February 1942', Supplement to the *London Gazette* of 26 February 1948, TNA ZJ 1/1029

Index